ENSOULING OUR SCHOOLS

A UNIVERSALLY DESIGNED FRAMEWORK FOR
MENTAL HEALTH, WELL-BEING, AND RECONCILIATION

Jennifer Katz

with Kevin Lamoureux
Foreword by Ry Moran

PORTAGE & MAIN PRESS

Portage & Main Press gratefully acknowledges the financial support of the Province of Manitoba through the Department of Sport, Culture & Heritage and the Manitoba Book Publishing Tax Credit and the Government of Canada through the Canada Book Fund (CBF) for our publishing activities.

Printed and bound in Canada by Friesens
Design by Relish New Brand Experience

IMAGE CREDITS:

Fig. I.1. George Couros/Sylvia Duckworth. Used by permission
Fig. 2.2 Glenbow Archives PA-3385-186
Figs. 6.8, 6.11, 6.12 Sheila Vicks
Figs. 1.4, 5.1, 7.10, 7.17–7.20, 7.26, 7.27, 8.5; Appendices C, D, E & G: Illustrations by Jess Dixon.
All others courtesy of the author.

LIBRARY AND ARCHIVES CANADA CATALOGUING IN PUBLICATION

Katz, Jennifer, author

   Ensouling our schools : a universally designed framework for mental health, well-being, and reconciliation / by Jennifer Katz with Kevin Lamoureux ; foreword by Ryan Moran.

Includes bibliographical references and index.
Issued in print and electronic formats.
ISBN 978-1-55379-683-1 (softcover).--ISBN 978-1-55379-743-2 (EPUB).--
ISBN 978-1-55379-744-9 (PDF)

   1. Inclusive education--Canada. 2. Educational sociology--Canada.
3. Teaching--Canada. I. Lamoureux, Kevin, 1977-, author II. Title.

LC1203.C3K38 2018   371.9'0460971   C2017-907837-2
                                                   C2017-907838-0

22 21 20 19   2 3 4 5 6

PORTAGE & MAIN PRESS

1-800-667-9673
www.portageandmainpress.com
Winnipeg, Manitoba
Treaty 1 Territory and homeland of the Métis Nation

For the three spirits who ensouled my life and whose light has passed –
my Aunt Sheila, Reb Zalman, and my father, Philip Katz – this book is for
you, and from you – it carries forward your light. This book is dedicated to
all the young people whose lives are touched by languishing mental health,
and the educators who pour out their hearts every day to try to be a part of
the healing – you are seen, heard, admired, and loved. And finally, as always,
for Jorel – whose life has ensouled mine from the day of his birth and inspired
so much of my work – I love you. **– J.K.**

Dedicated to the inspiring people of Aboriginal Youth Opportunities in
Winnipeg. Miigwetch for making the world a better place. **– K.L.**

Contents

Foreword

To fully understand this country we call Canada, we need to understand the impacts and legacy of trauma.

Many Canadians carry lived experiences with trauma, having fled other parts of the world seeking a better life, or having lived through traumatic experiences right here in this country. The world is, sadly, filled with stories of human-rights atrocities, cultural suppression, and denial of rights in all countries. Canada, as we know it today, is built upon the notion that the country is a safe harbour for people to flee to – a place that can provide a better life for themselves and their children, a place where they can find economic and social stability.

In the construction of this country, however, Indigenous peoples – the original inhabitants of this land – were not afforded that same level of safety as settlers. Residential schools tore children from their families, Indigenous peoples were forced onto reserves, and entire communities were relocated. All the while, the great riches of the land were being plundered.

Safety, in this context, needs be understood as much more than physical safety. Our schools today are working hard to create physically safe places for students – environments free from bullying and teasing. But, culturally, are they safe for Indigenous students?

The definition of safety for Indigenous students needs to include the safety of identify, culture, language, worldview, and approach and solutions to problems. Safety needs be understood as the pursuit and ability to self-determine one's future. Most important, safety in the context of Indigenous peoples means being safe to be, to think, and to act Indigenous. Any abrogation of this ability means the ongoing suppression and denial of Indigenous rights.

Central in the colonization of Canada was the creation of deep divides between Indigenous and non-Indigenous peoples. As Canada forcibly segregated Indigenous peoples from Canadian society, Canadians and the country as a whole lost the ability to learn from and hear the voices of the original inhabitants of this land.

At the same time, Indigenous peoples were forced to assimilate into Canadian society – they were told how to think, how to act, and how to live their lives. Colonial control and imposition stripped Indigenous peoples of their voice and of their right to determine their own future.

We now live in a country filled with Indigenous place names, but the meanings behind the words are hollow for the vast majority of Canadians. Words like

Manitoba, Saskatchewan, Ottawa, and *Canada* roll off the tongue without any understanding of the meaning behind those words.

We also live in a land that remains little understood. Fish, forests, and animals are seen through the lens of resource management and extraction. Our lakes are now polluted; the land is scarred; and populations of whales, bison, salmon, and countless other members of the animal family are a shadow of their past populations. As we lurch toward a highly uncertain future of climate change and environmental decay, we need to, more than ever, learn how to live respectfully with the planet and original mother. Sadly, the long history of colonization continues to frustrate this effort, and the process of reconciliation is a hurried attempt – perhaps far too late in our national history – to finally establish and maintain respectful relationships between Indigenous and non-Indigenous peoples.

To heal from these profound wounds of colonization, we need to understand how we have all been affected. Systems of oppression and colonization have operated on a global basis. Canada's treatment of Indigenous peoples and life is but one manifestation of a sick system of inequality and control that has been layered all over this planet.

Through this process of colonization and control, Canada has denied itself the ability to be a just and fair country – a national identity based upon the spirit and intent of treaties signed between Indigenous nations and representatives of the Crown; a country of respectful coexistence and peaceful relations.

The path forward is through acknowledging the wounds inflicted on this country on Indigenous peoples, on the land, and on families. This process starts with humility and respect – a solemn recognition that we have hurt Indigenous families deeply in the construction of Canada.

Acknowledging these wounds and scars presents us with a collective opportunity to become a deeper, richer, and more truthful society. It presents the collective opportunity where we will finally be able to learn from one another and where the forced assimilation and unjust attempts to dictate how Indigenous peoples ought to live their lives will finally be eradicated from this society.

When the Truth and Reconciliation Commission released its final report in 2015, we were given 94 Calls to Action to guide us in our healing journey. Central in this must be the recognition that the harms inflicted on Indigenous families and children will continue to reverberate for many generations to come. Unlearning the many ways we have been divided, subjugated, and collectively oppressed is also a central element in the successful implementation of these Calls to Action.

We cannot underestimate the complexity of the task at hand, nor can we afford to be naïve in our belief that it will not be deeply challenging on a personal, organizational, and societal level. This is a process of maturation that we are going through as a nation, and like all growth, it will at times be difficult and painful.

Guiding us on this path is the United Nations Declaration on Indigenous Rights. This declaration provides the framework for reconciliation across all sectors and levels of society. It will only be through adopting a rights-based approach to reconciliation that we can ensure we move beyond mere pleasantries and niceties to a state wherein Indigenous peoples are once again empowered and supported in being Indigenous. In the meantime, Indigenous families, languages, nations, and identities remain at risk of extinction.

Traditional knowledge keepers and Elders are fundamental in breathing meaning into these rights and must be cherished deeply by our collective society.

Our collective opportunity now is to make sure that education is no longer used as a weapon against Indigenous people – stripping and robbing them of their right to be Indigenous. Let us all work together to create education systems where we are finally given the opportunity to learn from one another in a spirit of mutual respect.

This is the path of reconciliation. This is our collective responsibility. This is what will transform this country into a nation we can all be proud of. I wish you the very best as you address the content in this book and apply it in your professional work. There is nothing more sacred or noble in life than sharing teachings with young minds, and I commend you for taking up the calling to teach our next generation of leaders.

Ry Moran,
Director
National Centre for Truth and Reconciliation
Winnipeg

Preface

I spent 30 years working in schools. I have been an educational assistant, youth worker, special-education teacher in a segregated setting, resource teacher, inclusive-classroom teacher, guidance counsellor, district consultant, author, editor, and presenter. I now serve as a professor of Inclusive Education at a major Canadian university, and work with government ministries, curriculum designers, school-district leaders, parent councils, school trustees, school-based administrators, and educators to support inclusive reform. In the last 12 years, I have travelled across Canada and the United States, providing professional development, conducting research, presenting at conferences, and co-teaching in classrooms from K–12. Why?

Because I believe in inclusive education.

Because I believe in inclusive societies.

Because I care about everyone – the adults and the kids.

When I was an adolescent, I worked with my Aunt Sheila, a psychiatrist who specialized in caring for children with autism and schizophrenia. She died young, at age 49, of lung cancer. She left me a card, asking me to "leave the world a better place than I found it." Her mentoring gave me the start I needed, and I have been trying ever since to pay forward that legacy.

My father, too, lit my path. He was an adolescent psychiatrist who taught at the medical school in Winnipeg. Dr. Michael Eleff, a protégé, colleague, and family friend, said that my father emphasized: "The therapist's task is to understand the patient and adapt his treatment to the experiences, beliefs, and values of the patient, not compel the patient to fit into a model of treatment which is foreign to the patient's worldview." I carried that forward into my teaching – believing that my job was to similarly adapt my teaching. A second teaching that all who knew and learned with my father was "the central role of the psychotherapist is in seeing the young person, not as a collection of symptoms and problems, but rather as who and what he or she might become in the future." That teaching, too, helped to form my identity as a teacher, particularly in my years in special education where a medical model of diagnosis, based on symptoms and labels that limited expectations for students' learning, was common.

In 1969, my father visited several residential schools. He was horrified by what he saw, and along with a few other doctors, called for them to be closed immediately. When the government didn't listen, he went to the press. The *Winnipeg Tribune* published a front-page story about it. My father told me he was sure something would be done, and when there was no reaction, he was devastated. He spent the rest of his life dedicated to supporting Indigenous youth, trying to help them cope with the legacy of the residential schools, the intergenerational trauma, and the racism that 50 years later still permeates Canadian society.

As part of my work, I have spent the last nine years working and learning with Indigenous peoples and communities. My experiences in that exchange have changed me as a person and as an educator. We have much to learn – about community, about spirit, about healing and educating the whole child from Indigenous Elders and educators. Unfortunately, we also have much to learn about coping with trauma, about suffering and its intergenerational impacts. On the positive side, we can experience the blessing of watching a people rise with resilience and renewed strength and spirit – and be allies to that healing.

One of my spiritual teachers, Rabbi Zalman Schachter Shalomi, challenged me and others to "ensoul our work" – to bring our spirit to what we do. He encouraged us to enact our values and involve our heart in our work life, not just our personal life, through the compassion, kindness, and mindfulness we were all working to develop under his tutelage. He talked about how, whatever we do, no matter the job/career, it could be ensouled. It could have meaning and purpose and serve others.

I have written this book because I want to do my part in reconciliation – with Indigenous peoples, and with the many, many students and teachers our educational system doesn't work for. I want to do my part, too, in response to my aunt's call to "leave the world a better place than I found it," and to Reb Zalman's call to ensoul our work.

I thought I was doing that when I developed the Three-Block Model of Universal Design for Learning (TBM of UDL), a holistic teaching model for inclusive education. The TBM includes programming for social and emotional learning (SEL) in Block One, inclusive instructional practices in Block Two, and systems change in Block Three. Research was showing us the TBM had significant, positive effects on social and emotional and academic learning. More and more teachers, districts, provinces/territories, and states were becoming involved. We had expert teams of facilitators being trained in several provinces. Teachers were sending me messages about the positive impacts they were seeing in their classes and students.

And then a tragedy happened. Two young people died by suicide. Their classmates and teachers were traumatized (I didn't meet the family, but don't mean to dismiss their loss and suffering). It all happened so quickly – in one weekend.

I heard a quote from a teacher that sent shudders through me: "I can't go back to a classroom with two empty desks."

The tragedy raised many questions for me. These questions had been in the back of my mind for a while – questions about trauma, mental health, and well-being. Questions about the purpose of schooling and why I, and others, became teachers.

In recent years, I had become more and more concerned by what I was seeing in schools related to the health and well-being of everyone – the adults and the students. Somehow, the road we have all gone down has increased stress and pressure and decreased joy and learning.

Teacher burnout rates are very high, as are youth mental-health needs. That may sound depressing, but it isn't. It's an opportunity. We have an opportunity to change course. Not to go backwards, but to move forward in a different direction. Research and experience can guide us now to what works – for everyone's well-being, and for improving learning.

I set out to learn – to expand my knowledge about what has been happening in our schools and what can be done about it. I listened to Indigenous Elders and educators; to researchers, scholars, and scientists; to psychiatrists, psychologists, and social workers; to educational leaders, teachers, and support staff; to families, students, and spiritual leaders. I also read, and I learned. As I often joke – I am not married and have no children, so I can choose to have no life ☺. My gift has always been my ability to see connections, synthesize, and weave together what seem like disparate parts into a connected whole.

In this book, I bring together all that I learned about education, well-being, health promotion, spiritual and peace education, Indigenous worldviews, and inclusive education to further ensoul my work. I weave together the scientific evidence, professional knowledge, and human intuition and insights in our field and my own experiences, to take us that next step toward an inclusive professional culture and system that cares, and educates, in the largest sense of the word.

As an inclusive educator and proponent of UDL, I always consider all of the students in our schools. I do not focus on one specific group of students as the old special-education model did, nor solely on students with specific mental illnesses. Instead, I focus on the learning community and how it can be designed to celebrate and teach to diversity. At the same time, it would be irresponsible of me to write about trauma and well-being in Canada and not consider Indigenous peoples and students and the issues of residential schools and the Indian Act. As an ally, I recognize it is my role as a non-Indigenous person to support and promote such consideration, but not to lead it.

I met Kevin Lamoureux in my work with schools in Manitoba. Participants in my workshops kept telling me that our work connected, and we should meet. So, I sought him out. We met, ironically, at a conference in Ottawa, the same day the Truth and Reconciliation Commission (TRC) was proclaimed on Parliament Hill. It was a momentous day – for the country, for me personally, and for my work. In the years since, Kevin and I have spent many hours talking about schools and schooling, reconciliation, inclusion, and well-being. Together, we have conducted workshops and led a conference, and we have shared our journey and passion to make the world a better place, despite the difficult moments along the way. When I decided to write this book, it was natural, then, to ask Kevin to work on it with me.

Kevin is the National Education Lead for the National Centre for Truth and Reconciliation, and the Associate Vice-President of Indigenous Affairs at the University of Winnipeg. He is an Indigenous educator and scholar, and someone I trust to make sure what is suggested in this book works for both Indigenous and non-Indigenous students. He is also a very busy man, so rather than ask him to co-author the entire book, I asked him to write the chapter on the TRC, give feedback on everything in the book, and advise me on the programming I was suggesting. We'd meet, and I would ask questions. I'd draft sections, and then I would send them to him for feedback. When we weren't sure about something, Kevin sought out Elders for information, advice, and wisdom. Without him, this book would not have been possible. Miigwech, Kevin.

In essence, this book is an expansion of Block One of the TBM. It takes a decided focus on mental health and social and emotional well-being. However, it also looks through that lens at instructional practice and how it connects to mental health.

In Part I, we'll start with the underlying premises of ensouled schools – schools that create inclusive learning communities, that are trauma informed, and that nurture health and well-being. Ensouled schools support the discovery of meaning and purpose in one's life, for both students and staff, ally in reconciliation, and, hopefully, raise a generation that will make the world a better place than they found it. We'll explore what we know, what the issues are, what the research says, and why it matters. In Part II, we'll go through the how – step by step.

For joining me on this journey, witnessing, sharing, and enriching it – Miigwech. Todah Rabah. Merci. Thank you.

Acknowledgments

First and foremost, I want to acknowledge all who live with challenges related to mental health. It is not an easy journey, and I hope this book contributes in some small way to the movement towards destigmatization and compassion.

To Kevin, my colleague, friend, and adopted brother – this is only the beginning of our journey, and to all of the PMP staff – Annalee, Catherine, Kirsten – thank you for continuing to support my work, and for the amazing work you do on behalf of Indigenous people and all educators.

This book began in 2012, when a panel of Indigenous educators presented to a group of teachers at a summer institute in Winnipeg. One of the women, a vice-principal of a northern school, told the tragic story of her son's death by suicide. She noted that at his funeral she was taken aback by the number of teachers who commented on what a good person he was, and then said, *"I shouldn't have had to wait until his funeral to hear good things about him."* The room was stunned into silence, and 120 teachers left there forever impacted, including me. That same group of amazing women educators became friends and colleagues – and so to all of the community of Norway House, Miigwech for your welcoming, sharing, and guidance.

The concept of "ensouling" was taught to me by my spiritual teacher, Rabbi Zalman Schachter Shalomi, who encouraged everyone to "ensoul your lives and your work." By that, he meant to bring your heart, mind, and spirit to every interaction in your life – whether with a sunset or a student. I spent many nights on Skype talking with him about what this meant for me and my work, and how I could contribute to the ensouling of our schools so that children's spirits were nurtured alongside their minds. We lost Reb Zalman shortly before his 90th birthday; this book is my small part of his amazing legacy.

I also lost my father in June of 2017. He was a powerful energy, and the world seems a little emptier without him. I am grateful for his modelling of respect for Indigenous cultures and people, wariness of anything ethnocentric or racist, and belief in the healing power of relationship.

To all of the members of the Manitoba Alliance for Universal Design for Learning (MAUDeL), and particularly that inner core who continue to sustain the organization – John Van Walleghem, Trevor Boehm, Jude Gosselin, Sherri Black, Alex Bertrand, Joan Zaretsky, Denise Smith, Deborah Dykstra, Val Wood, Sandy Turcotte, Karen Fraser, and Lesley Welwood – many thanks.

The faculty at UBC nurtured me through my beginnings as a teacher, my growth into a leader, and my days as a graduate student, and they now have welcomed me as a colleague. They are an amazing group of brilliant minds, open hearts, and inspirational leaders. In particular, to Marion Porath, Kim Schonert Reichl, Shelley Hymel, and especially Pat Mirenda – my eternal gratitude, respect, and love.

To all of the family, friends, mentors, and spiritual teachers who have guided my spirit, nurtured my heart, and enlightened my soul, my heartfelt thanks. Many thanks to my brother Laurence, my sister Vivi, my niece Jessica and nephews Zach and Jorel for their love and support. A special thank you to Reb Nadya, Reb Victor, and Reb Laura for helping me to connect my spiritual life with my profession, and guiding me on the journey – I am eternally grateful. To my soul family – Lynna, Lisa, Andi, Dafna, Kathyrn, Ida, David, Laura, Saida, Zana – my love and gratitude grow every day. Thank you for the inspiration and connection.

Finally, as always, and with everything I do – credit has to be given once again to the rock on which I stand – my mother. Now 87, she has seen a lot, triumphed, and become the wisest of elders. She remains friend, mother, consultant, social worker, advisor...spirit guide. There simply are no words – I am blessed.

Introduction

From the beginnings of public education, debate has raged about the purposes of teaching, learning, and schooling. Arguments have been made based on economics (to prepare the next generation of workers), philosophy (to produce democratic citizens), and communal values (to transmit the values of the local culture/society). All of these are unidirectional: they are the goals of adults for children and youth. Students themselves have no voice (an irony in the democratic model), and the balance of individual rights and collective rights is, therefore, lost. In a system determined to "school" a child, there is no room for self-actualization, self-determination, or, indeed, freedom.

Ask a teacher why they chose this profession, and the almost-universal answer is: "I wanted to make a difference for kids." Ask most youth why they continue their education, and their answers are often (apart from "because I have to,") to discover who they are, what they want to do with their life and their interests, and to form social connections and community. In truth, teachers become teachers for emotional, social, and spiritual reasons, and students come to school seeking emotional, social, and spiritual learning. Never have I heard a teacher answer the above questions with: "Because every student needs to know their times tables," nor has any student ever said: "Because I can't live a life of meaning until I have memorized the periodic table."

Ask any teacher to list the 10 most important things they want their students to leave school with, and they will write things like, "respect, empathy, self-confidence, leadership skills, critical thinking, risk-taker." No one ever writes, "passive, obedient, rote memorizer, conformist, good speller, teacher pleaser."

So, do our practices match our dreams? Will they help us raise the kind of youth we want to hand our world to – the kind who can improve the world we live in?

The current state of youth is concerning. The most recent data from Statistics Canada speak to a growing sense of anxiety and sadness in our students, occurring at younger and younger ages. Approximately 20 percent of children and adolescents, well over 800,000 children in Canada, experience mental-health problems severe enough to warrant mental-health services. Yet, 75 percent of them receive no care. This is not just adolescent angst. Twenty percent of elementary-school students reported being so sad every day for more than two weeks they stopped doing regular activities and wished they were someone else. This rose to close to 40 percent by high school.

Similar numbers of students rated their lives as having low meaning and purpose. The rates of depression and anxiety, clearly, are significant and far too large for any single school counsellor to address. Research, however, tells us that schools can play a significant role in the well-being of youth (Hymel, Schonert-Reichl, and Miller 2006). Given the numbers, it's going to have to happen in the classroom, with all the kids – universally designed mental-health programming.

Thus, it is critical that we create classrooms in which *all* students:

- feel good about who they are and what they have to offer
- feel connected to each other and treat each other with genuine respect and kindness
- are challenged to learn, develop critical thinking and perspective, and grow
- learn how to learn and work with diverse others

This is not new, or news. In 1994, representatives of 92 nations gathered in Salamanca, Spain, to discuss inclusive education under the umbrella of the United Nations. The resulting Salamanca Statement based its philosophy on the right to an education for all children. The framework adopted a guiding principle that schools (1994, 6):

> should accommodate all children regardless of their physical, intellectual, social, emotional, linguistic, or other conditions. This should include disabled and gifted children, street and working children, children from remote and or nomadic populations, children from linguistic, ethnic, or cultural minorities, and children from other disadvantaged or marginalized areas or groups.

The Salamanca Statement further recognized "the necessity and urgency of providing education for children, youth and adults with special educational needs within the regular education system" (viii). The delegates created an action plan to address this need, and stated that "those children with special educational needs must have access to regular schools, which should accommodate them within a child-centered pedagogy capable of meeting these needs" (30). The delegates asserted:

> regular schools with this inclusive orientation are the most effective means of combating discriminatory attitudes, creating welcoming communities, building an inclusive society and achieving education for all; moreover, they provide an effective education to the majority of children and improve the efficiency and ultimately the cost effectiveness of the entire education system (ix).

The Salamanca Statement compelled countries to implement inclusive education for all learners. However, it did not clearly define what was meant by the term *inclusion*. Surveys of definitions around the world appear to have several key components: (a) placement of all students in general education classrooms; (b) access to general curriculum and learning; (c) opportunities for meaningful participation, peer interactions, and social and emotional support and well-being. These qualities appear in definitions from such disparate places as the United States, Sweden, Russia, India, and Canada. Clearly, if the goal of the Salamanca Statement is "combating discriminatory attitudes," "creating welcoming communities," and "building an inclusive society," inclusive education must involve a social and emotional component.

How do we ensure that students meet diverse others in a context that fosters respect and exchange, rather than division and fear? Research shows that knowing oneself and one's environment is crucial to engaging difference positively. If we are insecure, we feel threatened by others who are different. Thus, devoting time to the development of students' self-worth, and explicitly discussing the importance of respecting the value of all people, is a critical piece to developing a more just society.

In traditional [industrial] models of schooling, standards and accountability were all-important to measure both student progress and teacher efficacy. This model of education – which focuses on standardized outcomes, statistics and metrics, and measurable curricula – is often referred to as an "accountability agenda." The further we have gone with "standards" and "accountability," the more we have sold our soul. Yes, we need to have a vision, and intellectual challenge is absolutely part of that. The classroom is a learning community, not purely a social community. But we want to stay true to what it is we really want students to learn, and no government exam will ever capture that. You can never capture the mind, heart, spirit, and soul of a child/adolescent on a paper-and-pencil test. Even when focusing on mind and cognition, true development of the mind of an intellect – one who seeks out learning, debates multiple perspectives, critically analyzes bias and purpose, formulates new and unique ideas and views, proposes solutions and designs products that are founded in both reason and prosocial outcomes – cannot be assessed with a test that has a right answer. Only a professional, well-trained, and dedicated teacher who spends hours every day in relationship with their students can do that.

Teachers, too, have souls. They care. They have families and children, lives and loves. Walking into schools today, you can see a level of stress and burnout like never before. One teacher described her job as "soul-sucking." It wasn't because she didn't like kids or teaching. It was precisely because she loved them, and didn't feel like she could meet their needs, or do her job well. The rates of teacher burnout are staggering. Forty-seven percent of teachers in Canada will leave the profession before retirement age. No other profession loses half of its practitioners prior to retirement age. We don't help children by burning out teachers. The result is increasing rates of anxiety in our youth, lower levels of learning and achievement, and higher levels of both teachers and students leaving our schools. We must bring back the heart and spirit of education; the love of learning and teaching; the sense of belonging, community, and connection.

It is time to ensoul our schools.

Are Schools an Archaic Institution?

Schools can be archaic institutions, but they don't have to be.

The initial motivation behind the formation of schools in modern times (as opposed to Ancient Greece, for instance, where learning was for learning's sake), was industrialization. There was the need for workers who had specific skills and knowledge, which led to a training program called schools. This belief system related to schooling has maintained a role, though a significantly reduced one, in students', parents', and teachers' beliefs about schooling when they have only experienced the traditional form. However, there are nuanced changes to the interpretation of the economic value. Students often cite "getting a good job," while parents and teachers will talk about "preparing kids to be successful in the work world." Within this is a subtle but important change – it is less about what industry demands, and more about what the child needs. Nevertheless, it remains an economic motivation, influenced by what makes students employable. Ironically, many of the skills defined by employers in the corporate world as essential for effectiveness in the twenty-first century work world – for example, working with a team, relating to diverse colleagues and customers, analyzing and generating solutions to problems, and persisting in the face of setbacks – are social and emotional competencies.

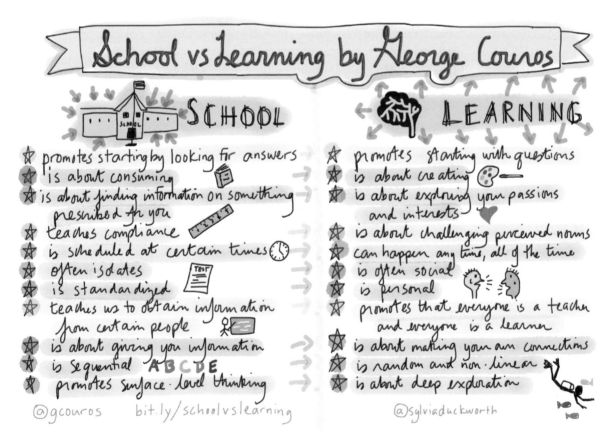

Figure I.1 Traditional Schooling versus Learning

Other purposes of schooling cited by teachers in the research and rated more highly than a strict economic function include teachers' desire to make a difference not only for individual students, but for society as a whole. Teachers cite:

> the desire to effect social change through education (e.g., help eliminate all forms of discrimination from society; provide a vehicle for social and economic mobility; a way for the poor to reach their potential); and development of an ethical and socially responsible citizenry as more important than economic purposes, though not exclusive of them (Widdowson et al. 2015).

Students tend to agree far more with the social purposes of schooling than with the economic. International research documents amazing similarities on students' perceptions of the purpose of schooling – learning, and developing social skills and personal skills. In fact, students who viewed schools as being about jobs and economics demonstrated a preference for work avoidance and the belief that success involves a commitment to surpassing others' achievement, luck, and impressing the teacher. In Widdowson's study, four categories of beliefs about the purpose of schooling were identified: (1) to learn and develop self-knowledge, (2) to develop life skills and social skills, (3) to optimize life chances and quality of life, and (4) to enable future employment and economic well-being. The most significant finding of this study was the strong consensus among stakeholders in the importance of learning for learning's sake. Attending school, sending children to school, and teaching in schools were not viewed as being about producing a workforce.

A spiritual function was also mentioned by parents, teachers, and students – parents and teachers wanted students to find happiness and fulfillment, while students said they came to school because "it was fun," and for learning about oneself.

In my own research, students in traditional classrooms described learning as a compulsory process, teacher dependent, and a means to employment. For example, student comments included: "It means trying stuff over and over again until you get it right." Students did not appear to be engaged. Rote memorization of facts was seen as boring, as noted by comments such as: "She tells us what to do and we do it, and when we're done, we give the sheet to her" and "Study. Answers. That's it." Comments such as: "I learn from teachers because they are older and they know better than us," and "Our teacher tells us what to do, and we go do it" reflect the authoritarian, teacher-centred perspective inherent in an industrialized paradigm. There's a boss, and there are workers.

When we introduce spiritual and social and emotional learning (SEL), there are changes to the students' perceptions of learning. Many more students discuss learning as a means to better opportunities later in life, making statements such as: "Learning is the first stage to your future," and "Learning is mandatory. Some people think it's something your parents are forcing you to do, but really it's to help you later on." Students comment on extending their definitions of learning beyond school subjects and into other facets of life: "Do your own stuff to get your mind healthy," "Sort of like encountering knowledge you haven't really encountered before and don't really have a lot of deep, concept or understanding of it. If that makes any sense," "Yah, it's kind of just you learn something new every day, and it might not always be about school, but you learn something new every day, and school is just another way to learn something," and "We develop skill sets that can be used in the future. And not just knowledge that sort of goes over your head but something that can just influence who you are as a person and how you react to the world around you."

Health Promoting Schools

The World Health Organization (WHO) promotes a movement toward holistic education called "Health Promoting Schools" (HPS). According to WHO: "A health promoting school is one that constantly strengthens its capacity as a healthy setting for living, learning and working." Health promoting schools focus on:

- caring for oneself and others
- making healthy decisions and taking control over life's circumstances
- creating conditions that are conducive to health (through policies, services, physical/social conditions)
- building capacities for peace, shelter, education, food, income, a stable ecosystem, equity, social justice, sustainable development
- preventing leading causes of death, disease, and disability: helminths, tobacco use, HIV/AIDS/STDs, sedentary lifestyle, drugs and alcohol, violence and injuries, unhealthy nutrition
- influencing health-related behaviours: knowledge, beliefs, skills, attitudes, values, support

Education ministries around the world, including many countries in Europe, Africa, and Asia, as well as in India, Canada, and the United States, have adopted HPS policy. However, while policy exists, and government initiatives have taken place, consistent implementation of a holistic educational paradigm has not been achieved. Often these initiatives appear as mixed messages to teachers, when the same governments also increase standardized testing, merit pay, and other practices that increase stress, are not aimed at healthy learning or environments, and pressure teachers into focusing on rote skills and curricula. Perhaps as a result, the healthy schools movement has often ended up relegated to being enacted through health curricula, focusing on physical and sometimes mental health, and given little time or importance. Although the following is recognized, it is rarely enacted on the full spectrum:

> Health promotion in schools is not just about encouraging children and young people to eat well and to exercise; it encompasses a much broader holistic approach. This approach is called the "whole school approach," which includes promoting the physical, social, spiritual, mental and emotional well-being of all pupils and staff (Physical and Health Education Canada).

Clearly, the purpose of schooling has changed, but in many cases, the pedagogy has not. Jones, Haenfler, and Johnson (2001) laid out what they called the "seven foundations of a better world": economic fairness, comprehensive peace, ecological sustainability, deep democracy, social justice, a culture of simplicity, and revitalized community. While many schools and government policies cite visions that align with these foundations, research shows there is rarely time dedicated to them, and often curricula, assessment practices, teaching methods, and school rules are not well aligned.

However, there is hope. We do know how to "do school" differently.

An alternative vision to the traditional industrialized version of schooling is offered through the Three-Block Model of Universal Design for Learning (the TBM of UDL), the basic theories and values of inclusive education, social and emotional learning (SEL), and health-promoting schools. This vision is also offered through Indigenous practices that draw in marginalized populations, move away from deficit models of students, and focus on developing student autonomy, self-regulation, and academic self-efficacy. Evidence shows that all children can have a school experience that develops academic and cognitive abilities, while also supporting them to become active contributors to a more just, peaceful, productive, and sustainable world.

The TBM of UDL was created in service to those goals and is the basis for curricula presented in this book. The model draws upon the philosophy of UDL – every child has the right to access our schools, an education, and the community of their peers. It seeks to create a true learning community – one in which teachers and students engage in deep, higher-order thinking around important issues and concepts, and in which students take charge of their learning and learn to be risk-takers, leaders, and team players. At the same time, the model provides students with the opportunity to develop their inner spirit – a sense of self-worth and connection to others, to the planet, and to something larger than themselves. The model pulls together the work of Rose and Meyer (2002), who developed the concept of UDL, key evidence-based strategies for inclusive education such as inquiry and differentiation, and the work of the Collaborative for Academic, Social, and Emotional Learning (CASEL), which promotes social and emotional learning in schools. The TBM is a synthesis of effective practices for inclusive classrooms and schools.

The TBM of UDL, as a holistic educational paradigm, also fits well with the whole-child worldview of Indigenous education and the concept of reconciliation. In 2007, The Truth and Reconciliation Commission of Canada (TRC) was formed to investigate the legacy of Indian residential schools. Out of its six-year investigation came 94 Calls to Action to bring about reconciliation, including several that focus on education. Reconciliation recognizes that in any conflict, all parties are affected. Each loses out on the richness that relationships could bring. The 2015 report of the TRC states: "It [reconciliation] is about coming to terms with events of the past in a manner that overcomes conflict and establishes a respectful and healthy relationship among people, going forward."

The premise of inclusive education, similarly, is that diversity, and the opportunity to interact in respectful ways with others, enriches our lives.

Systems and Structures

- Inclusive Policy – No "Except!"
- Visionary, instructional leadership
- Distributed leadership
- In-depth professional development
- Staffing for collaborative practice
  - Team planning time
  - Scheduling in cohorts/teams
  - Resource/EA allocations to classrooms
  - Co-planning/teaching/assessing
- Budgeting changed from segregated practices/ funding allocations
  - Assistive technology available to all
  - Multi-leveled resources
- School and district culture of care and inclusivity
- Curriculum designed for diversity
- Flexible learning environments

Inclusive Instructional Practice

- Integrated Curriculum – Cross-Curricular Connections
- Student Choice and Autonomy
- Flexible Groupings/Cooperative Learning
- Differentiated Instruction and Assessment
- Self-Regulated Learning
- Assessment for Learning/Class Profiles
- Technology
- Discipline-Based Inquiry
- Meta-Cognition
- Understanding by Design
- Problem-Based Learning
- Inquiry
- Social & Academic Inclusion as Guiding Principle for Tier 2/3 supports

Social and Emotional Learning and Well-Being:
Developing Compassionate Classroom Communities

- Developing Self-Concept
  - Awareness of and pride in strengths and challenges
- Sense of Belonging
- Self-Regulation
  - Goal setting and planning
  - Emotional regulation, mindfulness
- Valuing Diversity
  - Awareness of the strengths and challenges of others
  - Valuing of diverse contributions to community
  - Sense of collective responsibility for well-being, achievement of all
  - Empathy, perspective taking, compassion
- Democratic Classroom Management
  - Collective problem solving, recognition of rights and responsibilities
  - Promotion of independent learning, student choice and empowerment, leadership
- Positive Mental Health for Teachers and Students
- Resiliency and Distress Tolerance
- Indigenous Perspectives on Health, Healing, and Reconciliation
- Service Education – developing meaning and purpose
- Programming
  - Respecting Diversity Program (RD), Spirit Buddies, Class Meetings, Brain Unit, DBT, Mindfulness,
  - TRC programming

Figure I.2 Three-Block Model of UDL

Indigenous and non-Indigenous peoples stand to gain from positive and healthy relationships with each other, just as people with and without disabilities do, and just as our students do in interacting positively with each other. Thus, we believe every child who leaves our classrooms should know they have something of value to offer the world, they are unique and amazing, they matter, and they live in a diverse world with incredible beauty and majesty.

Inclusive education allows *all* children to discover a life filled with meaning and purpose.

In later chapters, we will discuss programming from the Three-Block Model of Universal Design (TBM of UDL), from peace education, and from mental-health initiatives that can help us to achieve our vision.

Weaving the Threads

Think of the structure of this book as being similar to that of a loom. The TBM has always been a weaving together of what we know is effective practice for inclusive education. The TBM is based on a belief, and now research evidence that says, to coin an old saying: "The whole is greater than the sum of the parts." When we weave together such practices as inquiry, differentiation, backwards design, and SEL – the impact for both students and teachers is exponential in power.

Implementing the TBM significantly increases diverse students' engagement, self-concept, belonging, prosocial behavior, and respect for diverse others (Katz 2012, 2013; Katz and Porath 2011; Katz, Porath, Bendu, and Epp 2012), including those of students with learning and behavioural challenges (Glass 2013). Research investigating academic outcomes suggests the TBM has a significant impact on the learning and engagement of all students, and the greatest impact on students with disabilities and students who are Indigenous. In fact, mean scores for Indigenous students indicated "the gap" between Indigenous and non-Indigenous students in academic achievement was completely closed – both groups of students in TBM classrooms achieved at significantly higher levels than either group of students in typical classrooms (Katz, Sokal, and Wu, in press). Teachers have indicated planning and teaching through this framework reduces teachers' stress, increases job satisfaction, reduces challenging behaviour, and improves teachers' self-efficacy related to inclusion (Katz 2014).

In our woven tapestry (see figure I.4), we highlight four important threads within the TBM. Each thread represents a critically important issue in twenty-first century schools, and has a body of research, well-known proponents, policy, and classroom-tested practices associated with it. In Part I, we will discuss each thread – what it is, what the research says about it, who is leading the way, and why the

> We believe every child who leaves our classrooms should know they have something of value to offer the world, they are unique and amazing, they matter, and they live in a diverse world with incredible beauty and majesty.

Figure I.3 Balancing Meaning and Purpose

Figure I.4 Weaving the Threads

thread is important for all educators to know. We will make connections between the threads; in the same way the TBM brought together instructional practices into a singular, practical framework, we can integrate each of these threads into the TBM and not feel like we are trying to do 50 things at once!

- Thread 1 (White) – Chapter 1: Spirit and Soul in Education
- Thread 2 (Black) – Chapter 2: Neurology, Trauma, Well-Being, and Mental Health in Our Schools
- Thread 3 (Red) – Chapter 3: The TRC and Indigenous Worldviews of Education for Well-Being
- Thread 4 (Yellow) – Chapter 4: Leadership for Inclusion and UDL

Of course, categories are always inaccurate. The three blocks all interact, the four aspects of the medicine wheel interact, and all four of the threads listed above interact. For instance, Thread 3, the TRC and Indigenous worldviews, include spiritual, emotional, mental, and physical elements. The connection is loose, therefore, but it made sense to link the spiritual aspect (and color of thread) to the chapter on spiritual education, the emotional aspect to the chapter on mental health, the mental thread to the chapter on the TRC (because it is about raising awareness, developing knowledge and understanding, and truth), and the physical aspect with leadership – because it requires action.

Figure I.5 The Medicine Wheel

- Threads 1, 2, 3, 4 (All) – Chapter 5: Weaving the Threads

In Part II, we propose practical, universally designed programming you can use with all students in your classroom) to address these threads, while connecting them to curriculum and school structures.

PART I

Ensouled Learning Communities:

Finding Meaning and Purpose in Schools and Schooling

Chapter 1
Spirit and Soul in Education

What Do We Mean by Soul/Spirit?

Experts in spiritual education generally agree that the spiritual dimension can be situated within the context of religion or within a secular context. In this book, we address spirituality through a humanistic, secular lens, but without dismissing the individual and communal values that may be associated with a transcendent faith. Spiritual education, whether taught through religion or in a secular context, is recognized as having multiple pathways to the same goal – that living a life of meaning and purpose can be supported through secular and/or religious values.

> Our soul is the core of who we are, our humanity, our essence. Soulful education is about self-actualization – discovering who we are, where our passions lie, and what gives our lives meaning and purpose.

An ensouled school recognizes the needs of all human beings for connection, appreciation, respect, and meaning. Staff and students alike become more engaged when they feel valued for who they are, are given the opportunity to learn and grow, and feel they have an impact on their world. Leaders in such schools recognize these needs as paramount to their role, and find ways to nurture both staff and students in their spiritual education journey. As such, leaders play both a visionary and a service role. They keep the big picture in mind while making decisions about what matters and is worth investing in, and they know how to provide the supports staff, students, and families need to achieve their goals.

Spiritual education embodies a holistic vision of children and youth – a belief that schools need to consider the heart, mind, body, and spirit. Modern medicine is beginning to focus more and more on the approach taken by holistic and ancient medicines – what affects the heart, affects the mind, body, and spirit. They are all connected.

So what does this mean for educators and education?

Before we define a holistic vision for ensouled schools, let's look at some of the theoretical/historical frameworks that may apply.

The History

Communities of Care

The concept of care as both a means and a goal for education is both ancient and modern. Aristotle spoke of *eudaimonia* as well-doing, and well-being as "living flourishingly," and a goal for every individual. Feminist teachings emphasized an ethic of care as being integral to education. In care ethics, relation is the core principle of education, and the caring relation is ethically basic to teachers. Nel Noddings' work on caring education had tremendous impact on the evolution of social and emotional learning in schools. She demonstrated the significance of caring and relationship both as an educational goal, and as a fundamental aspect of education. Noddings' 1984 work, *Caring: A Feminine Approach to Ethics and Moral Education,* is considered seminal for those wanting to emphasize the ethical and moral foundations of spiritual education.

The opposite of feeling cared for is feeling rejected, alienated, and unwelcome. Research has long shown that when youth feel their lives are not worthwhile, or if they become disconnected from their community or society, the experience of alienation that often follows can promote mental and emotional instability. Alienation can be social or academic. Socially, alienation results from a feeling of not "fitting in," of being different in a negative way that results in rejection and being unwelcome. Academically, alienation results from varying degrees of student estrangement from the learning process. When students have little power over their learning, when learning has little relevance to their lives and aspirations, or when they are devalued or marginalized, they are likely to engage in acts of resistance the system often terms as "oppositional." Or they may withdraw their assent for schooling altogether. Research shows that before leaving school (dropping out), students often disengage gradually, resulting in truancy, school failure, and disinterest in school-related activities. In such cases, dropping out represents the mismatch between student needs and expectations and school demands and benefits. Academic alienation occurs when students lack meaningful connection to their studies, when they see little relevance in the course content, and often, when they are effectively disconnected from other students through highly individualized forms of instruction that either require them to do a different activity than their peers, thus removing the opportunity to collaborate and participate, or remove them from the classroom altogether. Unsafe classrooms are therefore those that exclude students from social and academic success.

Figure 1.1 Stages of School Dropout

From the perspective of care ethics, a teacher's primary role is as "carer," responding to the needs of their students. At times, teachers will have to wrestle with the dilemma of a student's expressed need, and that of the curriculum, school, or class. In their role as carer, teachers are interested in students' expressed needs, not simply the institutional needs of the school and the prescribed curriculum. Relation becomes the critical lens – that which will maintain the relation determines the course of action. When teachers work very hard to help their students succeed, we often give them moral credit for caring. They seem to know what their students need and act faithfully on those beliefs. However, teachers have assumed these needs; the student has not expressed them. These teachers, therefore, have not established caring relations because they have imposed upon, rather than responded to, the needs of the student. For instance, a teacher who assumes a student is struggling to read a particular text and steps in to scaffold removes the right of the student to persevere through the text independently, seek out a peer to support them, or select another text. Such students may feel humiliated by the teacher's "support," or resent the inference that they are not capable of solving the challenge themselves, or on their own terms. At times, these teachers end up frustrated and stressed, because they believe they are doing everything they can to support their students and some students respond with negative behaviour. Care ethics, therefore, emphasizes the difference between assumed needs and expressed needs. From this perspective, it is important not to confuse the cared-for wants with those the teacher thinks students should want. Noddings counsels teachers to listen, not just "tell," and to not assume they know what the student needs.

Social and Emotional Learning

Social and emotional learning (SEL) is one aspect of spiritual education that, at its simplest, focuses on developing emotional and social competence. In its more complex iteration, SEL expands to consider meaning and purpose in the context of self-actualization, peace education, and social justice.

SEL and the Individual

The theoretical framework of SEL synthesizes the work of a variety of scholars within the fields of medicine, psychology, and education. Salovey and Mayer (1990) coined the term *emotional intelligence* and defined it as "a form of social intelligence that involves the ability to monitor one's own and others' feelings and emotions, to discriminate among them, and to use this information to guide one's thinking and action." Based on Salovey and Mayer's work, perhaps the more well-known theory of social and emotional learning was then put forward by Daniel Goleman and his colleagues at the Collaborative for Academic, Social, and Emotional Learning (CASEL). According to CASEL (Zins and Elias 2006, 1), SEL is defined as:

> ...the process of acquiring and effectively applying the knowledge, attitudes, and skills necessary to recognize and manage emotions, developing caring and concern for others, making responsible decisions, establishing positive relationships, and handling challenging situations capably.

The CASEL model, based on Goleman's concept of emotional intelligence, includes "five interrelated sets of cognitive, affective, and behavioural competencies": self-awareness, self-management, social awareness, relationship skills, and responsible decision-making. These five competencies include components of social and emotional development (well documented in the research) that influence both academic success and mental health as youth develop (e.g., achievement, belonging, self-worth, self-efficacy, and citizenship). Self-awareness involves recognizing and acknowledging one's strengths and challenges. Children who are self-aware are able to recognize their own emotions, and are aware of how they are perceived by others. Social awareness, on the other hand, involves the ability to take the perspective of others. Children with well-developed social awareness recognize that others have differing strengths and challenges. These children are, therefore, able to understand others' reactions to situations and suggest win-win solutions to problems. Children who have self-respect embrace their strengths and see them as tools for achieving their goals and overcoming their challenges. They willingly take risks and try challenging tasks. Students who are respectful of others demonstrate empathy and accept the relative strengths and challenges of others in relation to their own. They can work cooperatively with others, using their own and others' abilities appropriately. Socially, respect for others implies an appreciation for diversity.

In addition to the direct effects of SEL on factors such as bullying and trauma recovery, spiritual educators must pay attention to the social and emotional influences on academic learning. With rising rates of anxiety and stress among youth, it is no wonder teachers are reporting rising rates of students' inability to pay attention, retain information, or interact positively with peers and teachers. Thus, social and emotional issues will continue to create barriers to learning for youth unless successful SEL programming is implemented. Indeed, the ability to learn is affected by the joy associated with the experience of learning and the relational environment of school. "Involvement, motivation, self-esteem, hope, play, and the positive emotions experienced with the grasp of new concepts, all facilitate plasticity and learning" (Nelson et al. 2013, 245). It should come as no surprise, then, that SEL programs have been shown to affect academic achievement, even at the college level, including improving scores on standardized exams. Even when considering academic outcomes alone, inclusive, socially, and emotionally supportive classroom environments support positive outcomes for students.

SEL and Teachers

Implementing SEL programming in classrooms can have both direct and indirect positive effects on teachers who teach these types of programs, not just on their students. Teachers who have implemented SEL demonstrated lower levels of stress, and those with greater comfort in implementing SEL showed greater general professional commitment to teaching. Such positive effects suggest: "implementation of SEL nurtures teachers' own well-being" (Collie et al. 2011, 1045). Teachers who have well-developed social and emotional skills demonstrate greater enjoyment of teaching, and feel more self-efficacy. SEL programs that reduce challenging behaviour and improve achievement in the classroom are likely to further reduce teacher stress, given that student behaviour and failure have long been known to affect teacher well-being. These findings are significant, as many teachers worldwide experience high levels of stress – the main reason for career dissatisfaction and leaving the profession. As well, stressed teachers tend to have relationships with students that involve more conflict and less warmth. Moreover, these conflictual relationships are also associated with lower student engagement and achievement. When teachers and students learn about SEL and take part in its programs, teacher stress is lowered and poor, conflictual relationships between student and teacher are mitigated. Clearly, when teachers teach and practise SEL skills with their students, both teachers and students benefit.

SEL and the Community/Society

A second, broader theoretical basis of SEL comes from a social-justice perspective that explores issues of belonging as opposed to marginalization, conflict, and alienation in diverse school settings. In *Pedagogy of the Oppressed* (1993), Paulo Freire theorizes that the alienation of youth may be the single biggest factor in leaving school, disengagement, and the achievement gap. Freire suggests that because in traditional schooling students have little power over their learning, the content of the learning has little relevance to their lives and aspirations. Furthermore, students with disabilities, as well as those within cultural and sexual orientation minorities, are devalued or marginalized, resulting in youth who are more likely to engage in acts of resistance or to withdraw from school altogether. In schools with (a) a deficit view of students (i.e., the focus is on what students can't do, rather than on developing their strengths), and (b) teacher-centred instruction (i.e., students are expected to conform and listen passively, not given voice or choice or the belief that they are capable of having an impact on the world), Freire says, students often "succumb to a sense of fatalism. Enveloped in a culture of silence, they come to accept that this is the way things are meant to be and they lose their transformative capacities [the belief in their ability to effect change and make a difference in their world]," and, thus, disengage. A good deal of the causes of disconnection and powerlessness experienced by young people are rooted in major social divides based on class, ethnicity, and gender. Much like Noddings, Freire argues the need to incorporate the interests and concerns of students into the curriculum, because a spiritual education "challenges students to build a critical understanding of their presence in the world" and helps them acquire knowledge and resources to engage in social activism.

Teachers as Change Agents

One cannot be included if one does not belong. Noddings, in her work on the ethics of care, explicated the impact of relationships on teaching and learning. Despite power differentials, teachers and students affect each other's engagement and self-efficacy through their relating. Higher levels of belonging improve students' well-being and reduce the chances of future substance abuse, anxiety, and depressive symptoms. Positive relationships with teachers, instruction in resiliency and distress-tolerance methods, and positive classroom climates can also mitigate these negative impacts. Teachers, therefore, have the power to include the excluded by paying attention to unique needs and responding with an ethic of care. "Findings suggest a temporal sequence between positive feelings toward school as a protective mechanism for poor future mental health" (Lester, Waters, and Cross 2013, 159). Schools are effective socialization contexts in our culture and hold great influence in guiding social and emotional learning. Teachers can effectively facilitate children's social and emotional learning via classroom and school-based interventions, and teachers are therefore essential partners in building inclusive classrooms that truly celebrate diversity and allow all students to learn and grow together. This is the vision put forward in the Salamanca Statement.

In Part II, we will discuss programming from the Three-Block Model of Universal Design for Learning (TBM of UDL), from peace education, and from mental-health initiatives that can help us achieve this vision.

The Vision of Spiritual Education

In general, experiences of connectedness have been associated with the spiritual. It can be confusing to tease apart the difference between spiritual education and SEL. There are many shared values, concepts, issues, and foci. However, spiritual education places a larger focus on an existential perspective; that is, it goes beyond human relations to relations with all living things and the planet, with a purposeful or meaning-filled life, and with the conflict within, over a present reality and our ability to affect that reality. As Hay (1998, 12) contends: "Spirituality is what goes on when a person becomes directly and sensitively aware of themselves and of themselves in relation to reality." In other words, connection includes connectedness to self and connection to other in both the physical and transcendent sphere. Within schools, experiences of connectedness potentially enable individuals to rediscover and/or interact with the spiritual dimension by promoting a sense of self and place, as well as meaning and purpose. Indigenous perspectives on land-based and place-based education reflect this existential perspective. They recognize the importance of youth having a sense of who they are in the context of their natural environment. Being "a kid from the prairies," where winter survival and ice hockey are part of identity, for instance, shaped – and continues to shape – my values, experiences, and conceptual understanding.

Spiritual education is based on worldviews associated with many ancient and modern cultures that believe all living things are connected and deserving of respect. Even the most sophisticated science can neither prove nor disprove the holistic and complex interactions of all living beings on the planet, let alone the forces of the universe in general. Despite our desire to predict and control, we are limited by what we don't know, the technologies available to us, and the complexity of our natural world. Research may be our best hope for a given goal or vision. However, as a scientist, I know that denying phenomena just because we don't yet have proof is not science. Gravity, as has every other natural force, existed before we could measure it. We must entertain possibilities, seek to discover and innovate, and continue to recognize the difference between factual knowledge and wisdom.

Relationships with self and others bring passion and power to an individual's life and learning. Humans are social animals. Our initial instincts as young mammals are to fit in with the pack and model ourselves on adults as a means to survival. The awakening consciousness that takes us beyond purely instinctive living, however, begins with an external effort to embrace others who are familiar, and to connect to others who are different and unknown. Moving from tribalism to universalism requires guidance and support. Simultaneously, as adolescents explore their identity, there is a need to "go within" so the individual can discover new parts of one's self. The path leads to empathy and compassion at the outer level and to self-knowledge at the inner level. This growing sense of self in relation to one's proximal world, and to a role in the wider human and planetary community, provides a sense of meaning and purpose for the individual. It allows students to make sense of existential questions related to identity, place, and purpose – questions such as "Who am I?", "Where do I fit in?", and "Why am I here?"

Why Spiritual Education Is Critical in the 21st Century

Spiritual education is also connected to peace and social-justice education. Recognition that we are all connected gives rise to the understanding of equal rights. Scholars in peace and social-justice education suggest that rational, knowledge-based teaching is not sufficient to effect change in students' values, beliefs, and actions. Teaching about cultures and faiths around the world does not guarantee students' attitudes and prejudices will shift from what they currently believe.

> If prejudice, discrimination, and ethnocentrism can be learned, so too can peace, acceptance, and respect for diversity.

Inclusive education is directly connected to peace and social-justice education, particularly when one defines inclusion as being about all marginalized populations, not just students with disabilities. If prejudice, discrimination, and ethnocentrism can be learned, so too can peace, acceptance, and respect for diversity. As with inclusive education, there are many different approaches to peace education, but the unifying concepts remain human rights for all and the need to empower students to become agents of change. Schools and universities have significant impact on the ideas and information "known" by the populace. We can choose to have schools that promote human rights, peace, inclusivity, critical thinking, and innovation, or schools that reinforce "traditions" that continue a legacy of privilege for a minority.

Bringing It All Together

In ensouled schools, mental, emotional, and physical health and intellectual development (including academic achievement) are all connected within the concept of spiritual education. We cannot teach students human rights, inclusivity, critical thinking, and innovation or help them become powerful agents of change if we don't help them become literate and numerate, understand scientific concepts and discoveries, learn about human history and geography, or develop their ability to maintain their own health. For students to live a life of meaning and purpose, they need to see the complex web that is their world and find their place in it.

In the next three chapters, we will break down the pieces of this vision and provide more details about each remaining thread. Only then can we weave the threads together into a practical framework for classrooms and schools to achieve truly ensouled schools.

Chapter 2

Neurology, Trauma, Well-Being, and Mental Health in Our Schools

For the first time in more than 50 years, the worldwide prevalence of children's mental-health diagnoses has surpassed those of physical injury and illness. The annual direct and indirect costs of mental illness have surpassed $48.5 billion in Canada. According to Statistics Canada:[1]

- It is estimated that 10 to 20 percent of Canadian youth are affected by a mental illness or disorder – the single most disabling group of disorders worldwide.

- Today, approximately 5 percent of male youth and 12 percent of female youth, ages 12 to 19, have experienced a major depressive episode.

- The total number of 12 to 19 year olds in Canada at risk for developing depression is a staggering 3.2 million.

- Mental illness is increasingly threatening the lives of our children, with Canada's youth suicide rate the third highest in the industrialized world.

- Suicide is among the leading causes of death in 15- to 24-year-old Canadians, second only to accidents; 4,000 people die prematurely each year by suicide.

- Schizophrenia is youth's greatest disabler, as it strikes most often in 16- to 30-year-olds, affecting an estimated one person in 100.

- Surpassed only by injuries, mental disorders in youth are ranked as the second highest hospital care expenditure in Canada.

- In Canada, only one out of five children who need mental health services receives them (Smetanin et al. 2011).

Think about that. Can you imagine if only 20 percent of children who had a broken leg, measles, or even cancer got the treatment they need? Why is it that only 20 percent of youth with mental illness get the help they need? Do we not care? Or is the stigma so great that students and their families hesitate to seek treatment? Our experience tells us it's both. We care, but we have not, until recently, acknowledged the mental-health needs of our children. We believed it was a private family affair and something to be kept private. The stigma of mental illness remains significant.

---

1   See <https://cmha.ca/media/fast-facts-about-mental-illness>

Biologically, the separation of mental illness from physical illness makes no sense. All illnesses involve both biochemical and environmental factors. Genetics, organ malfunction, chemical imbalance, emotions, trauma, stress, and so forth affect cancer and heart disease, depression, and anxiety. If we take the example of diabetes, we are dealing with a malfunction of an organ in the body, the pancreas, not properly secreting the chemical it is supposed to, insulin. If insulin levels are only slightly off, then changes in diet, exercise, and behaviour may be sufficient to control the illness. If, however, the disease is significant, then we replace the missing insulin with insulin modern medicine has developed. If we look at ADHD, we are dealing with a malfunction of another organ in the body, the brain, not secreting a chemical it is supposed to, dopamine. If levels are only slightly off, then changes in diet, exercise, and behaviour may be sufficient to control the illness. If, however, the disease is significant, then we replace the missing dopamine with dopamine modern medicine has developed, called "methylphenidate" (Ritalin). If we look at depression, we are again dealing with a malfunction of the brain. The brain may not be secreting enough of the chemical serotonin, or it may lack receptors for it. If levels are only slightly off, then changes in diet, exercise, and behaviour may be sufficient to control the illness. If, however, the disease is significant, then we replace the missing serotonin with an antidepressant modern medicine has developed that blocks the serotonin reuptake. While the above is a very simplistic description of three illnesses, the point being made is valid. In all cases, an organ in the body is malfunctioning, causing a chemical imbalance, and modern medicine has developed ways of correcting the imbalance. Why is it then, that if a parent gives their child insulin to treat their diabetes, no one bats an eye, but if a parent gives their child Ritalin, they are accused of "drugging their child?" Why is there shame in taking an antidepressant, but not an antibiotic? Why do individuals feel stigmatized by seeking counselling, but not physiotherapy?

Indigenous Views of Mental Health and Well-Being

Canadian society has much to learn from Indigenous cultures. Traditional ideas of health in Indigenous cultures do not separate mental health from other aspects of well-being. Indigenous peoples' connections to the land and community (including all living beings around them) and everyday activities needed for survival include a spiritual dimension that maintain harmonious relations and balance (Health Canada).

Mino-Pimatisiwin

Mino-Pimatisiwin is most easily translated as "leading a good life." Some Indigenous Elders describe it as "walking in a good way." What is critical to understand is that the Indigenous worldview of well-being reflects the interdependent worldview of Indigenous culture. While "living the good life" in Western society is seen as an individual accomplishment, often based on monetary success, Indigenous views of well-being are a mixture of self-actualization and playing a valued role in one's community. In fact, among Indigenous peoples these two concepts are interconnected. They could not self-actualize without developing the gifts they had been endowed with from the Creator and contributing them to their community. This is not the same as destiny, which is individualistic. This definition of well-being and actualization is not a predetermined end goal, but rather a suite of gifts that one learns how to carry and use to serve.

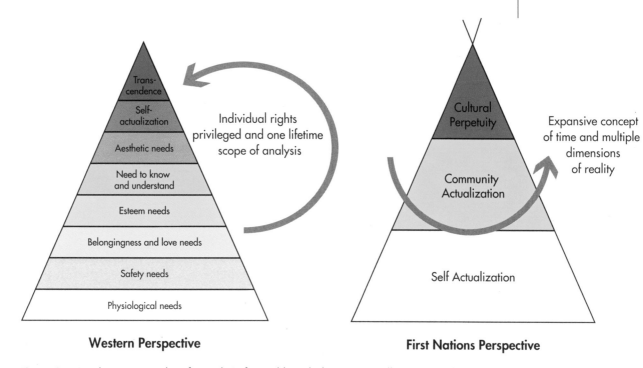

Figure 2.1 Maslow's Hierarchy of Needs (informed by Siksika Nation, Alberta). *Huitt, 2004; Blackstock, 2008; Wadsworth*

The clan system of government was also about personal relationships. Membership in a clan defined what role was expected of you, and your community counted on you to serve the greater good of the collective. Obligation was to the community over oneself. This was not thought of as self-sacrifice, but rather that "there is no me without the collective." Interestingly, it is now understood that Abraham Maslow's hierarchy of needs was based on teachings he received from the Kainai people in Alberta while doing research there. However, Maslow stepped further back than did the Siksika and stopped at the development of the individual; his triangle stops where the Siksika triangle begins. The triangle, shaped like a tepee was meant to have self-actualization as the foundation, with community actualization in the middle, and cultural perpetuity at the top. In other words, development of the self led to, and was aimed at, the strength and development of the collective. By contributing in this way, one's life contributes to a legacy that continues long after death – cultural perpetuity.

Mino-Pimatisiwin involves walking in a good way – toward being the individual you are meant to be. In pursuing that, moments of self-doubt, hardship, and trial become lessons that allow for an expression of a good life – resilience and the ability to use trial toward self-actualization.

Figure 2.2 Abraham Maslow with his anthropological team and Siksika interpreter, circa 1938

In contrast to the emphasis on the individual in many Western societies, the concept of the healthy person in Indigenous cultures relates to their role in the community, their impact on others, and the support of others for them. Interdependence, rather than independence, is valued. From a spiritual perspective, relations in Indigenous cultures include ancestral ties, which teach youth a respect for Elders and lineage, and in turn provide a sense of connectedness across time. Because of the trauma of cultural oppression and abuse, combined with this collective worldview, in Indigenous communities mental health is seen as a collective need for healing rather than as an individual failing. (In Part II, we will introduce programming to address this issue further.)

The Four Spirits

The four spirits, often represented through a visual such as the medicine wheel, reflect a contemporary view of Mino-Pimatisiwin. Although Western cultures relate to this with words such as *holistic* or *balance*, it is more than that. The 2D visual of the four spirits represents four separate concepts (physical, mental, emotional, spiritual), but these are actually intertwined. In fact, there are traditional teachings that differ from medicine wheel teachings (e.g., seven directions, which reflect a multidimensional view of human development, rather than four).

Indigenous peoples recognize you can't think about wellness without talking about the entire person. Being intellectually healthy but not spiritually healthy means an individual is not "walking in a good way." Some Indigenous Elders have articulated a developmental view that involves four stages of life (infancy, teenage, adulthood, senior/elder), each of which has four elements (mental, physical, emotional, and spiritual). Thus, emotional health for a teenager looks different than emotional health for an older person. Modern psychology recognizes this as stages, but Indigenous teachings were less defined and more of a continuum – a person could be in infancy physically, and teenage development intellectually. By Western standards, this is seen as "abnormal psychology" or "asynchronous," but among Indigenous peoples, this is a normal part of learning how to develop one's gifts.

The Circle of Courage

Martin Brokenleg developed a framework for exploring well-being that is based on the medicine wheel, which many schools use with their students. The circle of courage (COC) combines Indigenous beliefs about well-being and Mino-Pimatisiwin, and modern research on resilience. Brokenleg identifies four main human needs for growth and well-being: mastery, generosity, independence, and belonging. Mastery is developed when youth are given graduated levels of challenge and experience success, whether that is in the mental, physical, spiritual, or emotional realm. Students who experience constant failure and, therefore,

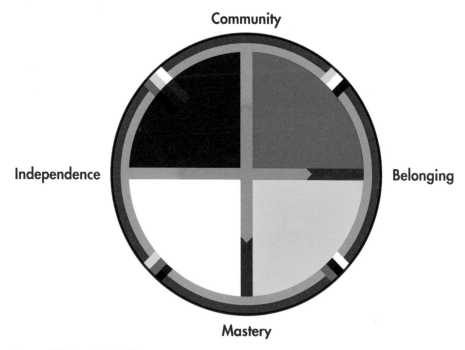

Figure 2.3 The Circle of Courage

lack self-worth and self-efficacy, are likely to demonstrate frustration, sadness, and anger – verbally, physically, and behaviourally. Generosity is nurtured in children when they learn to serve others, to appreciate the needs of the collective, and to place them ahead of their own. When students are made to feel they have nothing to offer, or when survival and trauma lead to a sense of isolation and the need to protect one's life, generosity is lost. Yet, it is generosity, the opportunity to help others, that can lift an individual out of trauma and create belonging. Independence in the COC is equated to autonomy and self-regulation. Adults are encouraged to guide, but not to direct. To learn how to self-regulate their learning and their relationships, children must be allowed to make choices, and mistakes. Finally, the sense of belonging is key in the COC. In youth, belonging is expressed through trust, friendship, and intimacy. Teachers must foster a learning community that accepts and values diverse learners to develop a sense of belonging. The circle of courage explores the needs of youth for positive development and can be used in schools as a planning tool to meet these needs.

Mental Health: Contemporary Western Views

In the rest of this chapter, we will use terms such as *mental health* and *mental illness*, because it is in keeping with the field. However, I challenge the reader to let go of any difference between mental health and health, and between mental illness and illness, and to consider the role of community and connection over the impairment of an individual.

The rest of the health field has not gone as far as eliminating the term *mental illness*. However, there has been a shift to recognizing the focus should be less on illness and more on health. For instance, the World Health Organization (WHO) defines mental health as "a state of well-being emerging from the realization of individual potential, ability to cope with normal life stressors, working productively and contributing to the community." Health Canada defines mental health as "a state of well-being that allows us to feel, think, and act in ways that enhance our ability to enjoy life and deal with the challenges we face." In both definitions, we see the balance of self-actualization and happiness, with the need for resiliency and the ability to interact with others, and less focus on illness from a diagnostic point of view.

Mental Health and Social and Emotional Learning (SEL)

At times, the two terms *mental health* and *social and emotional learning* (SEL) are used interchangeably in the literature, for understandable reasons. Both share a vision of living a life that is fulfilling to self and contributes to community. Let's have a look at the factors involved in the definitions of SEL and of mental health.

SEL	Mental Health (WHO)
Self-awareness	Realize individual potential
Self-management	Cope with normal stressors
Social awareness	Work productively
Relationship skills	Contribute to community
Responsible decision making	

Figure 2.4 SEL and Mental Health

A closer look at the above table reveals that SEL defines some of the key skills needed to achieve mental health. For example, to realize one's potential, an individual would have to develop self-awareness; to cope with normal stressors, one would need to develop self-management. In that sense, mental health is inclusive of SEL. However, mental health expands beyond it to include clinical illnesses, spiritual well-being, and more. Thus, when we refer to mental health we are talking about the big picture, and when we refer to SEL, we are focusing on some targeted skills to achieve mental health.

Positive Mental Health

Corey Keyes (2005) expanded on the dimensions of SEL and definitions of mental health with the dual continuum model of mental health. This model fits with WHO's recognition in 2004 that mental health is not simply an absence of mental illness, and incorporated both skills and the larger paradigm of mental health. In Keyes conceptualization of mental health, it is conceived as a syndrome, with measurable symptoms and diagnostic requirements. Keyes showed that data support the existence of two distinct continua (mental illness and mental health) and identified 13 "symptoms" of mental health:

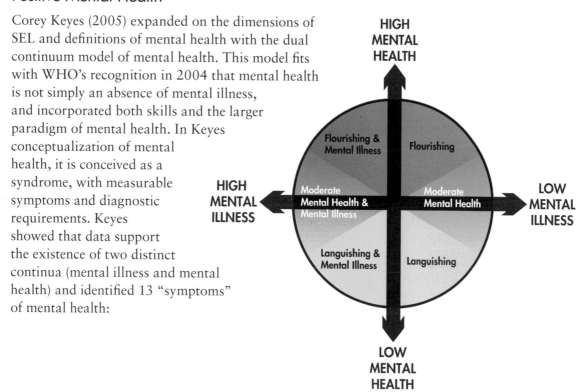

Figure 2.5 Dual Continua of Mental Health

- High emotional well-being, defined by 2 of 3 scale scores on appropriate measures falling in the upper tertile.
  1. Positive affect
  2. Negative affect (low)
  3. Life satisfaction

> Positive feelings about life, such as being "in good spirits," being hopeful about the future, and satisfied with the present.

- High psychological well-being, defined by 4 of 6 scale scores on appropriate measures falling in the upper tertile.
  1. Self-acceptance
  2. Personal growth
  3. Purpose in life
  4. Environmental mastery
  5. Autonomy
  6. Positive relations with others

> Six factors contribute to positive functioning (self-acceptance, personal growth, etc.): individuals feeling good about who they are, having goals and believing they are growing toward them, having positive intimate friendships and relationships, being able to meet their needs in their environment, and having a sense of personal power and choice.

- High social well-being, defined by 3 of 5 scale scores on appropriate measures falling in the upper tertile.
  1. Social acceptance
  2. Social actualization
  3. Social contribution
  4. Social coherence
  5. Social integration

> Individuals' experience of connection and belonging. Social coherence reflects a person's feeling of "fitting in"; that is, a sense that society's values and practices are coherent with one's own. Social actualization refers to an individual's perception of society as moving forward—the hope that "things will get better." Social integration and acceptance are feelings of being included and valued by your community. Social contribution refers to the perception that the individual is making an important contribution to society.

Symptoms of emotional well-being are determined based on participants' responses to questionnaires or interviews and relate to positive feelings about life, such as being "in good spirits," being hopeful about the future, and being satisfied with the present. In addition to these emotional states, Keyes wanted to quantify how individuals functioned in their lives, much as functioning levels are measured for depression, or disability.

Psychological well-being represents the intrapersonal, or internal, processes that an individual experiences. By contrast, social well-being represents an individual's experience of connection and belonging. Social integration and acceptance are similar to the sense of belonging referred to in the Three-Block Model (TBM) (see pages 53–55) – a feeling of being included and valued by one's community.

Similar to the specific criteria used for diagnoses of mental illness, Keyes proposed that individuals must exhibit at least 7 of 14 "symptoms of hedonia or emotional vitality" and "positive functioning" to be diagnosed as "flourishing in life." Furthermore, he proposed that under this new understanding of mental health, intervention programs must focus not only on decreasing the prevalence of mental illness, but also focus on helping individuals flourish and achieve a mental health state that includes "high levels of emotional, psychological, and social well-being." Thus, the focus of SEL expanded beyond the original five components (self-awareness, self-management, social awareness, relationship skills, and responsible decision-making) to address the larger goals of developing both the skills needed to flourish, as well as those required to mitigate mental illness. When distinguishing between happiness as short-term gratification and as longer-term flourishing, flourishing is presented as involving the search for meaning – a spiritual perspective.

The Pan-Canadian Joint Consortium for School Health (2013) elaborates:

> These positive mental health themes include: social and emotional learning, positive (strength focused) youth development, protective factors and resiliency, diversity, acceptance and understanding of student mental health needs, connectedness, strength-based perspectives, mental fitness and self-efficacy.

NOTE: In this text, we use the term *mental health* to refer to this expanded understanding of wellness, and the term *SEL* when referring to specific research, programs, and skills based on the Collaborative for Academic, Social, and Educational Learning's (CASEL's) model (see pages 15–16).

Languishing and Flourishing: The Implications for Youth

Languishing mental health is characterized by alienation, isolation, hopelessness, and the lack of a social support network. Youth who have friends and positive relations with significant adults are far less likely to have languishing mental health. In turn, adolescents who have close friendships and support at home and at school generally have higher levels of self-confidence and self-esteem. Similarly, according to Health Canada, opportunities for social interaction support the development of trust between people, a deeper sense of meaning in life, and an enhanced sense of coherence, control, and positive self-regard. These psychosocial factors then contribute to improved mental and immunological health. Flourishing mental health and positive self-esteem enable an individual to connect with and embrace a community of people. Belonging to a supportive community contributes to mental health by providing support in times of crisis, grounding in one's cultural roots, and opportunities for creativity.

So, how are our youth doing? Most students are doing well. Four out of five students report they rarely or only sometimes feel left out. That needs to be acknowledged. Nevertheless, 20 percent of our youth are suffering, and that's not okay. According to a WHO survey, approximately one in five boys and girls in grade 6 in Canada report that they often feel lonely or left out. A higher percentage of boys than girls feel they do not belong at school. This peaks in grades 8 and 9, where approximately 23 percent feel they do not belong at their school. Stress in youth is often first manifested physically, with symptoms such as headache, stomachache, backache, and dizziness. At other times, symptoms can be mental or emotional, including feeling low or depressed, irritable, nervous, and having problems sleeping. One in four grade 6 students in the survey reports having at least one of these symptoms daily, with no difference between girls and boys. Beginning in grade 7, a greater percentage of girls than boys report daily symptoms; by grade 10, the percentage among girls is 35.7 percent, or one in three girls.

And what is the number one source of stress? School.

Stress in school often presents as challenging behaviour, withdrawal, avoidance, truancy, and anxiety. Students with high stress levels react aggressively and without the ability to exercise judgment (see the next section on the effects of cortisol). While educators often assume that the stress comes from home, this denies the fundamental truth that, for many students, school is stressful. Students who struggle with the demands of traditional schooling, such as the abilities to read and write, sit still, process large amounts of auditory information, and navigate social and cultural expectations that may not be familiar to them, can find school extremely stressful and demeaning. Think about the one thing you find the hardest to do. Now imagine being asked to do it for six hours a day, five days a week, for twelve years. Don't complain, don't avoid the task, cooperate with your peers who find that task easy, and, oh, don't be oppositional! For me, that task would be sewing (I have very poor fine-motor skills). If I was asked to be a seamstress all day, every day, and a manager came by my workspace and told me to stop fooling around and finish what I was sewing, I'd exhibit oppositional behaviours, too!

The Role of Trauma, and the Promise of Plasticity

Today, neuroscience has much to contribute to classroom practice. Research has demonstrated that what happens in the mind affects the body, emotions, and spirit, which, in turn, influence learning. Our emotions regulate learning and memory. Our experiences affect us on every level. Studies in epigenetics and brain plasticity (see page 33) have provided additional promise, and questions, for the field of education.

Trauma

Trauma affects brain function. Chemical release during times of stress affects brain function and, over time, structure. When we perceive ourselves to be in danger, our brains release cortisol, a stress hormone related to adrenaline, into the bloodstream. It activates the fight-or-flight mechanisms of the brain in response to danger. Our heart rates rise, we go on alert, and we become totally focused on survival. Our brain shuts off the cortex (the part of the brain responsible for thinking and judgment) and uses only the lower, instinctual brain so that we can act quickly (e.g., throwing our hands up in front of our face to protect ourselves). This state of mind is called "fight or flight," because we look to escape the danger if we can, and otherwise fight for survival. It is an appropriate response when we are truly in danger (e.g., when in a car accident, or when chased by a dangerous animal). After the danger is gone, the brain stops releasing cortisol, and it is slowly metabolized out of our systems. Our heart rate comes down, our breathing returns to normal, and we can begin to think clearly and determine our next course of action.

Our brains are programmed to prioritize danger and safety messages, which makes sense. The problem is, our brains have not evolved to discern emotional from physical danger. Whether a tiger is chasing you, your boyfriend has broken up with you, or a pet has died, the brain's reaction is the same. It doesn't matter whether the threat is real or perceived – each results in cortisol release, fight-or-flight reaction, and, therefore, avoidance and/or aggression. A student who is worrying that they will be embarrassed in front of their peers because they can't read well, or that they will be bullied at recess, will react as if in danger. A teacher who thinks parents are being critical, colleagues or admin are not supportive, or has challenges at home, will respond similarly. As a result, students (and teachers) who are under chronic stress – who perceive themselves to be unsafe emotionally or physically – retain high levels of cortisol in their systems. These are the students who are constantly in avoidance or anxiety mode; who react to others looking at them, talking to them, or touching them; and who are aggressive and defensive over seemingly "minor things." Students in this state of being *cannot* "be rational" or "problem solve" – their cortex is not functioning well. No one reaches in on a cornered animal that is growling out of fear. We lower our voice and try to show that we are harmless and won't hurt it. So, why do we react to our students in aggressive, power-based ways and then act surprised that we "get bit"? Why do we react to an overwhelmed colleague with judgment rather than with compassion?

Long-term, ongoing stress or trauma leads to continuously high levels of cortisol. In turn, cortisol reduces the brain's ability to produce serotonin, a chemical responsible for mood and anxiety. As a result, ongoing levels of stress gradually wear down our ability to manage our emotions, and depression and anxiety are the result.

When students enter a classroom or school that feels safe to them, their cortisol levels will reduce. Regardless of what is happening to students at home or in the neighbourhood, if we create safe havens for them at school, they will be healthier and better able to learn. Even 10 minutes of meditation in a school day results in better outcomes both behaviourally and academically.[2]

But what about staff, families, and communities? Anxiety and stress look slightly different in adults – avoidance of stress in adults often presents as resistance to change or additional demands, aggression may be expressed as verbal conflict, refusal to interact/collaborate with peers, and more. The myth of resistance to change is a dangerous one. No one I know would resist a pay raise, an opportunity to travel, or other positive changes, even if there is stress involved and it requires significant effort (e.g., planning a wedding or a big trip). People resist change when they see it as overwhelmingly stressful in a negative sense, or when they

---

2   In the book *Teaching to Diversity*, we discussed programming to create safe spaces in which students' cortisol levels can be reduced. Programs such as Spirit Buddies, democratic classrooms, and the Respecting Diversity program all can help to reduce students' perceptions of danger in our classrooms.

believe themselves incapable of succeeding. So, how do we create safe, supportive environments on a larger scale? This is a critical question if we are truly to build inclusive schools. We will discuss this in detail in chapters six and seven, but a shift in our perspective must take place if we want to create schools of healing and well-being.

Complex Trauma

Most often we think of trauma as occurring due to a single, horrific event. However, researchers have begun to understand that ongoing exposure to high-stress events can also cause a form of post-traumatic stress that can have devastating effects on a child's physiology, emotions, ability to think, learn and concentrate, impulse control, self-image, and relationships with others. Complex trauma results in high rates of addiction, chronic physical conditions, depression and anxiety, self-harming behaviours, and other psychiatric disorders in later years.

Complex trauma results from repeated exposure to abuse, significant neglect, and fear for safety or survival on a day-to-day basis. Children who grow up in communities where food insecurity is common, where homelessness looms as a constant possibility, where domestic violence and addictions are common are likely to experience complex trauma. The constant fear results in damage to brain development, attachment and relationship skills, and more. The young of mammals naturally count on their parents to keep them safe and comfortable. When a parent cannot meet this need, a child's sense of safety and trust becomes threatened. They live their lives in survival mode, avoiding all possible triggers, and choosing survival over flourishing. We see these students in our schools on a regular basis, and wonder why they sabotage relationships, fight seemingly minor requests, and would rather be suspended than trust themselves or others. They are often very reactive to others' moods and behaviours – a teacher with a headache can result in a student reacting with aggression, because their perception of the teacher's facial expressions and tone of voice is that the teacher is unhappy or angry. In a home where an angry parent is dangerous, the survival reaction of the child makes sense. Unfortunately, these adaptations to a dangerous world often condemn students to a life of danger, because they may prevent positive relationships that would surround them with love, nurturing, and health.

Intergenerational Trauma

When trauma results from oppression over time and history, the negative consequences can be passed down to future generations. Intergenerational trauma has affected the health and well-being and the social disparities facing Indigenous peoples in Canada and other countries. In Canada, stress caused by the horrors of residential schools and the Sixties Scoop had significant impact on parenting, employment, education, and other aspects of Indigenous life and communities.

Intergenerational trauma can be seen on both individual and communal levels. For example, the trauma may be evident in a family where the parents or grandparents were forced to attend residential schools, and each subsequent generation of that family continues to experience trauma in some form. On a communal level, intergenerational trauma can be seen when a people have been oppressed or traumatized, and, thus, culture, parenting, and more affect the community across generations.

Direct survivors and intergenerational survivors of these experiences often transmit the trauma they experienced to later generations when they don't recognize their trauma or have the opportunity to address their mental health and well-being. Many self-destructive behaviours can result from unresolved trauma, including depression, anxiety, family violence, suicidal and homicidal thoughts, and addictions. Over time, these often-destructive behaviours become normalized within the family and their community, leading to the next generation suffering the same problems.

Epigenetics

There is a new field of neuroscience that I believe will inform, and transform, education in significant ways in the years to come. Epigenetics is essentially the study of the heredity of experience – how one's life experiences affect children through the transmission of genes and their expression. It has been shown that the children and grandchildren of Holocaust survivors have inherited certain responses to danger signals that concentration camp inmates were exposed to (e.g., the music of Wagner, which was played over the loudspeakers in Auschwitz). Some grandchildren of survivors will show stress reactions to Wagner's music, even if they have never heard it before and don't know what it is. As incredible as this sounds, it makes sense. How does a kitten know to be afraid of a dog? We have a system of passing on "danger" to our offspring, and now we realize that trauma experiences can be passed on.

This is important, because it means students whose parents have experienced trauma, or who have experienced trauma themselves, can also be affected, in terms of wellness, learning, and brain structure and function. The type and number of brain cells made, the formation of neural pathways, and the release and reception of neurotransmitters at synaptic connections occur in response to children's experience and genetics (Kessels and Malinow 2009; OECD 2007). A student whose family has had negative experiences with school may be entering our buildings feeling a sense of fear or dread and *not know why*. With the knowledge that students whose parents have experienced trauma, or who have experienced trauma themselves, can be affected in terms of wellness, learning, and brain structure and function, the importance of holistic educational systems greatly increases.

Think about it:

- What does this knowledge – that parents' trauma affects their children – mean for students whose parents had a negative school experience?
- What does this mean for Indigenous students, who likely have epigenetic cultural trauma embedded in their DNA?

If we know that beginnings may be difficult, and students need to feel safe in order for cortisol to reduce, how might this change what kindergarten, September, and morning start-up look like?

Neuroplasticity

There is some good news. Research has shown that because of the ongoing plasticity of the brain, the building of healthy peer and staff relationships at school is key to promoting long-term outcomes of health and well-being (Konishi et al. 2010; Troop-Gordon and Gerardy 2012). Trauma causes significant impairment in the brain, *but caring can lead to healing.* Despite early exposure to an environment of risk, brain pathways retain their plasticity to some extent, so an enriched environment in later years can promote well-being.

We have long known the impact of enculturation, socialization, peer modelling, and so forth. Neuroscience has begun to discover physiological systems that are responsible for these social connections and influences. Mirror neurons cause us to take on the emotions, habits, and patterns of those around us. Chemicals released by one person affect another, as in the case of pheromones. All illnesses are both physical and environmental (Polderman et al. 2015). Biochemistry and environment, genetics and life experiences, stress and grief, joy and resilience all play a role in cardiac disease as much as in depression, and early life experiences affect the later development of illnesses we term both *mental* and *physical.*

Neurocognitive research investigating the links between emotions and learning has demonstrated that for students to learn, the diversity of their needs must be recognized by teachers, and then classroom learning environments created that address social and emotional well-being and belonging (CASEL 2016). According to Hertzman (2012)

> Developmental systems theory is now the dominant paradigm in understanding children's development, and it is also now well established that the early experiences of children become biologically embedded. That is, experiences influence biological development (Nelson, Kendell, and Shields 2013, 241).

Youth who experience chronic stress incur changes in the structure and function of areas of the brain that then affect their ability to regulate emotions, process information, and remember. Cognitive functions, including neurocognitive processes, such as the ability to pay attention, retain in memory, and process language, are all mediated by social, emotional, and mental-health factors.

As teachers, we must be aware of our students' well-being. It is non-negotiable, and more important than any curriculum.

School-Based Mental-Health Services and Programs

Preventative programming can affect students' emotional resilience and well-being. In today's world, schools are the only institution that have access to all of our youth. Religious institutions do not, psychiatrists do not, family doctors do not.

As a result, schools are the only place where universal programming can occur. This reality has resulted in school-based SEL programs aimed at maximizing SEL while concurrently reducing the risks of maladaptive behaviours and mental-health problems. The conceptualization of what school mental health and SEL look like in application is emerging more fully, as an equitable partnership between schools, communities, and families. Unfortunately, the era of high-stakes testing and the pressure on teachers and schools to perform has often marginalized school mental-health programming. Yet, the need to create classroom environments that are safe for all students persists, and the evidence is mounting that doing so actually has more impact on academic achievement than many instructional practices do. For example, a large longitudinal study of SEL programs found that students who participated in such programs in grades 1 to 6 had an 11 percent higher grade-point average and significantly greater levels of school commitment, attachment, and completion at age 18. As well, school failure was reduced – 14 percent in SEL classes versus 23 percent of students in a control group. At age 18, students in the same study showed a 30 percent lower incidence of behaviour problems, a 20 percent lower rate of violent delinquency, and a 40 percent lower rate of heavy alcohol use when involved in SEL programming (Hawkins et al. 2005).

Improved mental well-being is associated with increased positive outcomes, including physical health, life expectancy, educational achievement, skills and employment rates, social interaction and participation, and fewer negative outcomes, including reduced health-risk behaviours (e.g., smoking and alcohol misuse), reduced risk of mental-health problems and suicide, and lower rates of anti-social behaviour and crime. Perhaps as a result, many governments around the world have proposed school-based mental health programming. In England, the National Institute for Health and Clinical Excellence promoted comprehensive mental-health programs involving both universal approaches (aimed at everybody) and targeted approaches (aimed at children at risk or with specific difficulties).

Often educators and governments that are proponents of the accountability agenda form of schooling look to Asian school systems that score highly on international tests. At what cost? Japan's Cabinet Office recently examined the country's more than 18,000 child suicides from 1972–2013 and found distinctly larger numbers of suicides at the end of August and beginning of September, as well as during the middle of April. The former coincides with schools reopening after summer vacation; the latter, as the Japanese school year begins. Pressure on our youth to perform and not disappoint has a cost. Japanese educators and government officials are now piloting universal school-based mental-health programming in an effort to address the suicide rate.

In Canada, as in the United States, the delivery of mental-health services in schools has been promoted and recognized as having the potential to fundamentally enhance the number of youth engaged in treatment. However, despite significant evidence for mental-health intervention in schools, implementation remains inconsistent within school districts in North America. Schools are the first line of defence in mental-health promotion. Mental-health concerns often first present as poor academic outcomes or behaviour in school, so teachers play a critical role in early intervention. Mandatory attendance at school and the natural setting of services may help address access issues, including transportation, time, cost, and cultural beliefs. As well, schools provide an opportunity for skills related to mental health, such as social skills, emotional regulation, and stress management to be practised, in a natural setting – for youth, school is the place where they will encounter many of the challenges socially and academically that are an everyday part of their lives, and where they will need to apply the coping skills being taught.

Traditionally, educators have debated whether their focus should be on knowledge development or on their role in the development of youth's social, emotional, and mental well-being. Modern science teaches us that this argument is moot, as cognitive function (including neurocognitive processes such as the ability to pay attention, retain in memory, and process language) are all mediated by social, emotional, and mental-health factors. Thus, even if one's goal is solely to improve academic achievement, the well-being of students has to be considered.

The challenge is that many teachers feel ill-equipped to provide universal supports or programming, let alone to recognize signs of illness. If we are to support the well-being of our youth and educators, training in and implementation of school-based mental-health programs is imperative. At the same time, teachers feel pressured to "get through the curriculum" and prepare students for exams. This reflects a lack of understanding that *investment in SEL and well-being will actually raise test scores more than another worksheet will*. Unfortunately, meeting children's mental-health needs is often viewed as the mission of some other agency. In turn, mental-health professionals do not always accept the criticism that their interventions for children must be more related to the core mission of school, which is learning. It is here where, once again, we must weave our systems of support together to best meet our vision for a holistic educational system. It may also involve the restructuring of some of our roles. For instance, psychologists are often used as evaluators, counsellors as academic advisors, and so forth rather than for their more professional skills supporting the well-being of staff and students.

Teacher Impacts

Implementation of school-based mental-health programming also affects teachers. Teachers exhibit high levels of stress and burnout compared to most other professions. Their unusually high stress levels have been linked to high incidences of both depression and anxiety. Research around the world, including in Australia, Germany, the United Kingdom, and Japan, have all found significant numbers of teachers meeting the criteria for having a mental-health problem – double that of the general population. High rates of languishing mental health in teachers in turn affect student learning and behaviour. A cycle of ill health is created, as factors in teachers' stress affect students. Thus, there is a need to address both student and teacher wellness in schools. Fortunately, training in school-based mental-health programs has shown to be positive. Teachers who implement programming for students in cognitive–behavioural strategies such as problem-solving, building social support and social skills, developing assertiveness and cognitive restructuring strategies to promote positive self-perceptions have shown reduced teacher stress and improved job satisfaction. Trainers in mental health are often positively affected, resulting in changes in attitude, emotional well-being, confidence, and self-awareness. However, training requires specific supports – not just professional development, but also coaching and appropriate human resources (e.g., counsellors or psychologists) – to help problem solve or provide feedback. Tyson, Roberts, and Kane (2009) state:

> With the high number of teachers seeking stress leave from work each year, and the increasing prevalence of internalising disorders in children and adolescents, this is an issue that needs to be addressed. Using teachers to run a mental-health program within the classroom could be a cost-effective way of promoting mental health for both teachers and students.

Changes in teachers' well-being might then have a positive influence on the climate of their classrooms, which, in turn, would affect students' attention, frustration levels, and acting-out behaviours.

Story 1: Ms. P

There is a heart beat underneath it all....
A few years ago I started becoming desensitized to the bad things that were happening to others. I avoided news stories that would tell of harm coming to people in the world and, in particular, children. Through all the vicarious trauma that I experienced at my old school of children going in the night and not getting that goodbye with them and being privy to CFS involvement in my students' lives, etc. In my second year of teaching, I was spending two nights a week tutoring one of my grade 5 students who was placed in the witness protection program with his family and shortly thereafter moved away with a new name and new life. I began to shut down. I know I did. In such a short time I stopped feeling deeply about not having that goodbye with my students, not being able to help them more because it was hurting too much. I placed it in a box. And it began to happen in my personal life too, but I just didn't realize it. When I did realize it the only way I could explain it to others was to say that I just wasn't feeling human. I wasn't feeling emotions as deeply as I knew I should and it was bothering me so much. This was definitely a small factor in seeking a change in schools.

I remember clearly the day that I was driving to work this year and began crying at the image of a bald child on the side of a bus. It was an advertisement for the children's miracle network and this child had clearly braved chemotherapy treatments. I realized at that moment that I had released my heart. Finally. Since then, big things and little things from world events to the feelings I have and the delight I experience from my own children have pulled on my heart.

Sounds silly now, but until this point I have attributed it to the simple act of changing buildings and removing myself from the vicarious trauma I was experiencing there that I don't experience "here". It is more than that. This change is because of the professional work that I have done with UDL, because it is always, always, always impossible for me to remove the personal aspect. Through this work I have grown as a person. I am a better mom, wife, teacher, and human. I love my kids, my husband, my students, and... I am learning to love myself more.

I have found my heart beat.

Impacts on Families and Communities

Clearly, the well-being of students affects their families. In early research, the term *family burden* acknowledged the effects a child with mental illness has on parents and siblings. Such effects included, but were not limited to, economic disadvantage (because one parent often had to stay home to be caregiver, costs associated with therapy, and potential costs related to violence or destruction), emotional stress, isolation (parents often report no longer being invited to family/community functions), and marital difficulties. More recently, the term *family impact* is being used, to remove the subjective perception of negativity inherent in the term *burden*. Families' reactions to anxiety, depression, and other mental-health conditions vary. Behaviours that one parent is distressed by and perceives as withdrawal, sadness, or nervousness, another parent perceives as sensitivity, introversion, and gentleness.

The economic costs of mental-health disorders to communities at large are estimated to be in the billions of dollars. These are in part direct costs, as when an employee takes stress leave, and indirect, as when a parent leaves the workforce, or is less productive at their job, because of the need to care for an unwell child. Social, emotional, and cultural costs are much more complex and nuanced. Socially, relationships between individuals, families, and communities may be disrupted due to languishing mental health or mental illness in individuals. Direct effects of behaviour, such as aggression or suicide, mix with indirect factors, such as disagreement over how best to respond to an individual with mental illness (e.g., jail/treatment, discipline/compassion). Families, communities, and governments must spend considerable resources responding to individuals: health-care systems, schools, police, and legal systems are all affected. One need only watch the news on any given night to witness tragedy caused by mental illness – and the impacts extend like a spider web to the doctors, nurses, teachers, police officers, and more who interact with individuals struggling with mental illness. At the same time, many of our greatest minds have at some time been touched by mental illness. It is impossible to quantify the influence of depression on Picasso's blue period or on Thoreau's writings, on Buddha's epiphanies or on Lincoln's speeches. Their impact on society is significant, despite, or perhaps because of, mental illness. Thus, while we look to reduce stress and support flourishing mental health, it is critically important we not dismiss or assume those who live with illnesses such as depression or anxiety need to be "fixed." What they *do* need is to learn how to manage these illnesses in their day-to-day lives.

Story 2: Ms. D – Resiliency in Care

School can be a protective factor in the lives of children in care. For many children who have grown up foster care, or as a ward of the Child and Family Services system, there is a recognition that school was a consistent and reliable safety net in life filled with uncertainty and tumult. Of course, for many educators navigating the complexity of the CFS system is a daunting and time-consuming task. Accessing records, getting permission slips signed, keeping track of kids after they have been moved from one home to the next, advocating for children to not be transferred out of a catchment area so that they can stay with their home-room friends and teacher; these are all difficult tasks. But as difficult as they are for teachers, they are nothing short of traumatic for children. Given the vulnerability of these children we believe that any contact between student and teacher, however short, is an opportunity to enrich their lives with those experiences that are most important to their success at school; namely belonging, care, compassion, a strong sense of efficacy and agency at school, consistency and reliability, and an opportunity to give of themselves and contribute in a meaningful way. No one knows this better than Chantelle Desorcy. Desorcy, who is currently a teacher in rural Manitoba, grew up as a child in care. Her story has very much informed the type of teacher that she has become, and is informative for us as a case study of working with children in care from a UDL perspective. As an Indigenous woman she first had the opportunity to engage with her own culture as an adult in University, something she believes children should have the opportunity to do much earlier on in life. In her own words…

Behind closed doors, there are worlds that have been shattered, truths hidden, lies, secrets, and darkness. But every door is made to be open, and eventually some light is allowed to trickle through. As I have survived and continue to live my life, I have chosen to come out beyond my room, and look back into the darkness not as a threat, but a reason to live.

As a child, you always look at life like there is another day. You don't stare watching your feet as you walk along, but you look up towards an adult, leader, mentor, or advocate. You don't understand that they may be doing the wrong thing; you look up at them to teach and to guide you, trusting your whole life to them. It is only until we grow up and look at society as a whole, do we then compare hardships, unfairness, betrayal, and morality. As a child you depend on those who are stronger than you, and those who have walked before you. You live every day knowing there will be a next, and dream of the future. My story is to inspire, not to bring hurt, anger, or pain. It is only because I once had eyes of a child, that I still survive today. With my story, I hope to remind adults of the perspectives we once had, and to remind our youth to keep our childlike focus because there is always a better future as long as we keep looking up.

I have no recollection of womb memories, but the story goes that I was beaten out of my birth mother four months premature. I was less than 30 centimeters long, and weighed 3 pounds. My birth father was violent, and affiliated with a Filipino gang, and my birth mother coped with cigarettes and alcohol. The effects on my physical body were noticeable, but my eyes were opened to life the moment I was born.

As we all get second chances at life, my mother had the same opportunity. Unfortunately she grew up in the system, and, well, history has a way of repeating itself.

At six and a half months, my two-year-old brother was pleading to 911 for help, for himself and his baby sister, because our mother was laying on the floor not far from me, bleeding, because she had been stabbed by one of our father's gang-affiliated friends. She ran out of chances, we ran out of time. We were permanently admitted into CFS.

As I turned 1, then 2, 3, 4, 5, 6, and 7, life is faded. Memories are gone except the few that taught me some critical lessons. Lessons that I never learned in school but in the wee hours at night when everyone else was sleeping. Here, in this moment of my life, I can look back as a teacher and understand what happens when you say to the student at the end of the day, "Bye, see you in the morning! Have a good night!"

As a child in the system every *bye* feels like the last time because you just may end up looking at your foster parent the wrong way – and get beat for it so bad you have to wait at home until the bruises lighten, or sent to another home. You hold onto the "see you in the morning!" because you get to have a chance to become a kid, a student, someone who can be a child, free... oh ever so free the next morning. And when you say – "have a good night", those words can help a child hold on in those late nights of being sexually abused, beaten, locked in a room with no food. Those end-of-the-day goodbyes are a child's lifeline for kids in care.

As a teacher, after a long day, you get caught up thinking about the child who chooses to crawl on the counters in the classroom instead of listening to the 100th different way you have shown them to do simple addition. As you sit and stare into the distance that night, on the couch, of why this student punches another student, or tries to bungee jump off the school play structure, or touch adults inappropriately, or says things that are just so not funny... You scream into your mind and wonder... *Why can't this kid be normal!!!* How much time and energy can we put into these children who just seem like they don't want to be there??? After so many ways of showing them how to read, or write, or do simple math, *how do they not get this!!*

And as any great teacher, after our poor-me, my-life-is-so-hard-as-a-teacher rant, you start to self-reflect. You start to question, "What am I doing wrong? What can I change to make this child change?" We start to blame ourselves and miss the big picture.

That child fights with their fists because that's all they've been taught how to communicate. The child lunges off of any play structure or plays life-threatening activities because they have never been taught how to have fun – how to play and what that even looks like. That child touches or speaks inappropriately because they have not processed what inappropriate looks like because they have not yet been shown what is appropriate. Touch to them is love, not dirty, sick, or sexual. And lastly, that child does not want to focus about how you can get 2 plus 2 in 50 different ways, orally, pictorially, symbolically, and with manipulatives because *they know.*

They have learned how to ration food because they don't know where the food will come from next. They don't need to understand money, because they will do whatever it takes to survive, to make their younger sibling happy, to get a gift for a friend because everyone else's parents bought brand new presents for a class party and, well, their cupboards may very well have a lock on them at home. That child knows what they need to survive, and in their perspective, to survive is the best knowledge you will ever need in life, and well, school – let's just say it is not a priority to get top marks, to earn a scholarship when they graduate, to win a paper award for good behavior.

School, for these children like myself, was a vacation and a chance to be a part of society. A place where I could have the chance to be who I wanted to be, or experiment with who I wanted to be like. And this is the reason why I chose this path to be an educational leader. I chose to be that one adult in that child's eyes that I can connect with. I can be that one adult, who says I look forward to seeing you in the morning – because I do. I want them to hold on, and I will make sure – everyday, that in the few hours with them, I can show them the light at the end of the tunnel. With my past, I can understand the path these children walk after school. I can make their time at school relevant because I know what is behind closed doors. Even today, as I do not walk in those shoes anymore, I find, on those really hard days when I am asking the same questions, and come to realize: Never once, as a child did my role models ask to change who I was, but modeled a life in which I could live. They modeled how I was supposed to be treated, how I should act in public, how to play and use my imagination. Today, after my educational degree, having two children, and being a teacher, I still suck at math. But I always look towards tomorrow as another day, and hope to see that child in the future, as successful as I am.

I remember my past through the eyes of a child. It has helped me survive today and will help me to help students tomorrow. You see, if I look back on my past through my eyes now, it stops me from living my life to the fullest. It steals my courage to move on. With eyes of a child, you see nothing but the future. You walk the circle of courage, seeing belonging and generosity in someone or anything, no matter what the situation is. You learn independence and you strive for mastery just so you can reach the next step. You never give up. Every day is not about survival but adventure and hope.

Chapter 3

The TRC and Indigenous Worldviews of Education for Well-Being

When European settlers to Canada decided they needed to "do away" with Indigenous cultures, we all lost opportunities – an opportunity to live in peace and harmony, an opportunity to learn from and with each other. There was, and is, much Indigenous cultures can teach us, and some of the problems we now face with the environment, the role of women, and the loss of community could have been avoided. To move forward with reconciliation, we must all educate ourselves about the mistakes of the past so that we can avoid making them again, and so that we, as educators in a country so very much in need of reconciliation, can work together with forgiveness and healing as our goal. Justice Murray Sinclair, commissioner of the Truth and Reconciliation Commission (TRC) has said forgiveness is not a necessary requirement to begin reconciliation work, as this might put unfair expectations on survivors of residential schools, the Sixties Scoop, and so forth. We recognize this truth, while continuing to work toward reconciliation and healing as our goal, in the hope that this communal work will create a better Canada for all.

While the TRC is a Canadian undertaking, the story of colonialism, discrimination, and residential schools, and the need for change and healing is a global one. The word *Canadian* or *Canada* can be substituted with the names of many other countries in much of what follows. One thing that separates the Canadian experience (or sets the Canadian experience apart) is the nature and legal effects of our treaties with First Nations. Understanding these treaties is necessary for efforts toward reconciliation in Canada.

Context and Relationship

On June 2, 2015, the TRC released its 94 Calls to Action as part of its final report to the people of Canada.[3] Participants in Ottawa witnessed many events and celebrations that drew Canadians together from across the country in a spirit of reconciliation. It was a powerful, inspirational experience. Here were people of all backgrounds and all faiths raising their voices in support of the survivors of Indian residential schools and their families. Here were people whose families originated

---

3   See <http://www.trc.ca/websites/trcinstitution/index.php?p=890>.

from other nations around the globe, who had since made Canada their home, and who were now gathered to hear difficult truths and to work toward reconciliation. Here there was no shame surrounding the abuses suffered in the past, and no silence; only a feeling of hope and optimism for a better future.

Many Canadians have either forgotten or have never learned about the partnership that founded Canada. Not every country can lay claim to that sort of history. Many nations, if we dig deep enough into their histories, are places that were founded on bloodshed, warfare, and human-rights violations. Certainly, Canada has its own history of colonialism and violence. But at its root, and in the founding documents that create the legal basis for our Confederation, it could not have been achieved without partnership with the First Nations of this land.

While this is not intended to be a chapter wholly about Canada's treaties with First Nations, it is worth noting that these treaties were originally made through the coming together of Indigenous peoples and new Canadians, as part of a new Canada, on behalf of generations of new Canadians who would later come to call these lands home. This is true for the earliest Peace and Friendship Treaties on the East Coast, which did not cede land, and continued with the post-Confederation numbered treaties, though that original spirit and intent was gradually forgotten or ignored as the young nation of Canada grew. As that spirit and intent was lost, and as newcomers and younger generations were denied the opportunity to learn about these treaties, the relationship between Indigenous peoples and settlers deteriorated. In fact, many government policies emerged with the deliberate intention of eliminating Indigenous peoples as cultural groups that had previously been so necessary to the survival and well-being of European settlers. Part of the truth we are being asked to explore by the TRC is the truth that our country is a treaty country, a country made possible through agreements between Indigenous peoples and settlers – agreements that are as sacred as they are legal.

One mistake many Canadians make when they are new to conversations about treaty agreements is their belief the treaties are so far in our country's past that their significance today is little more than theoretical or sentimental. If there was any introduction to treaties at all, the story we learned was one of bad deals signed in bad faith with Indigenous communities that were poor negotiators willing to trade away large swaths of land for trinkets and beads. Thanks to a growing emphasis on treaty education, emphasis in schools on Indigenous histories, and the testimonies of residential-school survivors, we are now being confronted with a new understanding of what it means to be Canadian. For many there is a grieving and natural frustration that comes with learning these stories for the first time – many feel robbed of a national identity that should have been their birthright. Non-Indigenous people are realizing how much has been hidden from them, and how much was lost when Indigenous cultures and peoples were segregated and marginalized. It is amazing how quickly Canadians will embrace a new national narrative when their own experiences are honoured and they are respected as potential allies. Reconciliation implies that all involved have been denied a relationship that should have always been theirs to begin with.

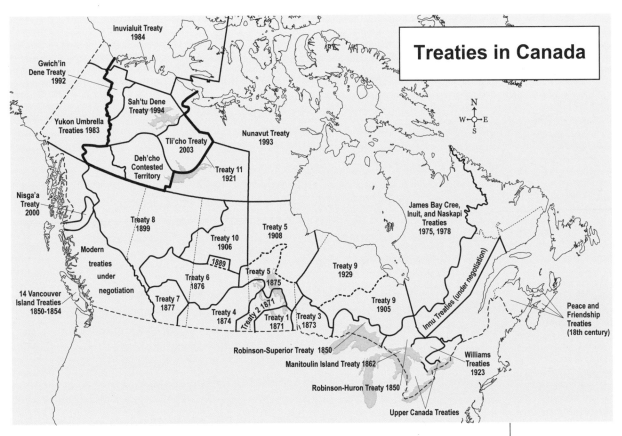

Figure 3.1 Treaty Territories of Canada

The treaties in Canada are still as legally and socially relevant today as the day they were signed. In Canada, we are all treaty people. What this means is that somewhere in our family or social history someone entered into an agreement on our behalf that guaranteed for us certain opportunities and obligations. What is special about our governments' treaties with First Nations peoples is that Canada is a nation founded on partnerships. The treaties set the legal framework for that relationship now and into the future. Contrary to the understandings, or misunderstandings, that many of us grew up with about treaties, there is nothing ancient, theoretical, or sentimental about our treaty identity. Treaties are enshrined in the "legal DNA" of Canada. For most Canadians, this should be a good thing. We can all enjoy a sense of belonging when we acknowledge "we are all treaty people" (a phrase coined by the Treaty Relations Commission of Manitoba to honour the legacy of treaties). We can also feel a great sense of relief in knowing that the treaties are enshrined in Canadian law. Today, many Canadians are just beginning to learn about how peace, friendship, military alliances, lands, and the resources upon that land were obtained through the numbered treaties. Many are just now learning how the treaties created a future for the people who would move here, the industries that would be created, the wars that would be avoided (as compared to our American neighbours whose Indian Wars lasted for 125 years), and the nation that would stretch from sea to sea to sea. Thanks to all of these, grounded in the support and partnership of Indigenous peoples, Canada has become one of the wealthiest and most successful nations in human history. Our country is the shining beacon of hope and opportunity that many people around the globe have left their homes to be part of.

For Indigenous people, their story didn't unfold anything like the way it should have, nor in the way those who signed the treaties intended it to. Indigenous people involved with these negotiations were shrewd negotiators who understood their bargaining position and used it to strategically and capably leverage for the best arrangements they could. Stories of First Nations and Inuit people as hapless participants in one-sided negotiations who traded away large swaths of land for trinkets are ridiculous fictions that have no place in the modern world. Likewise, no one at these negotiations bartered in the hope of laying the foundation for future cultural genocide, as happened to Indigenous groups.

Many people ask if these deals were signed in good faith. That's a very good question. Not all treaties were negotiated in the same contexts. For instance, the deal signed as Treaty One in 1871 occurred under circumstances very different from the later numbered treaties. In 1871, the majority of the population in Western Canada was still First Nations. First Nations people were still a vital part of the economy, and the ravages of disease had not yet played the role they soon would. Promises were made to First Nations people who sought to build happy, healthy, vibrant communities, thus, moving into the future as partners with Canada. However, the question is: Were the spirit and intent of the treaties' terms that were written into the contracts in English the same as those negotiated and understood in sacred ceremony between both signatories (who met face-to-face and often communicated through translators)? This question is unlikely to ever be answered to everyone's satisfaction. However, it is necessary to ask another question before moving forward. If these legal agreements created the framework for Canada, and for the possibility of culturally distinct communities that were happy, healthy, and vibrant, why did we end up where we are today?

The Canada of today is a place where too many Indigenous citizens struggle with adverse economic, social, and legal conditions – some of the same conditions from which refugees to Canada flee. In Canada today, Indigenous youth experience poverty at a rate greater than three times that of non-Indigenous children; 90 percent of children in care come from Indigenous families in some areas; the suicide rate for Indigenous youth is from four to eight times the national average; Indigenous youth are three times more likely to be the victims of crime; more than 1200 missing and murdered women have created a national crisis. Yet, many non-Indigenous Canadians still have no idea what their obligations are under the treaties, and many view First Nations people and their issues as a burden.

The Indian Act

The Indian Act, a unilaterally passed piece of legislation enacted in 1876 after the first numbered treaties were signed, has left a lasting impact on all Canadians.

Cindy Blackstock, a well-known Canadian scholar and activist, reminds us that Canada is the last Western industrialized nation to enforce federal race-based laws based upon blood quantum (Vowel 2016). What this means is that we collectively share a national identity where it will be impossible for many of our citizens to flourish and reach their potential as should rightly be their birthright in a country capable of so much more in terms of equity and opportunity. A full explanation and exploration of the Indian Act and its effects would be impossible here, though it will be necessary for all Canadians to become functionally aware of the damage it has created. For our purposes, let us suffice to say that the impact of the Indian Act cannot be overstated: it has undermined and affected every aspect of First Nations life in Canada since its inception shortly after the signing of the treaties.

The Indian Act dictates who is and who is not a legal Indian (Status Indian), and who is, therefore, entitled to treaty rights. The consequence of this is that, for generations, First Nations communities have been denied the right to determine who is and who is not part of their communities. The Indian Act has denied First Nations people title to the lands they live on, guaranteeing that it would be impossible to grow equity or capital on reserves. It has created separate and inferior healthcare, education, and child-welfare systems, all of which are essential for social, economic, and political well-being. It has denied First Nations people the right to leave their communities during times of sickness and poverty and has saddled communities with destabilized governance structures that are also woefully underfunded.

Perhaps the most egregious offense of the Indian Act was the creation and enforcement of a mandatory Indian Residential School system for First Nations children. This legacy saw more than 150,000 children taken away from their families and placed in schools administered by churches, destroying communities, identity, family ties, and, often, hope. Children who attended the residential schools suffered physical, emotional, sexual, and psychological abuse. At least 3201 children are known to have died at the schools. Evidence now suggests the full number may never be known, as children's bodies were buried in unmarked graves, and in some cases, in mass graves. Worse yet, some of these deaths were intentional – either due to severe beatings or deliberate exposure to disease and starvation (Fontaine, Craft, and The Truth and Reconciliation Commission of Canada 2015; Mosby 2013).

The Truth and Reconciliation Commission

The legacy of the residential schools is a long and dark one. Unfortunately, Canada has many examples of racial and cultural mistreatments, but the forcible removal of children from their families into such horrific conditions is perhaps the most disturbing example of cultural genocide in Canadian history.

More than 130 residential schools existed in the period from 1870 to 1996 (INAC). This experience of abuse, and of separation from family and culture, has had lasting, intergenerational effects. Children returned to their home communities traumatized by the abuse they had endured, ashamed of their culture, and not having had the experience of healthy parenting. They re-entered communities saddled by the Indian Act, which meant they could not own land, could not work, and were living on land that was not agriculturally productive – nor were communities near any resources that would allow for economic viability. Indigenous people required permission of the Indian agent – a government representative for the district – to leave the reserve, which was rarely granted. They faced racism and violence in towns and cities surrounding them if they did leave. Schools on reserve, funded federally according to the Indian Act, are estimated to receive 30 percent less per-student funding than off-reserve public schools receive (Drummond and Rosenbluth 2013). To this day, Indigenous students attend elementary schools that are chronically underfunded. Many schools have no computers or libraries, may lack heat or running water, and are staffed by uncertified teachers. After years of poor educational experiences, students are then expected to go to high schools off reserve and keep up with students from the town or city nearby.

The systemic racism of this legacy dooms too many Indigenous youth to a life of struggle that few manage to triumph over. To begin a healing process, with the support of the Assembly of First Nations and Inuit organizations, former residential-school students took the federal government and the churches to court. The settlement achieved as a result of this case was the largest class-action settlement in Canadian history. The agreement included financial compensation for survivors, and called for the establishment of The Truth and Reconciliation Commission of Canada.

The commission that was struck to gather information, record the stories of survivors, and make recommendations for healing shouldered a heavy burden of history and travelled a difficult journey. Listening to the stories of survivors took a toll on committee members, as Commission Chair Justice Murray Sinclair made clear when he said: "This has been a difficult, inspiring and painful journey... These were heartbreaking, tragic, and shocking accounts of discrimination, of deprivation, and all manners of physical, sexual, emotional and mental abuse."

For those involved, working on the TRC was both a labour of love and a test of resilience. Listening to the horror stories of people's experiences in the residential schools, and encountering constant racism and barriers to the process, required a heroic level of determination and care. To emerge from such an endeavour with a message of peace and healing, rather than anger and revenge, takes a highly developed spiritual essence.

The 94 Calls to Action that came out of the TRC are a road map to reconciliation.[4] Each recommendation represents a vital opportunity to redefine, reverse, or rewrite damaging aspects of the Indian Act. At the very least, the Calls to Action provide a basis to educate Canadians about what life in a Treaty country should look like in the future.

---

4   See <http://www.trc.ca/websites/trcinstitution/File/2015/Findings/Calls_to_Action_English2.pdf.>

It would be absurd to suggest that the damages created by the Indian Act haven't been most dramatic in First Nations communities; however, we are all living with the wreckage of colonialism. We all live with the social challenges created by the Indian Act. A society cannot be fully healthy, or reach its full potential, when certain citizens are denied rights and privileges on the basis of race and ethnicity. We have all been affected by the experiences of poverty in our communities, by soaring healthcare rates, and by concerns originating out of social inequity, crime rates, and abysmal education rates (it is estimated that as few as 30 percent of First Nations children coming from reserve will graduate from high school). So, too, have we all been affected by the suffering of our fellow Canadians (Richards 2014).

As well, many of us hear racial insults, jokes, and hurtful comments on a daily basis – perhaps not on the level of overt discrimination but on a much more pervasive and insidious level that some refer to as "micro-aggression" (Clark et al. 2014). Much of that racism originates from Canadians who have witnessed the wreckage of the Indian Act all around them and are horrified by it, but lack the education and awareness to understand the source and cause of what they are seeing. Justice Murray Sinclair once pointed out that while First Nations children were sitting in residential schools learning that their culture had no value or place in the modern world, the rest of Canadian children were receiving the same message about Indigenous people. This message was embedded into curricula, textbooks, lesson plans, and family conversations. In Canada, that ignorance has been passed down from one generation to the next and is nurtured by the "us vs. them" politics of the Indian Act.

Effects on Indigenous People	Effects on Non-Indigenous People
• Systemic racism	• Emotional consequences of carrying systemic racism
• Marginalization and discrimination experienced by minorities	• Guilt, shame, denial, animosity
• Effects of poverty on learning	• Thirst for healing
• Trauma, persecution	• Effects of poverty – crime, stress, addiction, mental health
• Impacts of the Indian Act	• Trauma of fearing the other, of seeing suffering
• Watching the wounds imposed on Mother Nature	

Figure 3.2. Recognizing the Shared Effects of Canada's Colonial History

The broken relationship between Canada's Indigenous and non-Indigenous peoples affects our children, not only in the economic and social sense, but in their education, as well. When Indigenous students struggle within our schools, non-Indigenous students bear daily witness to the suffering, frustration, and failures their classmates' experience. Resources and teacher time are spent dealing with problems, rather than with creating success. From a Universal Design for Learning (UDL) perspective, all of our students affect the community of care we are seeking to create, and what benefits some affects all. Unfortunately, what hurts some affects all, as well.

The Role of Schools and Teachers in Reconciliation

Education played a huge role in getting us into this mess, and education must play a huge role in helping us get out of it.– Marie Wilson, member of the Truth and Reconciliation Commission

As we think about reconciliation, we must ask ourselves two important questions:

1. Why are these Calls to Action being asked of us?
2. Would our communities and nation be better or worse off if these Calls to Action were fulfilled?

Much harm was done in the name of education, teachers, and schools. While today's teachers did not participate in that harm, we can be part of the healing.

> While today's teachers did not participate in that harm, we can be part of the healing.

However, for many teachers, talking about Indigenous issues can be overwhelming. The collective term *Indigenous* refers to First Nations, Métis, and Inuit people in Canada. But there are hundreds of First Nations, each with its own culture and history. Teachers fear making mistakes in bringing forward the perspectives of a culture and people that is not their own. Many teachers may also be learning about residential schools for the first time, even though they may see the impact of it every day, and feel unqualified to share these difficult stories of Canadian colonialism with their students. We acknowledge all of these barriers as fair and legitimate, but also want to encourage teachers to overcome them. To not do so is to perpetuate the silence and ignorance of non-Indigenous people for yet another generation. We encourage all teachers to educate themselves as much as they can; to seek out and connect with Elders who can support their own and their students' learning; to find resources related to Indigenous worldviews, treaties, subject-specific content, and residential schools; and to be willing to learn alongside their students in an open-minded way. We teach about ancient Egypt – and we weren't there, either!

Statistically, Indigenous students struggle academically more than their non-Indigenous peers. Today's Indigenous students may be intergenerational survivors – another legacy of residential schools. The TRC often heard survivors say their biggest regret was how their experiences affected how they raised their own children. Some parents – having no experience of child rearing in their own cultures – only knew how to parent using harsh discipline. Some did not know how to create a nurturing environment. Some abused alcohol or drugs to cope with the trauma of their residential-school experiences. We don't yet know the epigenetic impact of the residential schools, but it most likely influences students' experiences of schools and schooling.

Reconciliation in schools means educating for change, equity in education, and reclaiming identity for Indigenous students and for all Canadians. In bringing us together, reconciliation enriches the lives of all of us.

Education as a Way Forward

Educators have a particularly significant role to play in two of the TRC's Calls to Action:

62. We call upon the federal, provincial, and territorial governments, in consultation and collaboration with Survivors, Aboriginal peoples, and educators, to:

    - Make age-appropriate curriculum on residential schools, Treaties, and Aboriginal peoples' historical and contemporary contributions to Canada a mandatory education requirement for Kindergarten to Grade Twelve students.

    - Provide the necessary funding to post-secondary institutions to educate teachers on how to integrate Indigenous knowledge and teaching methods into classrooms.

    - Provide the necessary funding to Aboriginal schools to utilize Indigenous knowledge and teaching methods in classrooms.

    - Establish senior-level positions in government at the assistant deputy minister level or higher dedicated to Aboriginal content in education.

63. We call upon the Council of Ministers of Education, Canada to maintain an annual commitment to Aboriginal education issues, including:

    - **Developing and implementing Kindergarten to Grade Twelve curriculum and learning resources on Aboriginal peoples in Canadian history, and the history and legacy of residential schools.**

    - **Sharing information and best practices on teaching curriculum related to residential schools and Aboriginal history.**

    - **Building student capacity for intercultural understanding, empathy, and mutual respect.**

    - Identifying teacher-training needs relating to the above

In particular, the first three sub-points under point 63, emphasized above, rely on teachers.

While some teachers may not feel capable of developing the curriculum, we must all take part in implementing it. The only way forward is to learn about each other, about both the gifts and the mistakes of the past, in a mutually beneficial way. Resources are being developed across the country, and many are available online. There are also many novels, picture books, and videos teachers can use (see appendix A). Make it a fun, collaborative endeavour at your school! Although some of the content is difficult, the ultimate message is of the final point in the highlighted list above – creating a world of intercultural understanding, empathy, and mutual respect. What greater purpose is there for us as a profession?

Remember the second of our two questions: Would our communities and nation be better or worse off if these Calls to Action were fulfilled?

Chapter 4
Leadership for Inclusion and UDL

We have already defined a vision of inclusion: creating learning communities that honour the diversity in all our students. Now, let's explore universal design for learning (UDL) as a framework for achieving inclusive classrooms.

Universal Design for Learning

UDL is an educational approach based on the architectural concept of universal design (UD). UD was conceived in the 1980s by Ronald Mace (Messinger-Willman and Marino 2010). Mace sought to design architectural projects that were accessible to people both with and without disabilities. Subsequently, in the 1990s, David Rose, Anne Meyer, and their team at the Center for Applied Special Technology (CAST) extended these ideas into the classroom, adding the *L* (for "learning") to UD. They define UDL as a method of designing learning environments that are accessible to all students. The CAST team cluster their ideas around three main principles. First, the principle of "multiple means of representation" suggests that curricula should be presented in multiple ways to support students in understanding the content. Second, the principle of "multiple means of action and expression" promotes supporting students to use multiple and flexible modes to express their understandings and processes of learning. Third, the principle of "multiple means of engagement" supports students to sustain interest and self-regulate their learning. CAST's model initially focused heavily on the use of technology to support accessibility for students who faced barriers to their learning. For instance, a student unable to read a textbook could be given read-aloud software to provide them with access to the information. More recently, CAST has expanded beyond the use of technology to include social and emotional strategies.

The Three-Block Model of Universal Design for Learning

As with spirit, there are many paths to the same goal. The purpose of this book is to support schools in creating a healthy environment for all who enter them. The Three-Block Model (TBM) is one way of doing that (see page 8 for concept map). The TBM shares many common elements with CAST's model, particularly in its vision. Who could argue with the desire to help all students successfully participate in their classes? However, there are also some differences, perhaps mediated by the different contexts we work in (Canadian and American).

The TBM is based on four pillars and four visions.

The pillars are: self-worth, belonging, cognitive challenge, and social (interactive) learning. These form the theoretical underpinnings of the model. The four pillars are used as a decision-making filter. This means that educators make decisions about designing environments, programming, and interactions based on the ability to develop self-worth and belonging, provide cognitive challenge, and create opportunities for students to learn in interaction with each other (i.e., such learning experiences are not teacher centred, and not delivered through an educational assistant, with students segregated from their peers). If a school is considering adopting a program, it must assess its ability to develop one or more of the pillars, without doing the opposite – humiliating or stigmatizing students, segregating, dumbing down, or providing a program that denies students access to the general curriculum in interaction with their peers.

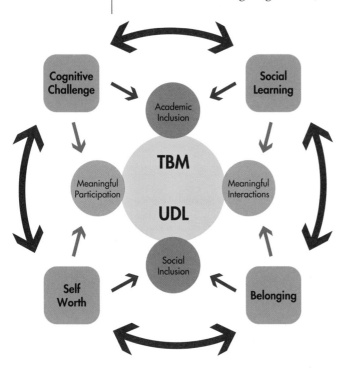

Figure 4.1 The Four Pillars and the Four Visions of the TBM

The four visions are what we hope to see in the classroom – social inclusion, meaningful interactions, academic inclusion, and meaningful participation. To be meaningful, interactions must go beyond tutorial, helper/helpee relationships to opportunities for students to interact as true peers and develop equal friendships. Meaningful participation implies that students who are included, particularly those with disabilities but also other marginalized populations, are involved in learning activities beyond a token role such as, for example, handing out the materials or colouring.

To have meaningful interactions, students must have a sense of belonging – of being part of the classroom and school community – and opportunities to interact with their peers with a vision to equality (i.e., developing authentic friendships, not just hierarchal relationships that involve being helped, or helping another).

Similarly, to meaningfully participate, students must have learning opportunities designed to provide multiple levels of complexity, so that students with varying skills, abilities, background knowledge, languages, and so forth, can work together with the knowledge that they are capable of doing so.

These pillars and visions do not apply only to students. All the adults in the school, from admin to teachers to support staff, matter, too. How do we help them feel a sense of self-worth in the context of this community? To do so, all staff need to feel they have something of value to contribute, that they are making a difference and are appreciated for it. Is it possible to create a sense of belonging and community, especially in large urban schools where staff disperse to many different neighbourhoods when the bell rings? I believe it is possible, and methods for doing so will be addressed in chapter 10. If educators can be supported to develop the spiritual dimension in their own lives, including in the workplace, they will be better able to recognize it in their students and be able to intentionally plan to support their students' growth and development.

What about families and community members? What do meaningful interactions look like in the context of teacher-family relations? Research has shown that parent involvement leads to positive educational outcomes, including improved student engagement, behaviour, test scores, and academic achievement (Anderson and Minke 2007). One of the most powerful factors shown to influence parent involvement is school staff's "beliefs as to why parents are not more involved." As teachers, we have to rethink our judgments about parents and acknowledge that we might be wrong. It's important to be aware of our prejudices. Ask yourself whether you are judging, and on what evidence? Families struggling to make ends meet are more likely to have both parents working at low-paying jobs, with little control over hours, often having to take shift work at night. As a result, involvement among low-income parents is limited in terms of time and/ or money. These parents may be unable to attend conferences with their child's teacher or a performance that involves their child. They may not be home in the evening to help their child with homework, or may not speak the language well enough. They may be unable to participate because their sociocultural values and practices conflict with those of the school (e.g., when a parent places significant value on religious ceremonies). They may need their child to look after younger siblings or work in a family business, each of which interferes with schooling.

Assumptions that parents don't care about their child's education, are controlling, or are unable to contribute to their child's education or the school community create a self-fulfilling prophecy. Parents recognize that they are not valued or are being judged, and retreat. In effect, our judgmental nature negatively affects the self-worth and belonging of parents, and so they believe they have nothing to offer. If we suspend our judgment, and ask questions instead, often we discover the barriers and fears behind parents' lack of participation. Furthermore, parent involvement has been shown to be significantly affected by parents' educational expectations for their child and their perceptions of the school empowering the parent, as when a school asks parents to share their knowledge and expertise, places value on a parent's goals for their child, or provides specific strategies a parent can use to assist their child. Thus, reporting to parents about their child's strengths becomes critical, because it can raise parent expectations, and empower parents to believe they have done something right.

The challenge is that many teachers feel ill-equipped to provide universal supports or programming, let alone to recognize signs of illness. Thus, if we are to support the well-being of our youth and our educators, training in and implementation of school-based mental-health programs, and holistic education, are imperative.

Leadership in an Inclusive Culture

Law, policy, and reforms to overall education have addressed the need for a move to inclusive education in every province and territory in Canada and every state in the United States, and, indeed, around the world. Despite this, a large number of students with disabilities continue to be excluded from the regular classroom. The role of school principals in this issue has changed. At one time, principals were seen as managers of a system, not responsible for determining vision or implementing evidence-based practices. More and more, however, principals are expected to embody educational and instructional leadership. As such, the responsibility of implementing law and policy related to inclusion and improving student outcomes now falls within a school leader's purview.

If inclusion is implemented through both policy- and evidence-based practice, then it is incumbent on school leaders to further its implementation. According to Fullan (2013): "the moral imperative in education consists of the deep commitment to raising the bar and closing the gap for all students." However, with so many different definitions of inclusion found in the field, there is a lack of consistency in policy and practice. Thus, the role of the educational leader becomes paramount in steering schools toward a shared vision. Often, leaders who are successful in moving their schools toward a more inclusive model do so by sharing a vision, taking a strong leadership position on what is expected, and then gradually releasing responsibility to a more distributed form of leadership that empowers teachers to assume leadership roles.

The impact of inclusive education has at times been negative on teachers (Brackenreed 2011). According to the Canadian Teachers Federation, 47 percent of teachers quit before retirement age, citing stress and lack of support as reasons. Many factors affect the perception that the demands on teachers are too great, and school leaders – including government, school-district personnel, and principals do not provide them with the support they need. Teachers often cite a lack of resources including staffing and teaching materials, and the seemingly endless list of programs they are asked to implement above and beyond the curriculum (e.g., anti-bullying, anti-racism, drug awareness, sex education). Global research demonstrates that teachers support the philosophy of inclusion (Ross-Hill 2009). However, they feel ill-equipped to teach diverse learners, and this becomes another source of stress due to their perceived inability to "meet the needs." In fact, a positive attitude has been shown to increase burnout, perhaps because those who believe strongly in the value of inclusion are most stressed by their perceived inability to make it work. For many teachers, it is the organizational climate that most affects their level of burnout. The feeling of being isolated, unsupported, and constantly having to overcome systemic barriers has the same effect on teachers that it does on students – alienation and disengagement. Losing one half of the workforce is destructive to everyone – the school community, the students, and the teachers themselves. It is, therefore, critical that a process for providing organizational support be identified. As leaders, school principals are expected to set direction, develop capacity, and redesign the school.

Effective Leadership for Inclusive Education

At all levels of leadership (including school-district and school-based administrators, consultants, and resource teachers), the challenge is to balance the need to develop teachers' capacity to implement inclusive education and meet the needs of diverse learners, with creating a supportive environment that recognizes the needs of all adults involved. School leaders, resource teachers, and consultants are critical facilitators – supporting teachers, who in turn, support those students who are otherwise marginalized or excluded. It is incumbent on leaders, then, to support both staff and students while holding high expectations for both. Leadership is especially important in schools serving diverse students; leadership for diverse populations needs to be practised differently. Prominent scholars in the educational leadership field, such as Mel Ainscow, Michael Fullan, Andy Hargreaves, Kenneth Leithwood, and Carolyn Riehl, suggest that developing teachers' capacity to teach in powerful ways and creating a sense of community are critical to leading inclusive schools.

Leaders who can build capacity in personally supportive ways are therefore likely to reduce teacher stress. One factor in doing this is the move toward collegial/collaborative decision-making and distributed leadership. Teachers must be empowered as active participants if systems change is to be sustainable. Effective leaders of inclusive education, then, must balance visionary, instructional, and servant leadership – prioritizing one over the other can create conflict. For instance, a principal who focuses on instructional leadership may be perceived as critical and judgmental of staff, resulting in resistance to change. On the other hand, a principal who focuses on servant leadership may hesitate to have the hard conversations that may be required to move teachers who struggle with change and shifting expectations to move forward. Thus, a leader who holds a vision of a healthy, inclusive school for all members of the community needs to strike a dynamic balance of supporting teachers while also maintaining the expectation for growth and participation in that vision. This sounds complex, but, in truth, it is the root of all education – teachers balance relationships and know when to push their students every day. So, too, must educational leaders.

Inclusive leadership requires building students, since teachers' attitudes and bel follows some consistent patterns, and aw assess progress and provide supports.

- **The Adoption Curve**

    Change begins with a small perce and pilot new ways of solving a pr the original inventors have design a slightly larger group of people, (learning about the innovation and people who line up to buy the nev projects or research, and regularly what might be ahead. Every scho

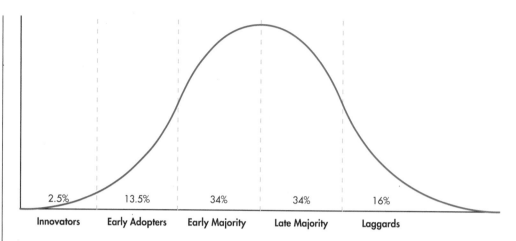

Figure 4.2 Rogers Adoption/Innovation Curve

to trying something new. When the early adopters begin talking about what they are doing and the results they are seeing, the early majority begin to get interested. These are people who are not afraid of change, but who wait and watch before jumping in. They want others to work the bugs out. They need evidence of efficacy, and then they will join in. The late majority are a little more hesitant, but will follow when it becomes clear "this is the way we are going." Finally, a small percentage of people are truly anxious about change. They will require significant time, effort, and support to bring on board (Rogers 2003).

· **Individual Change** (Majority of people)

As individuals, when we are introduced to something new, we follow a fairly consistent pattern. The start of change comes out of an awareness of an issue – the desire to "do better" at whatever we perceive as not being optimal. We investigate possible solutions, and gauge whether the effort

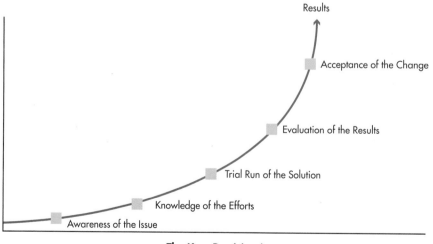

Figure 4.3 Individual Change Curve

will be worth it. Assuming we decide it is, we usually try the innovation, and watch the results carefully. If we see the change we were hoping for, we will then begin to adopt the change as part of our practice.

- **Individual Change** (Laggards)

  For some people, change is very anxiety provoking. They respond to any suggested change with fear. Often, the response to their fear is judgment from colleagues and leaders. We call them "resistant," "stuck in their ways," and other pejorative terms. In the same way we must stop responding negatively to students who show avoidance and anxiety, so too must we stop judging our colleagues. They may be adults, but that does not belie the possibility that they have or are experiencing trauma, that they lack self-efficacy or the ability to trust those around them. It is a normal reaction to anxiety and stress to want to deny ("Oh, this is just another fad"), become irritated ("What else are they going to add to my plate!"), bargain ("If they're going to add more stress, then don't expect me to…"), and become discouraged ("I just can't do this – I quit!"). If those around them respond negatively to their protests, these individuals are likely to stay in this place of fear and low self-efficacy, and become a difficult member of the staff and a negative influence on culture.

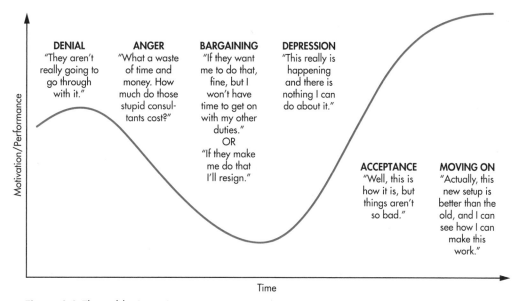

Figure 4.4 The Kubler-Ross Curve

Irvine et al. (2010) recognized "striving for authentic inclusion amidst the day-to-day tensions school administrators' face is not an easy task." Diversity creates complexity in community building, so leadership is especially important in schools that serve diverse student populations (Leithwood and Riehl 2005). The challenge for principals is that they must establish conditions that not only support teacher professional learning for student achievement but also equity and justice. Leithwood and Riehl describe the following priorities for the administrator striving to serve diverse populations that align well with the TBM of UDL.

Building Powerful Forms of Teaching and Learning

School leaders must support teachers to develop their vision and capacity for inclusive practice. As Sun and Leithwood (2015) note:

> Transformational School Leadership (TSL) emphasizes leaders' developing a compelling vision, providing individualized support and intellectual stimulation to staff, and engaging them in the achievement of shared goals. These leadership behaviors are intended to appeal to organizational members' basic values, build the organizations' capacities to realize those values, and enact practices aimed at achieving shared goals consistent with those values.

Professional Learning Communities (PLCs) are essential to inclusive education. Traditional methods of professional learning seat expertise outside of the teaching community in which it takes place. This creates the perception that "it takes an expert," and when the expert is not present, implementation is not possible. PLCs can develop educators' self-efficacy and change school culture, but they require specific conditions and supports such as (Wood 2007):

- developing and supporting teacher agency and voice
- discussing the benefits of teacher collaboration for well-being and instructional practice
- identifying enabling and constraining institutional and policy conditions, and flexibly approaching or changing them (i.e., there is more than one way)

Developing and Supporting Teacher Agency and Voice

The goal of PLCs is for teachers to work together to seek answers to their own questions and challenges related to instructional practice, develop a professional identity that encourages ongoing learning and collaboration, and build capacity through both knowledge rooted in educational theory and research and their lived classroom experiences. This kind of professional development re-conceptualizes teachers from workers to professionals – moving from workshops focused on instruction in techniques to developing professional knowledge and judgment.

Like any group process, PLCs require facilitation. They are new to many teachers who are used to outside experts providing workshops. Groups are likely to be made up of people at different levels of knowledge and comfort with change, and facilitators require coaching skills to create a safe space for dialogue and sharing.

Teaching diverse learners is challenging and ever-changing. This shift to professionalization is critical because schools are not assembly lines – the job changes day to day and year to year. Teachers and staff require an environment in which there is ongoing professional development supported by a sense of community, and in which innovation and risk taking are valued.

However, building inclusive learning communities requires systemic, school-based redesign to transform a special-education mindset. Human resources, such as the support of resource teachers, clinicians, and educational assistants move to push in services, working collaboratively with classroom teachers to support students in the classroom. Curricular resources refocus through a diversity lens: for instance, instead of spending thousands of dollars on a class set of novels or textbooks, multiple copybook sets at varied reading levels, technology, and hands-on materials are purchased. At the same time, research shows that administrators who made top-down decisions undermined teachers' faith that the learning community initiative was really meant to live up to the rhetoric. Leaders must, therefore, develop the skills of what Simon Sinek, in a renowned TED Talk, refers to as the ability to "communicate the 'why.'" That is, leaders who can help teachers to understand *why* the change is needed can support teachers to engage in a professional-learning journey toward effective inclusive practice. This differs significantly from a system in which professional development is decided by administrators, assumed to be the same for everyone, and defines teachers as technicians and teaching as the implementation of others' ideas. Educational history is gendered and ageist – young women became teachers straight out of high school, and older males were the managers. Given this history, it is not surprising that the legacy of it has resulted in a lack of professional perspectives regarding the role of teachers. It is time for that to change.

Discussing the Benefits of Teacher Collaboration for Well-Being and Instructional Practice

A safe and trusting environment is critical for all human learning – not just student learning. We cannot ask teachers to move from the isolation of their classrooms to publicly sharing their practice without ensuring they will be met with support and nonjudgment. Thus, professional learning communities cannot be effective without a safe and trusting environment. Leaders can develop such a culture through implementing many of the same structures that teachers do in their classrooms. Engaging in team building, running staff meetings using a structure similar to class meetings,[5] developing a staff profile of strengths and needs, and so forth, can be as effective with adults as they are with children.

Just as teachers should not work in isolation, schools likewise benefit from connecting with each other. Principals should interact with other school leaders in their communities to share innovative practices, resources, and solutions to problems within and across schools so that they are not constantly "reinventing the wheel." Scanlan (2009, 622) describes how serving students with disabilities is often "an isolated endeavor of individual school leaders working to reform a specific school rather than an effort undertaken by colleagues working across a system." School districts, therefore, play a critical role in scaling up change initiatives and ensuring sustainability. A clear vision and message must be sent

---

5   Information about effective class meetings can be found on p. 56 of *Teaching to Diversity: The Three-Block Model of Universal Design for Learning* (Jennifer Katz, Portage & Main Press, 2012).

across schools that inclusive practices are expected and permanent. Otherwise, inclusion will be seen as a passing trend that won't outlive the tenure of an individual principal.

Identifying Enabling and Constraining Institutional and Policy Conditions, and Flexibly Approaching or Changing Them

Teachers appreciate a leadership that facilitates the implementation of inclusive education and the creation of positive working conditions. For leaders, this means several things:

At the school district level, leaders need to create policy, budget resources, hire staff, and provide supports for their staff's well-being. Leadership goes beyond district-level issues. School districts that are successful at effecting change advocate for their teachers' and students' needs with government. Even if unsuccessful, this advocacy sends a message to staff that everyone is on the same team. School districts in which teachers perceive leadership as putting more barriers in their way, rather than doing what they can to make teachers jobs less stressful and more enjoyable, are doomed to failure. For instance, one district I worked with promoted the TBM as a framework for inclusive education, but then required teachers to (a) enter grades onto a website every two weeks so parents could see how their children were doing, and (b) assess students' reading on a benchmark scale and post students "progress." These requirements conflict with the premise of UDL – ranking students and expecting diverse learners to achieve a singular "benchmark" are inherently biased, deficit based, and damaging to students' self-concept. One teacher I worked with made statements like: "Well, I can't do UDL because I have to spend my time getting marks." Another asked: "Well, if they want us to pay attention to diversity and social and emotional learning, why are they publicly posting students' reading levels?" Good question. While it is possible to "do UDL" in a system that is focused on accountability, a mixed message to staff is disheartening.

At the school level, principals must mirror these same considerations. Principals must be seen by their staff as advocating for them, and doing their best to remove barriers that cause teachers additional work and stress. Flexibly using budgets, scheduling common planning times and collaborative opportunities, minimizing paperwork, and recognizing that fair doesn't mean everyone needs the same thing requires leaders who know their people.

Nurturing the Development of Families' Educational Cultures

Teachers and administrators face challenges adjusting to ever-increasing levels of diversity, but, in truth, these challenges pale in comparison to the challenges faced by diverse students and their parents. Parents see the potential in their children, the gifts they bring, and the community they bless. Parents of children with disabilities or who are disadvantaged in some way are not blind to the barriers their children face – but they also see the possibilities when their children are offered opportunity. For decades, parents of students with disabilities have been told that what was best for their child was intensive supports in small-group, specialized settings. These beliefs stemmed from a pedagogy of special education and disability – disabled students were limited in their possibilities for learning and required one-to-one intervention.

Families play a significant role in all three aspects of the TBM, and it is crucial that educators invite, value, and use the gifts families can offer not only to their children, but to the community as a whole. Parent involvement leads to positive educational outcomes, including improved student engagement, behaviour, test scores, and academic achievement. Home-school collaborations can positively affect a student's sense of self-worth and beliefs about self-efficacy. When students are valued for who they are and connected to their classroom, school, and communities, then families clearly influence this outcome. This requires that educators examine how they might influence family involvement, both positively and negatively. In doing so, they should consider the barrier that trauma might play. Parents who have had traumatic experiences with schools and schooling may not respond to the usual invitations. Educators may feel they have done everything they can to reach out and invite a family in, to no avail.

In the case of Elvin (Katz 2017), I arranged to meet his mother at a coffee shop. It was neutral ground, and the setting created a casual, social atmosphere that put his mother at ease. It wasn't a "meeting," it was "coffee." There, we sat and worked to change Elvin's program (i.e., his I.E.P.) from a deficit-based intervention focus to one that honoured Elvin and his culture. In time, Elvin came home happier and shared his experiences with his mother. A message from his teacher reflects the power a change in our approach can have:

> We recently had a team meeting to review Elvin's progress… it was the first time his mother and grandmother came into school, answered their phone, or communicated at all in the three years he has been here. I was frustrated that they didn't seem to care. Now I realize that was not true – we just had such a negative perspective about Elvin. We tried to couch it in concern and care, but really, I never valued his strengths. It was all about his behavior and what he couldn't do.

Communication with families is essential to student success. The work of leaders in creating an inclusive school community acknowledges the importance of family, community, mentorship, pride, and responsibility. Creating a culture of inclusion requires a strong emotional commitment from principals, teachers, and families. To participate in inclusive educational leadership needed to address diversity, leaders must commit to making actual change in social conditions of students and advocate for those who have not always fared well in our system.

Expanding Social Capital

The concepts of social capital, social value, and social-role valorization (SRV) are all related. In essence, the idea is to consider how we help all students to have valued roles in their classrooms and school community. Out of this comes a sense of pride for students and respect from their peers. It provides students with social networks and support, and a community that recognizes what they have to offer. One student I worked with told his mother it didn't matter if he went to school, his group didn't need his help with the project. This was a student with tremendous creativity, problem-solving skills, and constructive abilities (i.e., building models, puzzles, and so forth). Yet, because the "project" was purely verbal-linguistic in nature, he felt he was useless to his group. His peers are likely, under these circumstances, to devalue him as a group member, as he had devalued himself. Another student does not have a computer at home and has to look after younger siblings in the evenings, and so can't contribute to her research group's study. Another student helps the caretaker collect and sort the recycling, but he is the only one who does it, and he has a visible disability. Again, in all of these cases, social value is being removed from these students, and the ramifications of that are significant. In the classroom, all students should be provided work in which they experience success and from which they gain academic knowledge and skills that are socially and culturally valued by others. Students can all learn that every member of the classroom brings valued skills, perspectives, and background knowledge with them to their social relationships and academic learning.

At the secondary level, social capital expands from a focus on valued roles in school to students' social networks and roles for transition. When I left school, I had relatives who gave me my first job, and to this day, there are family members I can rely on in any number of instances. For many students, these networks don't exist. Leaders in high schools can implement mentoring programs, work placements, and other such community-based opportunities to help students expand their network and social capital.

Staff also need to see their role as valued. When I spoke to the bus drivers in one district and explained that they were some students' first connection every day, and could set the tone for that child's day, they were shocked – but it's true. What difference must a driver make who greets kids with a smile and by name, and plays some fun music on the bus, versus a driver who is angry, yelling, or ignoring the kids? Anyone who works in schools knows how important the school secretary is to our relationships with parents, as well as with students. The disrespect sometimes given to teaching assistants, itinerant teachers, and teachers themselves affects school culture.

The TBM of UDL emphasizes developing students' higher-order thinking, and involving all students in activities related to the general curriculum (Katz 2012). As excellence for all is the goal of UDL, it seems an appropriate framework for providing school leadership with a coherent pedagogy for supporting inclusive education. In the model, a Response To Intervention (RTI) framework is used to create teams that co-teach and provide service delivery to all students in the regular classroom, using such inclusive practices as differentiation, inquiry, and other evidence-based strategies. However, implementation of a comprehensive framework for inclusive education requires significant professional development, and the guidance of a transformational leader.

Chapter 5
Weaving the Threads

From Distress to Success

The greatest danger of the dialogues about reconciliation, inclusive education, and mental health is that they stay just that – dialogues. Without action, they become nothing more than talking points that breed further frustration, and, unfortunately, likely lead to beliefs that they are not possible. Many teachers support inclusive education, and understand the importance of reconciliation, but get tired of rhetoric and policy without an actual "how-to" plan for implementation. Healing generations of trauma and exclusion, whether one is thinking of the treatment of Indigenous peoples, the exclusion

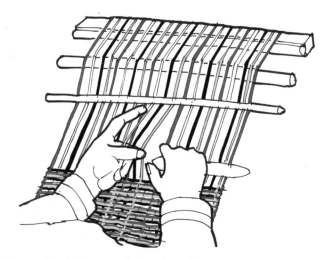

Figure 5.1 A Tapestry of Mental-Health Programming

of students with disabilities and other differences, or institutionalization and the stigma of mental health, is a complex process and does not come with easy or instant answers.

So, how do we move from discussion to action?

Aside from the obvious complexity of resolving centuries of trauma, discrimination, and exclusion, there is also the concern about the well-being of teachers. Just how much can we add to teachers' plates? We have already discussed the concerns over teacher retention rates and burnout. How can we now ask teachers to become involved in such complex, and difficult, issues?

The answer comes in what we know about *connection*.

We know trauma and exclusion affect both the perpetrator and the victim. Our classrooms become happier places for teachers to teach when they are happier places for students to learn, and vice-versa. There is no getting away from this interdependence. Students, teachers, families, and communities are all affected by the experiences of our youth in school. Students who feel unwelcome, unsafe, and alienated disengage from learning, and often become disruptive in the classroom. The cycle of unsafe classrooms moves from student stress/disengagement, to challenging behaviour, to teacher stress, to suspension or punishment and further alienation of the student, to student fear and disengagement. And the cycle continues. So, the question is: Is there a way to create inclusive classrooms; address the Calls to Action of the Truth and Reconciliation Commission (TRC); and address the well-being of students, teachers, and their communities?

I believe there is, and in the rest of this book I outline how that can be achieved.

We begin by recognizing the places of connection needed to address these complex issues. These connections are crucial, because they mean specific changes can be made that will address *all* of the threads, rather than trying to implement separate programs for everything, and overloading teachers.

The Connections

It's All About Relationships

When we build safe spaces in which everyone feels a sense of self-worth and belonging, we create the opportunity to develop spiritual well-being in its fullest sense, address issues of discrimination and exclusion, and create learning communities in which both teachers and students are more likely to take risks, innovate, and achieve. That is, when students, teachers, families and/or communities are stressed, there are widespread impacts. Communities that are struggling are more likely to be divisive and filled with conflict, which in turn creates more struggle. If we seek ways to reduce stress and increase joy through positive relationships, we will be fulfilling the TRC call to "Build student capacity for intercultural understanding, empathy, and mutual respect," addressing well-being and resilience for everyone, and improving readiness for learning.

Neurology

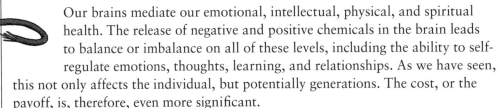

Our brains mediate our emotional, intellectual, physical, and spiritual health. The release of negative and positive chemicals in the brain leads to balance or imbalance on all of these levels, including the ability to self-regulate emotions, thoughts, learning, and relationships. As we have seen, this not only affects the individual, but potentially generations. The cost, or the payoff, is, therefore, even more significant.

Designed for Some, Of Benefit to All: Reconciliation as Reflecting the Values of UDL

There are two important ways in which our innovations must be based on an understanding of this big picture:

1. It has to happen with *all* students.

You cannot make the world more respectful of diversity if you only talk to minority populations. Everyone must learn to see value in the minority. Segregated special education doesn't work, because without involving general education teachers and students without disabilities, inclusive education can never be achieved. Similarly, the healing of the intergenerational trauma of Canadian Indigenous peoples (or any other persecuted minority population), cannot happen if they walk in a world that continues to embrace systemic racist practices and interpersonal violence. Nor can the needs of students with languishing mental health be addressed in an environment that perpetuates stigma and isolation. Our classrooms and schools must become places of spiritual transformation, intellectual inspiration, and community actualization. Everyone matters, and everyone is needed – this is a *moral imperative*. If we don't care about the well-being of our students and each other, what do we care about?

2. It has to be based on core, fundamental values of inclusion and reconciliation.

   • Every child who lives in a community has the right to go to school in that community, and to be welcomed.

   • Every member of that community, including staff, families, and students, has a valuable contribution to make, and deserves to be treated with kindness and respect.

   • Humanity is a mosaic, and we must find a way to see the beauty in each piece and how each piece connects to create a work of art

   • The original pieces of that mosaic in Canada, Indigenous peoples, still hold foundational wisdom and beauty we can all benefit from.

The connection between all of the pieces – spiritual education, the TRC, mental health, and leadership lies in the above values, and so too does the programmatic intervention. When we create learning communities that truly value the diversity of humanity and recognize the importance of well-being (including, but not limited to, intellectual) – we will help our students to develop their spirit, heal the wounds of our history, and lead our society into a new and healthier age. For this to happen, we must do the following:

   • Recognize things aren't as they should be.

   • Understand this reality creates difficulties for all of us.

   • Commit to the idea that the solution involves all of us.

   • Make decisions for programming that involve learning and healing on individual and collective levels.

   • Be inspired by the opportunity to contribute, knowing that those who do will be affecting everyone.

We can acknowledge the mistakes of the past – our history of discrimination against Indigenous peoples, the mistreatment of people with disabilities in institutions, and so forth, without needing to be guilty or ashamed. What is not acceptable is to continue to perpetuate systems that are racist and discriminatory. We can acknowledge that we have many students and teachers with languishing health who need support to achieve a state of well-being and have not, until now, been provided with those supports free of judgment and stigma.

All of this may sound idealistic – and it is – but it is also realistic.

No one teacher can save the world. But our schools nurture the development of every child in our society. We have a broad reach in changing the next generation's way of living and learning. The ancient Talmudic teaching, "he who saves a life has saved the world," has resonance in today's classrooms.

On a less esoteric scale, we can consider that if each of us makes a difference in one child's life, we cannot predict the legacy of this deed across generations.

The essential question here, then, is: How do we move from distress to success?

By distress I don't mean everything is dark and terrible; rather, how do we continue to grow and develop in ways that benefit all of us, and stop doing the things that are causing harm?

The Science and the Art of Ensouling Our Schools

Ensouling our schools will require both that we be intentional about our pedagogy based on research – we are a profession, after all – and we stay focused on our values and what we care about. Teaching is a science and an art. The field of neuropsychology informs our practice about teaching and learning, mental health, and child development. Science connects the ideas of spiritual education, reconciliation, mental health, and leadership because it informs our understanding of what happens when we are stressed, isolated, and feel unsafe, and what happens when we are happy, connected, and feel safe. Leaders who create safe and caring schools and classrooms for staff and students will support the spiritual, emotional, physical, and intellectual well-being of all. Below is a diagram of what I call the "Dual Pathway." The choices we make about the environment we create have powerful outcomes, as you can see.

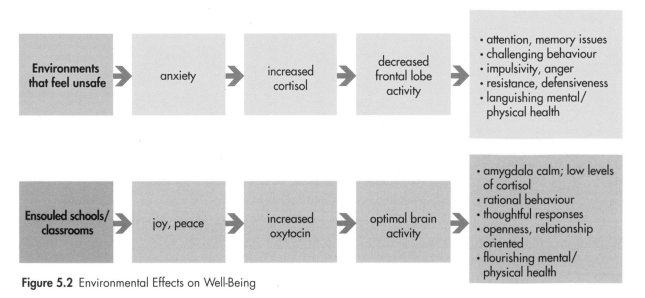

Figure 5.2 Environmental Effects on Well-Being

A third pathway could be added, one that recognizes the impact of trauma:

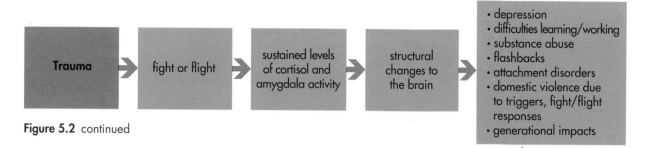

Figure 5.2 continued

The Gift of Plasticity and the Hope of Reconciliation: We Can Grow and Change

In the past, we believed the brain stopped developing after a certain age. However, modern science has revealed that brain plasticity is far greater than we knew (Nelson, Kendall, and Shields 2013). The brain continues to grow, form new connections, and develop new pathways throughout our lifetime. If the former was true, the impacts of trauma would be permanent. Thankfully, because the brain is plastic, individuals who are experiencing languishing mental health, trauma-related mental illness, and concomitant behavioural challenges can hold out hope for healing. Research has documented changes in brain structures when trauma occurs, but it has also documented changes in brain structures when the same individuals are placed in caring, safe spaces; are connected in healthy, positive relationships, and are taught strategies to mindfully manage their triggers (McEwen and Gianaros 2010). We used to think the brain couldn't change, and we may still often feel that schools, racism, and society can't change, but none of that is true: We didn't use to include students with autism in our schools, but we do now. It used to be illegal to marry someone of another race or the same gender, but it's not now. Women didn't used to have the right to vote; now we run for office.

The gift of plasticity and the hope of reconciliation are that we can grow and change!

Framing Well-Being

In previous chapters, we discussed a number of models related to well-being, including positive mental health, the Four Spirits and Mino-Pimatisiwin, and the Circle of Courage (COC). We explored definitions of mental health that identified key characteristics of well-being, including those of the World Health Organization (WHO) and Health Canada. All of these definitions contain some common characteristics, which can be grouped into three categories: intrapersonal characteristics, interpersonal characteristics, and spiritual or existential characteristics.

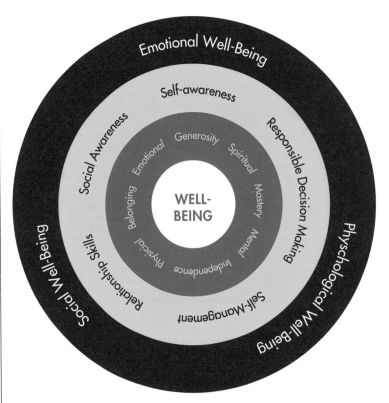

Figure 5.3 Connecting the Frameworks: Dual Continuum, SEL, Four Spirits and the Circle of Courage

- **Intrapersonal characteristics.** The prefix *intra* means "within." Intrapersonal qualities are those that lie within the individual (e.g., resiliency, self-worth, self-regulation). Any attempt to develop well-being, whether in schools or therapeutically, must support these internal skills and processes.

- **Interpersonal characteristics.** The prefix *inter* means "between." Interpersonal qualities are those that affect our sense of connection with and ability to relate to others. Sense of belonging, social skills, cultural identity, respect for diversity, generosity, and so forth are interpersonal qualities that affect both an individual's and a community's well-being.

- **Spiritual/Existential characteristics.** These characteristics link the individual to something larger than themselves. A person's sense of connection with nature, humanity, and purpose in life has been shown to have significant impact on well-being, perseverance, and resiliency.

It is possible, then, to once again pick up our loom and weave these frameworks together. By looking at these three aspects of well-being, we can incorporate all of the aspects of the medicine wheel, COC, and positive mental health with WHO and Health Canada's definitions of well-being.

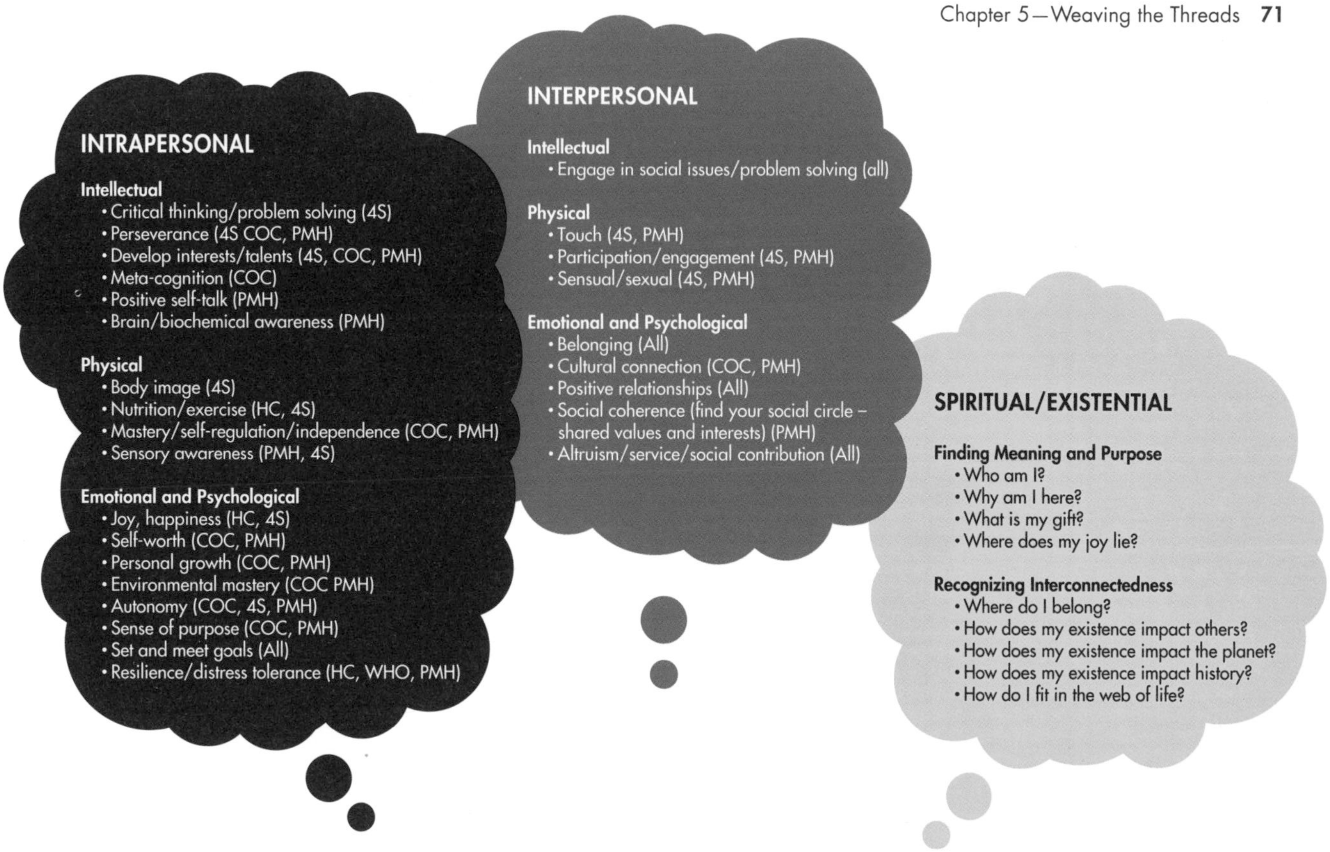

INTRAPERSONAL

Intellectual
- Critical thinking/problem solving (4S)
- Perseverance (4S COC, PMH)
- Develop interests/talents (4S, COC, PMH)
- Meta-cognition (COC)
- Positive self-talk (PMH)
- Brain/biochemical awareness (PMH)

Physical
- Body image (4S)
- Nutrition/exercise (HC, 4S)
- Mastery/self-regulation/independence (COC, PMH)
- Sensory awareness (PMH, 4S)

Emotional and Psychological
- Joy, happiness (HC, 4S)
- Self-worth (COC, PMH)
- Personal growth (COC, PMH)
- Environmental mastery (COC PMH)
- Autonomy (COC, 4S, PMH)
- Sense of purpose (COC, PMH)
- Set and meet goals (All)
- Resilience/distress tolerance (HC, WHO, PMH)

INTERPERSONAL

Intellectual
- Engage in social issues/problem solving (all)

Physical
- Touch (4S, PMH)
- Participation/engagement (4S, PMH)
- Sensual/sexual (4S, PMH)

Emotional and Psychological
- Belonging (All)
- Cultural connection (COC, PMH)
- Positive relationships (All)
- Social coherence (find your social circle – shared values and interests) (PMH)
- Altruism/service/social contribution (All)

SPIRITUAL/EXISTENTIAL

Finding Meaning and Purpose
- Who am I?
- Why am I here?
- What is my gift?
- Where does my joy lie?

Recognizing Interconnectedness
- Where do I belong?
- How does my existence impact others?
- How does my existence impact the planet?
- How does my existence impact history?
- How do I fit in the web of life?

Figure 5.4 Three Aspects of Well-Being

We can begin to plan learning communities that support well-being. We know that we need programming that helps students develop an internal sense of self-worth, mastery, joy, and purpose. Students will need to know themselves as learners and develop skills and a mindset that seeks peace and joy, rather than conflict and stress. At the same time, they will need to learn how to manage stress and distress, as life will undoubtedly present them with a range of challenges. We need to build communities that provide members with the opportunity to build positive relationships, create a personal and cultural identity while respecting the diversity of others, and develop generosity and altruism. Finally, we will need to help students explore their spiritual connection with other living things, the planet, and the collective – and find meaning and purpose in their lives.

And so we begin.

PART II

How to Build Flourishing Learning Communities

Chapter 6
Classroom-Based Programming for Social-Emotional Learning

In this section, we review three educational frameworks that interact to create inclusive educational pedagogy: RTI, UDL, and SEL. The goals of each are to create inclusive classrooms and schools that support the well-being and learning of all learners and their teachers.

Response to Intervention

Response to Intervention (RTI) is a framework for designing learning environments, instruction, and systems that are inclusive of diverse learners with diverse needs. RTI is based on three tiers of intervention that provide services – evidence-based instructional strategies of increasing intensity – to help ensure the academic growth and achievement of all students (Katz 2013.

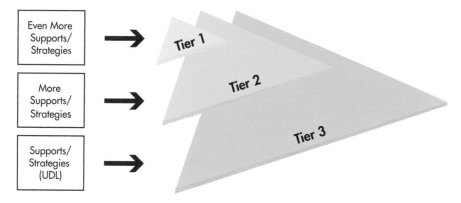

Figure 6.1 Response to Intervention (RTI) Model

RTI promotes the use of evidence-based practices, with constant assessment for learning. In other words, Tier 1 is the program that takes place in the classroom for all students, where teachers use effective instructional practices and assess their students to determine whether they have understood the concepts and mastered the skills taught. If students are struggling, teachers can differentiate their instruction to determine whether the students learn well through an alternative modality or medium (e.g., technology, visual supports), or ideally, universally design the learning environment so that *all* students benefit. Students who are still struggling after teachers have redesigned the learning environment and instruction to the best of their ability, are referred for additional levels of support, called "Tier 2 instruction." Tier 2 instruction can be delivered through one-to-one teaching or in small groups by the classroom teacher or a resource teacher, in the classroom or out.

The tiers in RTI represent layers of support. They are *not* necessarily related to geography. Tier 2 does not mean automatic pull-out, and Tier 3 does not mean referral to segregated programs. Tier 3 is the level at which an individual education plan (IEP) is created with a support team, parents, and the student, and it is intensive. Like Tier 2, Tier 3 can be delivered one-to-one or in small groups by the classroom teacher or resource teacher, in the classroom or out. Thus, a student with significant emotional and behavioural challenges can still be part of classroom academic life, but may also have individualized goals and programs and specialized supports. On the other hand, a student with a visual impairment may have to leave the classroom to learn Braille, or for mobility training. RTI reduces the number of students requiring special services, builds capacity in teachers to design instruction for diverse learners, and provides what the student needs to be successful in the classroom. RTI does *not* weed students out.

While RTI is not geographical, it is sequential. Programming for any and all students begins with Tier 1 instruction. Before we use pull-out programming, modifications, or any other alternative supports, we need to consider three questions:

1. Would all students benefit from these supports?
2. Can the supports be delivered in the classroom?
3. How will the supports affect the targeted students?

Let's take an example. A teacher begins the year by introducing expectations to the students. He works with the class to develop some rules for conduct, and does some "get-to-know-you" activities. As the term moves forward, he notices two students are struggling with anxiety. They do not answer questions in group discussions, need constant reassurance that what they are doing is okay, and frequently decide their work is not good enough and want to start over. As well, one of the students experiences headaches and stomachaches, and is beginning to miss significant school time as a result.

A common reaction for the teacher would be to consult the guidance counsellor. Many times this action results in students being sent to the counsellor to learn strategies for managing anxiety. Universal Design for Learning (UDL) and RTI use a different process as demonstrated below:

1. Would all students benefit from these supports?

   All students will, at some point in their lives, experience anxiety. So, yes, all students would benefit from learning strategies for coping with anxiety.

2. Can the supports be delivered in the classroom?

   This is an opportunity for co-teaching. Why not have the counsellor come in and support the teacher in this programming for all students? This builds capacity and understanding in the teacher and in the targeted students' classmates, who can now support the students with anxiety when issues arise.

3. How will the supports affect the targeted students?

   We always want to consider issues related to stigma, privacy, and self-concept. Delivering anxiety programming in the classroom normalizes the experience of students with anxiety, thereby reducing stigma. Students realize they are not alone in their experiences; everyone sometimes has anxiety. For students who want privacy to discuss a personal or traumatic event, let them know one-to-one counseling is available. This is why RTI is not geographic – most often we want to deliver supports to all students in the classroom. But there are times for individualized programming.

Universal Design for Learning

As discussed in chapter 4, the concept of universal design comes from architecture and the field of design and engineering. Universally designing a building means making sure diverse persons can enter and make use of the building and its services. The addition of ramps, specialized washrooms, elevators, and other technologies allows elderly persons with walkers, people in wheelchairs, parents with strollers, and able-bodied people alike to enter and use the building. Designing the cockpit of a plane or car with stationary seats, steering wheels, and controls limits who can use it. The invention of adjustable seats, periscoping steering wheels, and controls on the steering wheel made cars much more widely accessible to a variety of users.

In UDL, the metaphor of accessibility is extended to the physical set-up of learning environments and in the design of the social and emotional climate and the learning activities. A classroom with rules that include "sitting still" and "being silent" is inaccessible to a number of students, as is a novel study that assumes all students can read at the same level and pace. On the other hand, a rule like "think and contribute," "be respectful of others' learning," or "support your learning team" is flexible enough to take into account the student who needs to move, but can learn to do so without distracting others. Students working in cooperative teams can complete challenging tasks through universal differentiation (i.e. tasks are differentiated for all students, not just particular individuals). Formats such as literature circles, for example, provide flexibility and give different students choices in text and in ways of expressing their understanding. In such teams, students whose strengths are verbal-linguistic learn alongside students whose strengths may lie elsewhere.

There is more than one way to universally design a learning environment. Just as architects' buildings will look different, so, too, can frameworks and classrooms. The originators of UDL, the Center for Applied and Special Technology (CAST), have a framework they use to plan learning environments called the "Three Principles": multiple means of engagement, multiple means of representation, and multiple means of action and expression. Teachers using this framework to engage diverse learners in areas of interest teach through a variety of modalities, and allow students to represent their learning in a variety of ways.[6]

The Three-Block Model of Universal Design for Learning (TBM of UDL) uses three blocks: (1) Block One creates compassionate learning communities, (2) Block Two provides inclusive instructional practice, and (3) Block Three provides systems and structures. Teachers who use this framework consider the social, emotional, and mental-health needs of their students; teach and assess in inclusive ways; and consider policy, resources, staffing, and other systemic variables to create more inclusive schools and classrooms.

Each tier of RTI can be universally designed. Tier 1, the classroom program, can be designed to meet the needs of a diverse range of learners, or it can be designed in traditional ways that only support students who are able to learn through verbal-linguistic, whole-class pedagogies. Additional supports in Tier 2 and Tier 3 can similarly be universally designed. In a UDL paradigm, these

6   For more on these principles, visit <www.cast.org>.

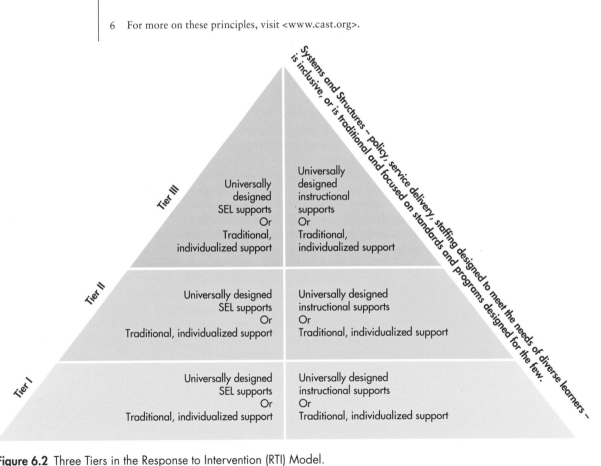

Figure 6.2 Three Tiers in the Response to Intervention (RTI) Model.

supports are offered to all students, within the classroom, to the greatest degree possible. In a traditional paradigm, supports are seen as targeted to particular individuals based on deficits, and are generally offered outside of the classroom.

Each concept covered in the three blocks – social and emotional programming, inclusive practice, and service-delivery models – can be done in traditional ways, or be universally designed.

Tier I of RTI in the Three-Block-Model of Universal Design

Tier 1 of RTI represents the instructional program that all students in the class receive. In a UDL classroom, Tier l means the classroom is designed to accommodate diverse learners, and the program is designed so that most students will be successful. It *is* possible! (See *Teaching to Diversity*, in which I describe how to design such a classroom.)

Current research in education often uses a statistic called "effect size" to determine if a program is worth doing. An effect size means that the program made a difference – but how big a difference? John Hattie, an educational researcher who has analyzed many educational strategies (e.g., differentiated instruction, cooperative learning, assessment for learning), uses effect sizes to rank the most effective educational strategies. Hattie argues there is no point in implementing strategies with an effect size of less than .4, because they have the same effect that traditional educational programs do. Our research shows that TBM classrooms increase student achievement profoundly, with effect sizes over 2.0, much larger than most strategies discussed in Hattie's book, *Visible Learning*. This holds true even for students with significant disabilities; for them, the effect size is not as large, because achievement comes a little slower – but, at .80, it is still very large. All of this takes place in a context that, research shows, also improves teachers' job satisfaction and self-efficacy. (Although there has been criticism of Hattie's meta-analyses, overall, the measure of effect sizes is well respected in measurement and research.)

The first block of the TBM of UDL, then, addresses the social and emotional needs of students in inclusive classrooms. And just as the three tiers of RTI can be universally designed, each block of the TBM could be divided into the three tiers. That is, Tier 1 of block 1 would be the social and emotional programming done with all the students in the classroom. Tier 2 might be some additional social skills supports or strategies, and Tier 3 would be individualized supports aimed at mental health, delivered either in the classroom or out. In Tier 1 of Block One, teachers implement practices to create democratic, caring classrooms that encourage multiple means of engagement (e.g., self-regulated learning). These practices include: holding regular class meetings to develop prosocial problem-solving skills, providing authentic choice and voice through the teaching of self-regulation, and developing empathy and collaborative skills. Students are encouraged to contribute to the creation of a positive learning community in which individual and group rights and responsibilities are balanced.

As part of Block One, teachers begin the year or semester with a strategy called "Respecting Diversity" (RD). The RD program involves nine lessons that support students as they develop awareness of their own learning profiles (i.e., how they learn best and what is challenging for them), as well as respect for their classmates' diversity, complementary skill sets, knowledge, and experiences. Developing an understanding of one's unique learning profile allows students to become aware of how they learn best, recognize their strengths, make choices for academic activities, and understand how they can make valuable contributions to their classrooms, communities, and future careers. In the RD program, social awareness and respect are taught through curricular and collaborative tasks that require multiple skill sets and background knowledge. These tasks allow students to appreciate diversity as they come to understand how students with different learning strengths, experiences, and background knowledge can contribute to a complex, multidimensional task.

In Block Two of the TBM, teachers use a five-step planning and instructional framework that weaves together evidence-based inclusive instructional practices. The five steps are as follows:

1. Create a one-year plan that integrates curricula across subject areas (e.g., match geography in social studies with ecosystems in science, then choosing related literature, writing activities, and math activities).

2. Determine the essential subject-area understandings or "big ideas" for each unit.

3. Transform the essential understandings into questions to spark an inquiry process.

4. Develop rubrics to assess mastery of the essential understandings, and guide instruction that allows for multiple means of expression.

5. Plan differentiated instructional activities to support diverse learners, using multiple means of presentation and engagement.

Teachers are also taught to use instructional strategies designed to meet the needs of all students: innovative classroom design, varied student groupings, and multimedia and adaptive technologies. In addition, the TBM emphasizes mastery of complex concepts, with scaffolding through cooperative teamwork and differentiated instruction. As part of this practice, teachers use Bloom's Taxonomy to build curricular rubrics that reflect multiple developmental levels of understanding. TBM teachers are encouraged to use the rubrics regularly (e.g., daily or weekly) as tools for formative assessment and student feedback.

Block Three of the TBM addresses the systems and structures that must be in place to support inclusive classroom practices. This includes funding based on classroom needs rather than on individual student needs, assigning assistants to classrooms rather than to students, and providing staff assignments that facilitate collaboration and co-teaching. School and district leaders, policy makers, and government personnel are encouraged to develop inclusive education policies and curricula, establish hiring practices that emphasize skills for teaching diverse learners and support collaborative cultures in schools. Teachers become leaders within a professional learning community through activities that teach collaborative and consultative skills; effective communication practices for collaborating with families, clinicians, and paraprofessionals; and strategies for developing professional growth plans.

Social and Emotional Learning: Block One of the TBM

In *Teaching to Diversity* (Katz 2012), I introduced three strategies for developing social and emotional learning (SEL): RD, Spirit Buddies, and Class Meetings (see below). Each strategy goes beyond SEL and addresses many factors in the development of well-being.

Strategies	Aspects of Well-Being		Specific Target
Respecting Diversity Program (RD)	Intra	Intellectual	self-awareness, self-regulation, development of interests and talents
		Physical	awareness of kinesthetic strengths/goals
		Emotional/ Psychological	self-worth, hope, self-regulation
		Spiritual	sense of purpose: What is my gift?
	Inter	Intellectual	respect for diversity, perspective-taking, collaborative and cooperative skills, common language
		Physical	
		Emotional/ Psychological	belonging, generosity, class culture, positive relationships
		Spiritual	meaning: What do I have to offer?
Spirit Buddies	Intra	Intellectual	
		Physical	movement, cortisol reduction
		Emotional/ Psychological	self-worth, being "seen"
		Spiritual	impact on others
	Inter	Intellectual	
		Physical	
		Emotional/ Psychological	belonging, social coherence, positive interactions
		Spiritual	

Figure 6.3 Strategies in the TBM: Targeted Outcomes for Well-Being

Strategies	Aspects of Well-Being		Specific Target
Class Meetings	Intra	Intellectual	awareness of needs, values, and wants; mastery, autonomy, independence
		Physical	
		Emotional/ Psychological	expression of feelings, needs
		Spiritual	personal integrity, values
	Inter	Intellectual	critical thinking, problem solving, perspective-taking
		Physical	
		Emotional/ Psychological	social contribution, belonging, positive relations, cultural connection (how we do things here)
		Spiritual	values of community

Figure 6.3 (continued)

Strategy One: The Respecting Diversity (RD) Program

The RD program consists of nine lessons. The goals of RD are to develop specific components of self-awareness, social awareness, and respect: self-efficacy; goal-setting; emotional resiliency; perspective-taking; empathy; valuing diversity; and creating a positive, inclusive classroom climate. The RD program has self-regulation as a goal throughout: students develop a sense of who they are and how they learn well, set goals for themselves, learn to check in with themselves and seek help from others, and develop self-efficacy. Research indicates that the RD program significantly increases students' self-respect and their respect for others (Katz and Porath 2011). Helping all students understand their strengths, as well as their challenges, improves classroom climate. Helping students understand the advantages of having diverse learners in a classroom community enables them to develop emotional resiliency and acceptance of others.

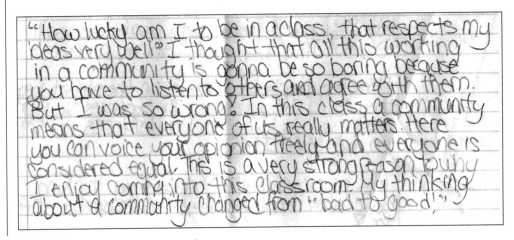

"How lucky am I to be in a class, that respects my ideas very well" I thought that all this working in a community is gonna be so boring because you have to listen to others and agree with them. But I was so wrong! In this class a community means that everyone of us really matters. Here you can voice your opinion freely and everyone is considered equal. This is a very strong reason to why I enjoy coming into this classroom. My thinking about a community changed from "bad to good."

Figure 6.4 One student's journal reflection

Traditional curricula and instruction focus on a narrow range of techniques, primarily text-based, for teaching and learning. They, therefore, create an educational disadvantage by favouring the students who are verbal-linguistic over other students (Gardner 1995; Hearne and Stone 1995). Students who do not learn best through text (who are not verbal-linguistic) face a struggle to learn in ways that do not best fit with their learning strengths. For instance, a student whose strength is visual-spatial (and who may one day become a great architect) might feel incapable because they cannot write as well as others – art, after all, is generally considered of secondary importance in the curriculum. Introducing students to the concept of multiple intelligences (MIs), which recognizes all intelligence categories as equally valid and valuable, helps create a climate for student self-acceptance and acceptance of others. As Elias (2004, 58) states: "Working through multiple intelligences is more than just pedagogy. It represents finding windows into the souls of children and ways to reach them in powerful and meaningful ways."

Introducing Multiple Intelligences to Students

Introducing students to the concept of multiple intelligences allows them to explore their own interests, interests and talents, abilities, feelings, and strengths that describe their current learning profile. As well, they experience the diversity of intelligences in the learning profiles of fellow students who make up their school community.

Helping children understand their strengths and challenges leads to more accurate personal insight (Levine 2002). As they begin to appreciate the advantages of having diverse learners in a classroom community, they develop emotional resiliency and acceptance of others (Shepard 2004), and respect for themselves and for others. The strategy can be used in inclusive classrooms from K–12, in resource-room settings, and in one-to-one counselling situations, with some adaptations.

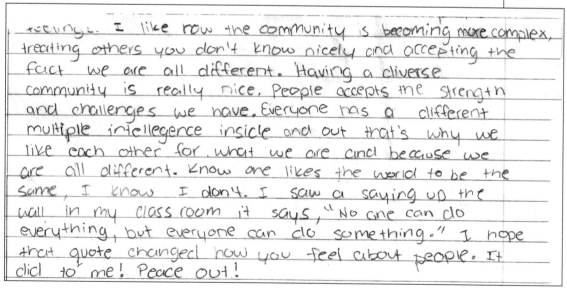

Figure 6.5 A student's reflection on multiple intelligences.

In secondary schools, teachers face the dilemma that students might repeat the same lessons several times if all teachers (in each discipline) undertake RD. Some secondary schools I worked with found one of these solutions helpful:

- Solution 1: For the first few days in September, teachers postpone implementing the planned regular class schedule; instead, they place the students in homerooms – if necessary, ones created for RD – and work through the nine lessons (see pages 86–99). Then, when the regular class schedule starts, all students have the vocabulary and thinking with which to approach study units designed for universal learning.

- Solution 2: Teachers create a homeroom period at the beginning or end of each school day, and, for a few weeks, use those periods to work through the RD program.

Verbal-Linguistic	Verbal-linguistic intelligence is the capacity to develop verbal skills and sensitivity to the sounds, meanings, and rhythms of words. Verbal-linguistic people demonstrate strength in the language arts – listening, speaking, reading, and writing.
Visual-Spatial	Visual-spatial intelligence is the ability to visualize in detail, the capacity to think in images and pictures, accurately and abstractly. People who demonstrate visual-spatial intelligence learn best visually and by organizing things spatially. They enjoy charts, graphs, maps, tables, illustrations, art, puzzles, and costumes – anything eye-catching.
Logical-Mathematical	Logical-mathematical intelligence is the ability to think conceptually and abstractly, and the capacity to discern logical or numerical patterns. People who display this type of intelligence have an aptitude for numbers, reasoning, and problem solving.
Bodily-Kinesthetic	Bodily-kinesthetic intelligence is the ability to control one's body movements and to handle objects skillfully. Bodily-kinesthetic people experience learning best through activity: games, movement, hands-on tasks, and building.
Musical-Rhythmic	Musical-rhythmic intelligence involves the ability to produce and appreciate rhythm, pitch, and timbre. Musical-rhythmic people learn well through songs, patterns, rhythms, instruments, and musical expression.
Interpersonal	Interpersonal intelligence is the capacity to detect and respond appropriately to the moods, motivations, and desires of others. Interpersonal learners are noticeably people-oriented and outgoing, and they do their learning cooperatively in groups or with a partner.
Intrapersonal	Intrapersonal intelligence is the capacity to be self-aware and in tune with inner feelings, values, beliefs, and thinking processes. Intrapersonal people are especially in touch with their own feelings, values, and ideas.
Naturalistic	Naturalistic intelligence is the ability to recognize and categorize plants, animals, and other objects in nature. Naturalistic people love the outdoors, animals, and field trips. They notice details such as characteristics and behaviours in the natural world.
Existential	Existential intelligence describes the sensitivity and capacity of a person to probe the deep questions about human existence, such as how we got here, why we die, and the meaning of life. Existential people want to know why what they are studying is important in the bigger picture, and what the philosophy is behind ideas and expectations.

Figure 6.6 Multiple Intelligences

Plan for Respecting Diversity Program

RD offers nine lessons teachers can use to explore and discuss how multiple intelligences apply to teaching and learning UDL. They can also use the lessons to introduce students to the vocabulary and concepts of multiple intelligences. The lessons are sequential and designed to help students become aware of their own and others' learning profiles, and to help build a positive learning climate in the classroom. Teachers should work through them, in sequence, at a pace that their students find comfortable.

Working with Young Students

Teachers can use the lessons for all grade levels, with personal adaptations appropriate to their students and their grade. The amount of scaffolding provided and the language level used will differ for younger students. For instance, when asking students to make predictions (lesson 1), older students can do this in written form. However, teachers might have children in kindergarten and grade 1 turn to a partner and talk, or place a sticker with their name on it on the chart next to their strength. Teachers might choose to do the surveys (lesson 2) for children in the early years as an activity for a parent night, with older students as buddies, or in small groups with teacher facilitation. When discussing careers with younger children (lesson 4), focus on "community helpers" familiar to them – firemen, police officers, doctors, librarians, and so forth. For lessons 5 and 6, some pre-teaching of group work could be helpful, particularly when working with one group at a time.[7]

---

7   Chapter 5 in *Teaching to Diversity* (Katz 2012) gives some possibilities, or lessons, on cooperative learning skills.

Lesson 1: What Does "Smart" Mean?

Rationale

This lesson introduces the language to describe *intelligence*, to discuss different levels of intelligence, different interests, different abilities, different feelings, different strengths, needs, and values. As students expand their ideas of what *smart* means, they understand there are many ways to acquire and demonstrate one's knowledge and abilities, and each way is equally valuable in contributing to one's overall intelligence. The ways (or modalities) may overlap, but it is helpful to distinguish among them.

Well-Being Foci

self-worth, hope, sense of purpose, common language

Materials

student journals, chart paper, chart-paper stands, coloured markers

Process

1. Brainstorm. Ask: "What does *smart* mean to you?" As students respond, record their answers on chart paper as a web. As you write, begin to group the responses into MI categories (e.g., group "can read well," "knows lots of words," "can spell accurately" together because they are all part of verbal-linguistic intelligence). Use a different coloured marker for each intelligence to make each stand out visually.

2. When the students run out of ideas, ask questions such as: "What other ways can people be smart?" "How do you learn best?" "What things are you good at?" (If a student says "hockey," for example, group it with other sports, eventually identified as bodily-kinesthetic intelligence.)

3. Prompt students until you have listed examples of all nine intelligences, filling in as necessary (e.g., "Does anyone here play piano?" "I have a friend who likes to draw.").

4. Introduce the nine MIs. Discuss each separately. Circle phrases from the students' brainstorming session that relate to that intelligence, and discuss what activities or skills help define this group of people. Name the intelligence by saying something like: "You're right, some people are word smart, they are good at _____ (e.g., spelling, writing, reading). We say these people have 'verbal-linguistic intelligence.'"

Discussion and Journal Reflection

Have students reflect on the following question and draw or write their response in their journal: What strengths do you think you have?

Tiered Supports

Students with significant disabilities can listen to the discussion and communicate their likes and interests by using visual aids or matching their classmates' pictures to pictures of activities they like.

Figure 6.7 Kindergarten students' brainstorm of what "smart" means.

Figure 6.8 After students did some brainstorming about what it means to be smart, the teacher discussed the different intelligences to them and had them reflect on which intelligence they felt was their strength. A few students shared theirs with the class.

Lesson 2: Who Am I as a Learner?

Rationale

In this lesson, students respond to a survey designed as a tool for metacognition and reflection on their interests. Individual demystification allows children to develop self-perception and a realistic self-concept by recognizing their strengths, needs, and values; they increase self-efficacy as self-awareness grows. As well, journal reflections give students a chance to identify and recognize their emotions, and evaluate their reactions regarding their learning profile.

Well-Being Foci

self-worth, self-awareness, sense of purpose

Materials

student journals, Multiple Intelligence Survey (see appendix B) at the appropriate level for your students (provide each student with a copy, but do not make this a reading task), and including Part 4, Intelligence Profile graph.

Process

1. Tell students the survey is not a competition. Have them think about each statement and decide as best they can whether it describes them, or how they think or feel. Read the instructions for Part 1 of the survey with the students.

2. Remind students that everyone has strengths and challenges. Emphasize that it's okay. If you don't make this emphasis, students will answer according to what they think you want them to say, not what they actually believe. With the students, read each statement in each section of the survey aloud, and have them put the number 1 on the line if they believe the statement is true for them most of the time, or leave it blank if the statement is not true or not very often true.

3. At the end of each section, have students add the 1s and write the total. Tell them it is not important how many statements in each section they have marked

4. When students have finished the nine sections (90 statements), have them transfer all their totals to the table in Part 2, then shade in the portion of each column that matches their totals in the bar graph in Part 4. To avoid students comparing scores, tell them the scores don't matter. What *does* matter is their relative strengths and challenges.

Discussion and Journal Reflection

Have students reflect on the following questions and draw or write their responses in their journal: Were your predictions of your strengths correct? Were there any surprises for you? Why do you think this happened? (e.g., Survey is wrong; Had not thought myself good at that.) How do you feel about your learning profile?

Tiered Supports

Students with disabilities can use visual aids, PicSyms, or PECS (Picture Exchange Communication System) to communicate their likes and interests. Participation depends on the student's level of functioning and degree of training with PECS, which has to be determined on a case-by-case basis.

Lesson 3: Community Brain

Rationale

This lesson follows up on what the students have learned about their strong interests and abilities. It develops students' awareness of social relationships and of the skills that foster a sense of community – their interdependence as members of their community. All students have a chance to be the helper at times, and at other times to ask for help, which reinforces the idea that everyone has strengths and challenges. Students can use a positive framework to manage cooperative relationships, to develop communication with their peers, and to foster social engagement and inclusion.

Well-Being Foci

self-worth, sense of purpose, sense of belonging, respect for diversity, generosity, class culture, positive relationships

Materials

Plasticine (enough for each student to contribute to the model of a brain), paper "flags" or sticky notes and toothpicks (for students to make flags. With very young children (K–1), prepare the flags in advance, or have a parent volunteer present to help.)

Process

1. Work together to create a model of the brain from Plasticine. Give each student a piece of the Plasticine to roll into a snake. Then, have them add their strip as you build up the layers into a multi-fold brain.

2. Have students write their name and dominant intelligence strength on a flag. Holding their flag, bring students together into a circle. Tell students they will be placing their flags into the brain. First, though, you have two important points to make:

Figure 6.9 Colour-coded Brain Anatomy

   • "Everyone in this room has something to contribute, something to be proud of. Whatever you wrote on your flag shows us what you have to contribute to the community." Give examples of actions characteristic of someone with a particular type of intelligence. For example: "If you are 'interpersonal,' you can be a friend to a new student or to one who needs someone to hang out with at recess. If you are 'bodily-kinesthetic,' you can coach others in your skill. We all have strengths and challenges, so all of us will be helpers sometimes, and 'helpees' at other times. When you need help in an activity we are engaged in, look for someone with strength in that area."

   • "This is a commitment to our community and to yourself: When someone asks you for help with a task, leadership means you will not make fun of them, nor will you do the task for them. But, you will help them learn how to do what you are able to do, or to understand what you have learned."

3. Have students place their flag in the appropriate area of the Plasticine brain.

NOTE: Be sure to call on your students for help at times (e.g., to draw on a chart for you, or to fix something), using the brain model.

Figure 6.10 All Kinds of Brains!

Tiered Supports

For students who are significantly disabled and who may have marked only a few statements in any category of the survey, consider what emotions they evoke in other students. For instance, do they make others smile? Are they willing to interact with others? If so, their profile might be "interpersonal."

Indigenizing the Lesson

Indigenous cultures recognize important moments to the community with ceremonies. One teacher recognized the importance of this lesson, so she turned it into a ceremony. She laid out a table with the community brain, and added candles and flowers. Students prepared the flags, and a treatise called "Community Commitment" was written and signed by the class. You can find out more on her blog https://sheila-vick.com/

Figure 6.11a, 6.11b Community Committment Ceremony

Lesson 4: Diversity, Intelligences, and Careers

Rationale

This lesson develops self-motivation and resiliency by building hope for students; they see there will be opportunities for success and even fame, regardless of their learning profile.

Have students explore career options and life paths open to those with diverse learning profiles. When students can identify role models who have learning profiles similar to theirs and who have been successful, they may begin to develop self-efficacy and emotional resiliency.

Well-Being Foci

self-worth, hope, sense of purpose, belonging, generosity, develop interests

Materials

chart (from lesson 1; see figure 6.7), photographs of public figures and people in different areas of work, the arts, and community endeavours (collected by you and/or students)

Process

1. Have students sit in a circle around the chart created in lesson 1. Discuss the range of activities involved in different types of work done by well-known people in your community. Ask: What strengths might each have in one or more of the intelligence categories?

2. As you go around the circle, brainstorm careers for each category. Identify some well-known people who have strengths in each field: a popular radio presenter (strong verbal-linguistic abilities); a soccer coach (strong bodily-kinesthetic abilities); and so forth. It is critical, during this discussion, to point out to students that, no matter the nature of their profile, they can be successful in whatever work or career they choose to pursue and train for.

3. If students need help, hand out photographs of public figures they may recognize, or figures in settings that help identify their field (e.g., sports; music; technology; sciences; local, provincial, national politics). Have students discuss that person's career and what their learning profile (strengths and challenges) might be.

4. As an extension, have students research and write a brief biography of someone with a profile similar to their own. This task might help them see that someone just like them can be successful.

Figure 6.12 One teacher gave students pictures of careers and had them sort them by intelligences.

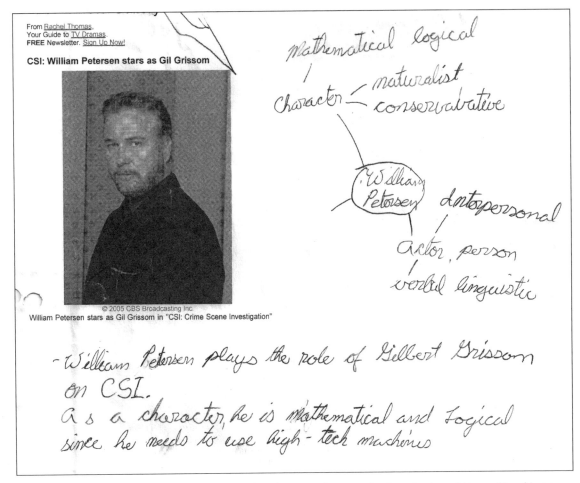

From Rachel Thomas,
Your Guide to TV Dramas.
FREE Newsletter. Sign Up Now!

CSI: William Petersen stars as Gil Grissom

© 2005 CBS Broadcasting Inc.
William Petersen stars as Gil Grissom in "CSI: Crime Scene Investigation"

Mathematical logical

Character — naturalist — conservatative

William Petersen — Interpersonal — actor, person — verbal linguistic

- William Petersen plays the role of Gilbert Grissom on CSI.
  As a character, he is Mathematical and Logical since he needs to use high-tech machines

Figure 6.13 A student's web for a biography of a television character he thought shared his profile of being logical-mathematical and interpersonal.

Tiered Supports

Students who are significantly disabled can take part in the discussion and brainstorming. When writing biographies, have them work with a partner who has similar strengths (e.g., they both enjoy music), or they can find out about other persons with disabilities similar to their own (e.g., autism, Down syndrome).

Lesson 5: Interdependence in Learning Teams

Rationale

In this lesson, we focus on respect for others and respect for diversity. School-age children are naturally egocentric; they think everyone should know, like, and believe what they do (e.g., "How could you not like hockey? What's wrong with you?") We cannot teach students to value diversity until we teach them to see that their life and the world are better for it. As students become aware that a community actually requires diversity to function, they learn to value people who are different from themselves. This focus helps create social awareness of the value of diversity and helps students develop respect for others.

Well-Being Foci

sense of purpose; belonging; generosity; respect for diversity, class culture; positive relationships, perspective-taking, collaborative and cooperative skills

Materials

nine paper slips, each with a different MI written on it, and placed in a small container

Process

1. Place students in nine groups. Have a student from each group pick a slip of paper (intelligence) from the container. Each group is to develop and write a role-play, based on the MI selected, which they will perform. Prompt students by asking:

   • What if everyone were (e.g., verbal-linguistic)? What would the world be like?"

2. Have all groups perform their role-plays. Ask students the following questions, and discuss as a class:

   • What are the pros and cons of everyone being the same? (e.g., everyone would be talking; there would be no roads, no cars, which would lead to chaos and disorganization)

   • How does diversity benefit a community? How do diverse others support our lives? (e.g., someone builds our houses; performs on TV, programs computers). You want students to see how diversity benefits *them*.

3. Have students write and perform a second role-play. They can focus on the same intelligence, or you can place the slips back in the container and ask them to redraw. This time, ask the students to create role-plays answering the questions "What would the world be like without people who have strength in (e.g., musical-rhythmic)?"

Discussion and Journal Reflection

After all groups have performed their role-plays, discuss: What would be missing from the world and from your life if other people did not have likes and abilities different from yours?

Here our goal is to have students recognize that they would be missed if they were not exactly who they are, and that they would miss other students with different abilities than them.

Ask students: Why is diversity necessary? How would your life be more difficult without it? (e.g., "I would have to build my own house"; "...make my own music.")

Have them draw or write their responses in their journal.

Lesson 6: Valuing Diversity

Rationale

In this lesson, students reflect on the advantages and disadvantages of working with others who may be similar to or different from them. The ability to work with diverse people is important. For instance, a technology company might have different departments – software, programming, graphic design, marketing and promotion, and sales. Within each department, employees will share many of the same strengths, but to create a successful product, the developers will have to collaborate with others who have different strengths, such as graphic designers and programmers.

Students, too, must learn to negotiate with their peers about when and how to choose and work with partners and group members, whether they have similar or differing learning profiles. By doing so, students build explicit awareness of the value of diversity, explore the pros and cons of working with similar and different types of learners, and see value in all. Students develop social awareness and relationship management skills.

Well-Being Foci

sense of purpose, belonging, generosity; respect for diversity, class culture, positive relationships; perspective-taking, collaborative and cooperative skills

Process

1. Break the class into groups according to MI strengths in learning profiles (i.e., all the kinesthetic learners work together, and so on).

2. Assign a topic to each group. Prompt students by saying something like: Show me what you know about _____. Choose a curricular topic the class is going to study, and use this as a formative assessment to see what your students know. Tell students they must use at least two intelligences in their presentation (e.g., draw and write; act and speak).

I think that I have changed very much this year. Grades don't matter to me as much as before and now it just matters to me how much I try my best. I also learned to think for myself and have the courage to speak my opinion if I didn't agree with someone. I also became more confident in participating in class activities and I learned to help others and be a leader the right way. I've made many new friends in this class, some I never thought I would become friends with and I always enjoy doing group work. I can now work better with people and cooperate more. Although not everyone in this class is my "best friend" I really value the things we do as a class because when the whole class is laughing and playing together it gives me a happy feeling. I'm very excited to go to highschool next year, but it's sad to know that I'm leaving this class behind.

Figure 6.14 A grade seven student's journal entry about making friends and working with diverse others.

3. Discuss: What were the advantages and disadvantages of working with people of like mind/ learning style to you? (Possible response: "Well, it was easy to decide what we wanted to do, but then everyone wanted to draw and no one wanted to write.")

4. Re-arrange the students into groups of mixed intelligences.

   - Assign a second topic (e.g., Show me what you know about _____).

   - Tell students they must use at least two intelligences in their presentation on the topic selected (e.g., Draw and write, or act and speak).

   - Discuss: What were the advantages and disadvantages of working with people with mind/ learning strengths different from yours? (e.g., Possible response: "Well, it was hard to decide what we wanted to do, but then it was easy to divide the labour.")

   Discuss: We have to be able to work with and relate to both people who think like us or do what we do, and people who think and work differently. Sometimes, it is useful to work with people who have the same interests as you, and, sometimes, it is useful to find partners or team members who have complementary skill sets. You cannot have a hockey team made up only of goalies.

Lesson 7: Goal-Setting

Rationale

This lesson develops students' self-awareness, particularly their ability to set goals, to plan and organize, to recognize the need to develop strength in these areas, and to challenge themselves in areas of weakness. They begin to share goals as they learn to count on others for help, accept that they can be vulnerable, and become the kinds of friends who can be strong for each other. This, in turn, creates a sense of interdependence.

It is vital that we allow, encourage, and expect students to set goals in areas of strength. Too often, we imply that goal-setting is all about getting better "at what you're not good at." But greatness is achieved by setting goals in areas of strength. If someone had said to Mozart: "You are good enough at music, but you need to work on your spelling," the world would have lost a great talent! Give students the opportunity to reflect on what is important to them and to set goals in their strengths. Help them learn to use their strengths to overcome challenges and explore stress-management techniques for dealing with challenge goals.

Well-Being Foci

sense of purpose, respect for diversity, generosity, class culture, positive relationships, sense of belonging perspective-taking, collaborative and cooperative skills

Process

1. Discuss the process of setting goals.
   - It is important to set goals in both strengths ("How are you going to develop your talents?") and challenges ("What do you want to get better at?").
   - Emphasize setting goals in one's strengths! Tell students: "There would be no Mozart, no Lebron James if someone had said to them: 'You're already good enough in music/basketball. You really need to work on _____'"!
   - Students tend to write goals they think their teachers or parents want to hear (e.g., "getting better at math.") Remind them: "Goals must matter to you, or you won't work toward them."

2. Goal #1
   - Have students each set a goal in their strength. How will they develop their talent? (If a strength is athletics/hockey, what do they want to get better at? Conditioning? Stickhandling?) Have them make a plan for how they will do that.

3. Goal #2
   - Discuss goals in areas that we find challenging – the areas we cannot improve on our own. (Goals in challenge areas require community support. You have to plan who will help you, how they might help you, and how you can gain their support.) Have students set a goal in a challenge area. Ask: What is important to you? Make a plan, and decide who you need help from.

4. Class discussion
   - Gather students in a circle. Ask them, one at a time, to share their goals. After the student has shared, ask: "How can we help you?" It is important to have students articulate how their peers can help them, as this builds trust and teaches students how to communicate their needs. Emphasize that everyone in the classroom community is responsible for supporting everyone else to reach their goals.

Story 3

I had a breakthrough with one of my grade 2 students who has low self-esteem and shuts down because he thinks he is not smart. We were setting our goals for our challenges and he just shut down because he didn't think it was okay to have any challenges. After a few different tactics, I asked him who he thought was the smartest kid in the class. He named a profoundly gifted student. I knew that that student's MI graph looked similar to his, with marked highs and lows. So I asked the gifted student if it was okay to share his graph with the other student. He was shocked that the smartest kid in class had a graph that showed great strengths and great challenges like his did. I could see his shoulders come down and he was in disbelief. We talked about the idea that it is not how smart you are but *how you are smart*. He then picked a goal to be able to work on by himself (intrapersonal). I asked him what was hard about working on his own, and he said "spelling." We talked and decided that his plan of action would be to just put down what he knows in words and not worry about the spelling, that I and other students would remind him that his ideas are more important than spelling, and that in periods other than writers' workshop he could show his understanding in other ways, using the multiple intelligences. Even during writing workshop I could see that he took some of the pressure off of himself and put in extra effort. He was so pleased with his accomplishments. It's a start, but it truly made my week and his!

Lesson 8: Social Influence

OPTIONAL: for older students

Rationale

In this lesson, students develop an awareness of common misconceptions about what intelligence is, and they are made aware about the diversity of learning profiles. Students explore concepts such as societal bias and its influence on individuals. They also explore societal views of intelligence, and reflect on how society's views have influenced their own view of themselves and others.

Well-Being Foci

respect for diversity, generosity, class culture, positive relationships, perspective-taking

Process

1. Have students create their own survey on MI. They can pose one or more questions that explore definitions of intelligence (e.g., Which of the following activities is your favourite? Who do you think is the smartest, Mozart or Shakespeare?). Students can then survey classmates, friends, other students in the school, teachers, or family.

2. Tally the results.

3. Record the results, using a variety of graph types.

4. Discuss:
   - What does this say about how we view intelligence and the distribution of intelligences? (e.g., We think Einstein is smarter than Michael Jordan, but more people are bodily-kinesthetic than logical-mathematical. Or: Out of 50 people I surveyed, 48 said verbal-linguistic was more important than naturalistic).
   - Would the results be different in another culture? (i.e., Is bodily-kinesthetic intelligence viewed more positively than logical-mathematical intelligence in some societies?)

Discussion and Journal Reflection

Have students reflect on how the culture and society in which they are growing up has influenced how they think about themselves and others. They can write or draw their reflections in their journal.

Lesson 9: The Brain and Disabilities

Rationale

In this lesson, students develop social awareness of and empathy for the challenges that people with disabilities face. We try to encourage students to reflect on their personal, moral, and ethical responsibilities within diverse communities. At the same time, we must make students aware that someone with a challenge in one area does not mean they are challenged in all areas – people with mental or physical challenges can be capable in many ways. It is important to help students become aware of the relationship between the intelligences and some of the disabilities their peers and classmates may have. Research into the outcomes of the Respecting Diversity (RD) strategy indicate students find this discussion to be one of the most powerful.

Well-Being Foci

respect for diversity, generosity, class culture, positive relationships, perspective-taking, collaborative and cooperative skills

Process

1. Discuss with students the following: We all have strengths and challenges, but what would it be like to have a severe challenge in any one of the intelligences?

2. Work through each intelligence, noting associated disabilities, and the potential abilities. (e.g., If you are quadriplegic and in a wheelchair, does it mean you are not intelligent? No, because you can be smart in these other ways…..) Then, have students work with partners, or in groups to role-play what it would be like to be:

   • Verbal-Linguistic: learning disabled, hearing impaired, mute

   • Visual-Spatial: visually impaired

   • Logical-Mathematical: dyscalculia

   • Bodily-Kinesthetic: physically challenged, ADHD

   • Musical-Rhythmic: tone deaf

   • Interpersonal: conduct disorder, nonverbal learning disability (NVLD), autism spectrum disorder

   • Intrapersonal: anxiety disorder, mood disorders, autism spectrum disorder

   • Naturalistic: phobias

   • Existential: developmental delays; challenges with conceptual understanding, higher-order thinking

Discussion and Journal Reflection

Have students reflect on the following questions and draw or write their responses in their journal: If you had a severe challenge in one of the nine intelligences, what other activities could you do to prepare for a career? As a person without disabilities, what could you do to support community members with disabilities?

Story 4: Ms. D

Sometimes, I have explained disabilities using the metaphor of the brain as a city. I tell students your brain is like a city – it has roads carrying information in and out of it. For all of us, some roads are six-lane highways, and some are bumpy gravel roads with construction on them. In other words, we all have some roads that work well, and some roads (i.e. ways of learning/gathering information) that don't work as well. We talk about disabilities as a road that is closed, or very slow to travel on.

I **teach French Immersion kindergarten and last year I had a boy with autism in my class.** Several people at the board office level were totally opposed to him being in my class because his language development is behind. I implemented the Respecting Diversity program and we made our class brain. I talked about the 12-lane super highways, the bumpy roads, and the roadblocks. At one point, Timothy was hitting and spitting quite a lot and the children were complaining about it. I decided to have another discussion about multiple intelligences. I asked what would happen if someone had a roadblock on the visual-spatial part of the brain, and a few other scenarios. I also asked what would happen if someone had a bumpy road in the interpersonal part of the brain. What could happen and how could we help that person? I didn't use any names but I could see that the children got it. The other children's reactions to Timothy changed after this and they saw him in a different light. I want to share a letter I received from Timothy's mother. Because of working with you I was able to see Timothy not as a pathology to be dealt with, but as a person with strengths and challenges, like the rest of us. Here is the letter:

> Dear Madame,
> We are so grateful!!! Thank you for your creativity, enthusiasm and amazing teaching skills. Thank you for your patience, steadiness, and your endeavor to search for the brilliance and gifts in each of your students. We know that Timothy would not be where he is today without you! We are thrilled to pieces that from a boy who would not willingly put pen to paper, we now have literally hundreds of drawings taped all over our house....a beautiful imagination that is being expressed! We have a boy that has opened his world to us! We can laugh over Timothy's jokes, discuss wild adventures, and listen to why he is having a bad day – we do not take this for granted, we cherish every word. There really aren't enough words to express our gratitude! Thank you and God Bless.

This is the best teacher gift I have received.

Strategy Two: Spirit Buddies

As I read the literature on SEL, I thought about how spirit and connection could be injected into our classrooms. The RD program is a good start, but we must find ways to maintain the feeling and the daily connection on an ongoing basis. Unfortunately, some students make no connections before their arrival at school. No one has said: "Good morning," or asked: "How are you feeling today?" or sent them off with: "Have a good day." Some students, too, are not greeted by anyone upon their arrival at school. They don't have friends waiting for them on the front steps or in the halls, and they enter our classrooms each day in relative obscurity. Often, these students express a feeling of being invisible – they believe no one notices them and no one cares.

How do we change that? How do we ensure every child starts every day on a positive note, experiencing a sense of connection and belonging? I learned a practice called "Spirit Buddies" from Rabbi Shefa Gold, a spiritual teacher, and I began incorporating it into my classroom: For 15 minutes at the beginning of each day, students connected in small groups of Spirit Buddies to greet and welcome each other, check in, and start the day in community. This provided an opportunity for the cortisol of students who arrived at school stressed to settle down. In my class, I put the students into groups of three, and gave them the first 15 minutes of the morning to meet. This gave me time to take attendance, collect any monies and forms, and handle other necessary administrative tasks, and greet the students. This practice creates community – everyone knows someone, has a support network, and is welcomed to the shared space every day. If someone is or has been absent, their buddies can check on them or fill each other in on happenings when they return. Because my students were also working on active listening skills, part of the English Language Arts curriculum, I asked them to take a few minutes each to share, and then just chat. Their buddies were not to interject their own stories, but they could make supportive comments (Like, "Wow, that's cool!" or "Are you okay?"), and they had to focus on really listening to each other. The amount of time the class spends as Spirit Buddies can be less than 15 minutes, but the sharing proves to be a vital part of building a sense of community. Now, in my university courses, I continue to implement this practice, and get a lot of positive feedback about it; for example, students who attend the course from outside the city are grateful for the chance to make connections so they do not feel completely isolated. At every grade level, at every age level, humans seek a sense of belonging and connection. Fifteen minutes at the beginning of the day can go a long way to achieving this feeling.

Spirit Buddies has been used in some schools across classrooms or grades. For instance, in one K–6 school, there had been considerable conflict between the grade 6 students, the oldest kids in the school, and the grade 5 students – the grade 6 students were making sure the grade 5s knew they were the boss. The teachers decided to put the students into Spirit Buddy groups that mixed grade 5 and 6 students every morning. The resulting connections significantly reduced the conflicts.

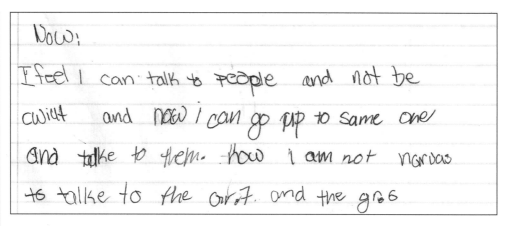

Figure 6.15 A student with an intellectual disability reflects on how spirit buddies has supported her.

Spirit Buddies helps foster students' sense of belonging and social coherence; initiate positive interactions; and increases students' self-worth, Students want to "be seen," and have an impact on others. Spirit Buddies helps students achieve these goals.

Strategy Three: Creating Democratic Classrooms

A democratic classroom is a vital ingredient in implementing UDL: Such an environment allows students to take ownership of their learning and to develop pro-social problem-solving skills. It also encourages student autonomy which, research shows, is integral to an individual's development of intrinsic motivation and self-efficacy (Hu and Zhang 2017). To create a democratic classroom environment students need to be involved, on a regular basis and in developmentally appropriate ways, in shared decision-making that increases their responsibility for making the classroom a good place to be and learn.)

Creating democratic classrooms involves the following:

1. Rules and Logical Consequences: A clear and consistent approach to discipline fosters individual responsibility and self-control. The rules and consequences are decided at class meetings, and then consistently implemented.

2. Guided Discovery: Practise instructional pedagogy that encourages inquiry, heightens interest, and teaches care of the school environment. This philosophy of teaching requires students to take ownership of their learning and teachers to step back and let students take on leadership.

3. Academic Choice: Devise approaches to give children choices in their learning that help them become engaged, self-motivated learners.

4. Classroom Organization: Implement strategies for arranging materials, furniture, and displays to encourage independence, promote caring, and maximize learning and positive social interaction for all students.

5. Family Communication Strategies: Devise ways for involving families as true partners in their children's education.

Five characteristics of a democratic classroom are:

1. Students and teachers work together to make students' learning a contribution to their community.
   - praise for students across intelligences, social behaviour
   - service projects

2. Students demonstrate their learning in public settings and receive public feedback.
   - in-class presentations
   - presentations to other classes, parents

3. Students have escalating degrees of choice, both as individuals and in groups, within the parameters provided by the teacher.
   - Students have input into schedule, grouping structures, methods of learning, and representing understanding.

4. Students actively work with problems, ideas, materials, and people as they learn skills and content.
   - A problem-based learning approach, in which students work in teams to figure it out

5. Students are held to a high degree of excellence in both their academic objectives and their social contributions to their larger community.
   - Students rise to high expectations, so expect your students to support each other, work together, and learn at deep levels.

Seven principles of a democratic classroom are:

1. The social curriculum is as important as the academic curriculum.

2. How children learn is as important as what they learn; process and content go hand in hand.

3. The greatest cognitive growth occurs through social interaction.

4. The set of social skills children need to be successful academically and socially includes cooperation, assertion, responsibility, empathy, and self-control, among others.

5. Knowing the children we teach – individually, culturally, and developmentally – is as important as knowing the content we teach.

6. Knowing the families of the children we teach and inviting their participation are essential to children's education.

7. How the adults at school work together is as important as individual competence: lasting change begins with the adult community.

A democratic classroom contributes to character development, because it provides an ongoing forum where students' thoughts are valued and the needs of anyone in the group can be addressed. Students learn how to consider the needs of others, voice their own needs in appropriate ways, and find solutions that are mutually acceptable. Empowered students are motivated to assume a degree of social responsibility, as they recognize how their contributions, either positive or negative, affect others in their community. Democratic classroom management creates a support structure that develops moral reasoning by strengthening the sense of community and holding community members accountable to practise respect and responsibility. Democracy mobilizes the peer culture on the side of virtue; that is, democracy creates a positive peer pressure that models pro-social behaviour.

Class Meetings

The Class Meeting is the best means of creating a democratic classroom environment. Arrange a face-to-face circle for the meeting to emphasize interactive discussion and problem solving. Class Meetings should be scheduled weekly in elementary schools that students attend all or most of the day, although a meeting can be called at any time by a community member. In September, students call a lot of meetings, in part because of the newness or sense of power, and in part because the community is still forming. It is vital for the teacher to respond. This sends the message to students that how we treat each other and how we feel about ourselves is more important than anything else. We will stop reading, teaching math or science – whatever we are doing – to resolve an issue that makes students feel emotional or social stress. The novelty of Class Meetings quickly wears off, but students will have received the message that the classroom is a safe place for resolving conflict peacefully. As the school year goes on, students are often able to resolve challenges without input from teachers. In a secondary-school setting, Class Meetings may be scheduled less often, perhaps once a month, but the process is the same.

Class Meetings teach students the skills of problem solving in social situations, and involve students in their learning community. The teacher sets safe and reasonable parameters for ideas and solutions.

The Class Meeting procedure goes as follows:

1. Students sit in a circle.

2. In turn, students go around the circle giving compliments and expressing their gratitude for the good that has happened in the community. For example: "I would like to give a compliment to _____ for helping me when _____," or "I am thankful for _____."

3. Students go around the circle a second time, raising issues in the community with the sentence frame: "I would like to change _____."

4. Students are not allowed to mention names when raising issues. Instead of saying: "Jack is yelling," say: "I would like to change how noisy it is during _____."

5. Students brainstorm possible solutions to problems raised, and discuss the advantages and disadvantages of each solution. I have had students role-play their solutions so they can see what the outcomes might be.

6. Students can try solutions as long as doing so is safe. If a solution doesn't work, students learn how to revisit their thinking, and try Plan B. With experience, students become more realistic. Students cannot learn if the teacher is always in control.

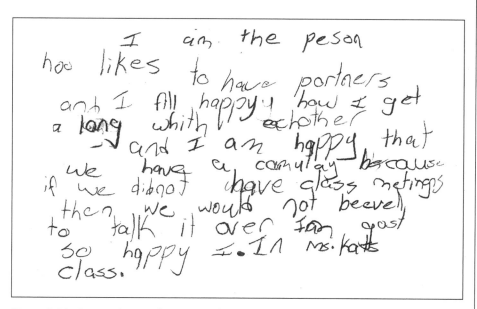

Figure 6.16 One student's reflection on class meetings.

Chapter 7

Addressing Mental-Health Needs with All Students

Children know when their parents are in conflict. Similarly, students are aware when teachers and staff are in conflict. A healthy school begins with a healthy staff culture that builds a healthy school culture.

Leaders need to consider how the programming used for students can also be used to build healthy district, staff, and school cultures. In turn, teachers need to consider how this programming can build classroom culture that is health-promoting and supports learning.

If the goal of Tier l is to design classrooms that meet the needs of the greatest number of students possible, we have to consider what social and emotional learning (SEL), mental health, and Indigenous education look like in UDL classrooms. As with social and emotional programming and instructional practice, universally designed Indigenous education means the programming is offered to all students, both Indigenous and non-Indigenous. Universally designed Indigenous education develops respect for Indigenous peoples and cultures and knowledge of Indigenous history and treaties, and focuses on reconciliation. Both Block One (SEL) and Block Two (inclusive instructional practice) affect students' and teachers' well-being. The link of well-being to SEL (Block One) is obvious and direct, but we also have to realize that our instructional practices (Block Two) affect well-being. All the social and emotional programming in the world won't help if students feel stupid and experience constant failure. Teachers' well-being is also then affected, because teachers don't want to see their students struggle and/or fail. Failure leaves teachers feeling ineffective, and it often leads to increases in challenging behaviour in the classroom.

In this chapter, we will discuss how to design a learning environment for student and teacher well-being.

A Framework for Well-Being

Research over several decades has revealed key factors in well-being. In chapter 2, we discussed many different frameworks for well-being. As weavers, if we pull these different frameworks apart and focus on the threads, we can see many connections in the concepts within that allow us to weave a new tapestry that is a synthesis of all of these frameworks.

There is an intrapersonal, interpersonal, and spiritual component to each framework. The Circle of Courage, Four Spirits, and positive mental health all focus on aspects of well-being that are about our relationship with ourselves, aspects that are related to our relationships with others, and aspects that connect these in a spiritual way. Well-being gives our life meaning and purpose, and allows us to see the interconnections within ourselves, with others, and with the planet.

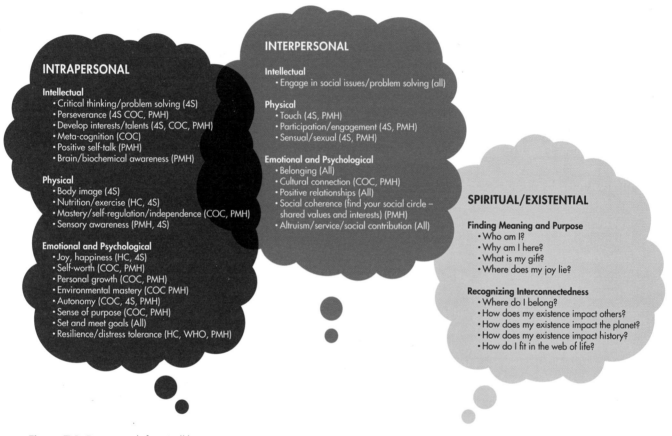

INTRAPERSONAL

Intellectual
- Critical thinking/problem solving (4S)
- Perseverance (4S COC, PMH)
- Develop interests/talents (4S, COC, PMH)
- Meta-cognition (COC)
- Positive self-talk (PMH)
- Brain/biochemical awareness (PMH)

Physical
- Body image (4S)
- Nutrition/exercise (HC, 4S)
- Mastery/self-regulation/independence (COC, PMH)
- Sensory awareness (PMH, 4S)

Emotional and Psychological
- Joy, happiness (HC, 4S)
- Self-worth (COC, PMH)
- Personal growth (COC, PMH)
- Environmental mastery (COC PMH)
- Autonomy (COC, 4S, PMH)
- Sense of purpose (COC, PMH)
- Set and meet goals (All)
- Resilience/distress tolerance (HC, WHO, PMH)

INTERPERSONAL

Intellectual
- Engage in social issues/problem solving (all)

Physical
- Touch (4S, PMH)
- Participation/engagement (4S, PMH)
- Sensual/sexual (4S, PMH)

Emotional and Psychological
- Belonging (All)
- Cultural connection (COC, PMH)
- Positive relationships (All)
- Social coherence (find your social circle – shared values and interests) (PMH)
- Altruism/service/social contribution (All)

SPIRITUAL/EXISTENTIAL

Finding Meaning and Purpose
- Who am I?
- Why am I here?
- What is my gift?
- Where does my joy lie?

Recognizing Interconnectedness
- Where do I belong?
- How does my existence impact others?
- How does my existence impact the planet?
- How does my existence impact history?
- How do I fit in the web of life?

Figure 7.1 Framework for Well-being

In the clouds illustrated above, specific factors (e.g., belonging, self-worth, autonomy) are shared across frameworks. These are the factors we focus on in our programming, because they are critical to well-being. Initially, the Three-Block Model (TBM) focused on the interpersonal and intrapersonal aspects of well-being, specifically self-worth and belonging, and programming was created to address these goals. However, a tragedy at a local school showed us that even students with high self-worth and belonging can, in a moment of acute distress, make tragic decisions. It became clear we were missing something. People can feel good about themselves, have friends, and so forth and still not know how to cope with acute distress (e.g., death of a loved one, breakup of a relationship). Psychiatrists refer to the ability to cope with acute distress as "distress tolerance." It is an aspect of resiliency, but one we rarely address. Positive self-worth and a strong sense of belonging build resiliency – "coping with the everyday stresses of life," as Health Canada puts it. However, self-worth and belonging are not sufficient to support students with acute crises.

The key is to realize we are not just talking about extreme trauma (war, abuse, or other incident we would all find traumatic). We must also realize there are experiences that might traumatize one individual and not another. Particularly in adolescence, students have heightened sensitivity, and can find the effects of a breakup with a best friend or partner so distressing that some have ended their lives. We cannot decide what another individual finds traumatic. Thus, we need to add distress tolerance to our understanding of resilience, and to our programming.

Intrapersonal wellness, interpersonal wellness, and spiritual wellness are interrelated. Someone who has strong self-awareness and emotional regulation is more likely to sustain positive relationships, and vice-versa. Similarly, the Four Spirits – physical, emotional, mental, and spiritual wellness – affect each other. We have two organizers we can use to build some kind of framework to understand such a large concept as well-being.

1. A framework that explores intrapersonal, interpersonal, and spiritual aspects of well-being, their links to Indigenous worldviews and the Truth and Reconciliation Commission (TRC), and programming that supports them.

2. A chronology of the school year or implementation – where to start, and how to then carry forward.

What is presented in the rest of this chapter is a holistic framework for health-promoting schools and classrooms. Note that I say framework and programming – not program: this is not scripted or rigid. I believe strongly in the professionalization of teachers. The framework provides support, information, and strategies – no one knows your students and your community like you do. All programming can be done in K–12 except where noted. How it is scaffolded, the complexity of the conversations, and the time allotted varies for different age groups.

Sustainable implementation will require:

- Leadership: Leaders will need to hold the vision, support teacher professional learning, and involve the community.

- Teacher professional learning: Teachers will need to have a base knowledge of inclusive education and UDL. I recommend teachers be familiar with the instructional design elements laid out in the book *Teaching to Diversity*. Teachers will also need support, professional learning communities, and time to implement the framework we are suggesting here.

- Recognition: Recognize what the specific needs of your community are.

- Believe in yourselves as professionals. Select what makes sense for you, and adjust as needed.

As we look to develop a school and class culture that fosters well-being for students and teachers, we need to be clear about our focus, and what is required:

- Intrapersonal Well-Being. Students and teachers need to develop:
  - personal definition of well-being
  - awareness of brain functions, and signs of flourishing and languishing
  - knowledge and practices related to physical health (e.g., nutrition, exercise, sleep, hydration)
  - self-worth
  - metacognitive abilities
  - self-regulation, mastery, independence
  - personal identity (awareness of strengths, challenges, goals)
  - resiliency and distress tolerance
  - hope
  - joy
- Interpersonal Well-Being. Students and teachers need to develop
  - generosity/altruism
  - positive relationships
  - sense of belonging
  - sense of connection to the land, their culture, and their social niche
- Indigenous Worldview and the TRC
  - recognition of the negative impact of racism and discrimination including historical wrongs involving the treaties, Indian act, and residential schools
  - sense of purpose related to healing and bringing people together
  - appreciation of the benefits of Indigenous worldviews for all people
- Spiritual Well-Being
  - sense of purpose
  - belief in the meaning and impact of their life
  - skills for spiritual connection (e.g., meditation, mantras)

To make programs about distress tolerance and the bigger picture of mental health and well-being, as well as the Calls to Action of the TRC accessible to all of our learners, we need to redesign existing resources. We want all students to be active participants in all of the activities. This is especially important for programming related to well-being (as compared to a curricular lesson), because this is what creates the classroom climate, and the interpersonal and intrapersonal skills on which we will rely to have a positive school year. This is about health and well-being, something far more important than any subject-related skill.

Universally designing these programs for well-being requires similar processes to curricular universal design: focusing on the big ideas and essential understandings, facilitating student inquiry into the concepts, and differentiating the means of instruction and student response. Role-plays, case studies, bibliotherapy and videotherapy, visual representations, and so forth can bring programming to life, engaging students and helping them to make connections and remember the content.

Mental-Health Literacy

At times, mental-health literacy has focused on student and teacher awareness of signs and symptoms related to mental illness. While it is important for students and teachers to recognize when they, or others they know, are languishing, an inclusive perspective focuses on a Tier 1 level – classroom-based programming. Strength-based perspectives mean we want to work toward well-being preventatively.

> Mental health literacy has been defined as the knowledge, beliefs and abilities that enable the recognition, management or prevention of mental health problems. (Canadian Alliance on Mental Illness and Mental Health [CAMIMH] 2007)

Mental-health literacy in inclusive schools means that our students need to explicitly be taught how the brain works and what is involved in well-being. Students explore different cultural beliefs and practices related to well-being, and develop an internal locus of control – they learn how to self-regulate rather than be externally controlled. In a learning environment, self-regulation incorporates both emotional self-regulation – the ability to work collaboratively; persevere through challenges; and manage frustration, anxiety, and anger – and academic self-regulation – the ability to monitor attention, strategies, and outcomes of learning. We will begin by thinking about self-regulation of well-being in the emotional sense.[8]

Now's (My Progress):
- Goal was "To Get the Rick Hansen" winning the Rick Hansen was a goal. It was something I really wanted to win but as the year went by I learned that it didn't matter if you didn't win an award. The important thing is if you've done something from your heart and feel good about it – then you don't need any award to be recognized for it. This has really changed my thinking. Earlier, I wanted every "nice" action of mine to be recognized– but now I feel the best way to help others is by doing it when your heart tells you to: not when an adult is present so that he/she can see what you are doing...

Figure 7.2 A student reflects on shifting from being reward oriented to an internal locus of motivation.

---

8   Teachers who want more information about MHL, or wish to go deeper with their students, can go to <teenmentalhealth.org>.

In mental-health literacy, students need to know:

- how the brain works
- the components of mental health
- how to maintain well-being
- how to be a friend

The Brain Unit: Mental-Health Literacy the UDL Way

The Brain Unit consists of seven lessons. As with the Respecting Diversity (RD) program, the brain unit lessons can be extended into great depth, or can be completed in a workshop format. The intention is to help all students develop the following:

- an understanding of how the brain works
- a personal definition of well-being, and strategies for maintaining it
- an understanding of mental illness, respect and compassion for those who live with illness, and the ability to be a friend to someone with a mental illness
- the ability to recognize signs of mental illness within oneself and know how to get help

To complete these lessons, you will need to do the following:

- Familiarize yourself with the structures of the brain on the diagram for teachers in appendix C, including the lobes (parietal, temporal, occipital, and frontal), levels (brain stem, cortex), emotional and memory centres (amygdala, hippocampus, cerebellum, and corpus callosum). Appendix F reviews the parts of the neuron (dendrite, axon, terminal button, synapses). As well, learn about key chemicals (e.g., neurotransmitters, and the hormones cortisol and oxytocin). These are discussed in Lesson 4, page 118.
- Gather materials such as chart paper, markers, Plasticine, Lego, or some other constructive material.
- Reproduce brain diagram for students found in appendix C, and the sensory diagram in appendix D.
- Select age-appropriate video clips for your students from YouTube, Edutopia, or other sites related to:
  - parts of the brain
  - neuron communication
  - fight-and-flight mechanism
  - famous people living with mental illnesses

Program	Aspect of Well-Being		Specific Target
Brain Unit	Intrapersonal	Intellectual	self-awareness, self-regulation, develop interests and talents
		Physical	awareness of how the brain functions, physical outcomes of chemical responses, and importance of sleep/nutrition/exercise
		Emotional/ Psychological	self-worth, hope, self-regulation, expression of feelings, needs
		Spiritual	sense of purpose: what is my gift?
	Interpersonal	Intellectual	respect for diversity, perspective-taking, collaborative and cooperative skills, common language
		Physical	
		Emotional/ Psychological	belonging, generosity, class culture, positive relationships, impact on others
		Spiritual	meaning: what do I have to offer?

Figure 7.3 The Brain Unit: Targeted Outcomes for Well-Being

Assessment

The Brain Unit is not meant to be assessed through evaluation or grading (unless it is being done as a science/curricular unit. If so, see the rubric in appendix E.) We don't care whether students memorize every part of the brain and its function(s), as long as they understand the big ideas (essential understandings). We will talk about assessing well-being on page 159. For now, what matters is whether or not students can do the following at the end of the unit:

1. Identify their emotions and ways they can manage them.

2. Create a personal definition of well-being and plans for maintaining it.

3. Articulate strategies for creating positive thoughts and reducing stress and cortisol.

4. Show compassion and demonstrate support for anyone struggling with well-being.

Lesson 1: Parts of the Brain

Essential Understanding: The brain has specialized areas for different kinds of information and functions.

Essential Question: How does the brain work?

1. Brainstorm with students: What do you know about the brain? Sort information into categories such as physical structures, functions, interesting facts.

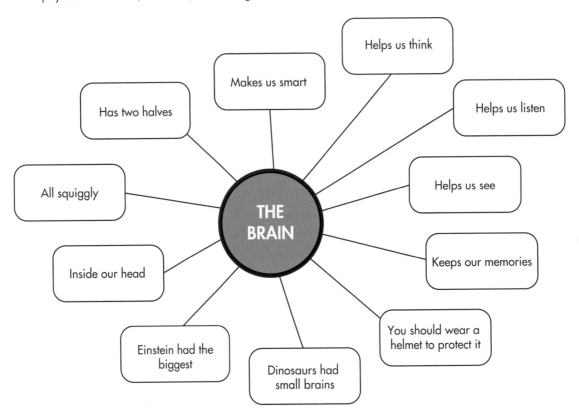

Figure 7.4 Brain Brainstorm

2. Show students visuals of the brain – preferably a mix of 2D and 3D (see online or in reference books, or you can make one out of Plasticine).

3. Explain that different parts of the brain perform different functions, but they all communicate with each other. Like a sports team, different parts of the brain do different things, but they all have to work together to play the game.

4. Introduce students to the hemispheres and lobes of the brain, and the levels (brain stem, cortex).

5. Provide each student with a copy of student diagram from Appendix C. Have them label the parts of the brain discussed. Note that they will be continuing the discussion in the next day's lesson and adding to the diagram at that time.

6. Give students Plasticine, and have them each make a small model of the brain.

Central Nervous System

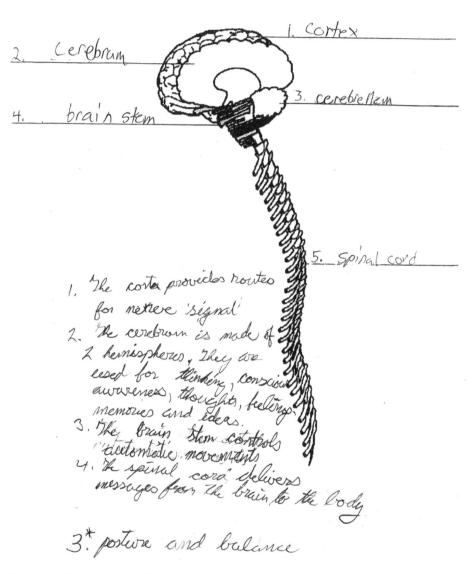

1. Cortex

2. Cerebrum

3. cerebrellum

4. brain stem

5. Spinal cord

1. The cortex provides routes for nerve 'signal'
2. The cerebrum is made of 2 hemispheres. They are used for thinking, conscious awareness, thoughts, feelings, memories and ideas.
3. The brain stem controls "automatic" movements.
4. The spinal cord delivers messages from the brain to the body.

3.* posture and balance

Figure 7.5 Student sample from the Brain Unit.

Lesson 2: Cross-Section of the Brain

Essential Understanding: The brain has specialized areas for different kinds of information and functions.

Essential Question: How does the brain work?

1. Review lesson 1.
2. Discuss the function(s) of each lobe:
   - parietal: motor cortex
   - temporal: hearing
   - frontal: thinking, judgment
   - occipital: vision
3. Show students a cross-section of the brain. Have each student add to their diagram from lesson 1. Together, label the spinal cord, cortex, amygdala, cerebellum, hypothalamus, and corpus callosum.
4. Discuss the function(s) of each part:
   - spinal cord: carries messages to the rest of the body
   - cortex: where thinking occurs
   - amygdala: regulates emotions by releasing chemicals into the brain
   - cerebellum: balance and coordination
   - hippocampus: memory
   - corpus callosum: connects the two hemispheres
5. Have students re-form their brain model to include internal structures and label the parts.

Lesson 3: Neurons

Essential Understanding: The brain is made up of small cells called "neurons" that are responsible for communicating messages within the brain.

Essential Question: How does the brain communicate?

1. Build a brain out of Lego or any constructive material that has connecting parts. (There are many examples online you can refer to).

2. Show students a diagram of a neuron (see appendix F). Explain that each section of the brain is made up of small cells called "neurons" that act like wires. They carry messages from one part of the brain to another. Explain that each Lego piece represents a neuron, and that electricity passes through the neurons, and then triggers the release of chemicals that travel to the next neuron, and start the process over again.

3. Show a video that illustrates the communication from one neuron to another. See resource list in appendix A for some suggestions.

4. Have students represent brain communication. Some possible ways include:
   - Use dominoes and a marble track. Have the dominoes fall, trigger the marble, which rolls across a space, and causes the next line of dominoes to fall.
   - Have students act it out. In small groups, have students pass a ball hand to hand within their group, then throw the ball across a space to the next group of students.
   - Sequence images to show the steps.
   - PBS provides some additional great activities.[9]

---

9   See: http://www.pbs.org/newshour/extra/lessons-plans/nobel-prize-medicine-honors-discoveries-cells-move-cargo-neuroscience-lesson-plan/>.

Lesson 4: Neurochemistry

Essential Understanding #1: The brain has chemicals called "neurotransmitters" that control emotions, attention, memory, and general well-being.

Essential Understanding #2: Thoughts and perceptions cause the brain to release chemicals, and the chemicals affect our feelings.

Essential Question: Why do we have feelings?

1. Discuss the three chemicals (neurotransmitters) that affect emotional well-being and what each controls:
   - serotonin: anxiety and mood. Low levels of serotonin are linked to anxiety and depression.
   - dopamine: energy and pleasure. High levels of dopamine are associated with high energy and pleasure.
   - norepinephrine: focus and alertness. High levels of norepinephrine are associated with greater ability to concentrate, stay alert, and feel energized.

2. Explain that when we think, the brain releases chemicals. There are two important chemicals, in addition to neurotransmitters, that the brain can release:
   - cortisol: stress hormone. Cortisol increases heart rate, breathing, body temperature, and reactivity. When we are afraid or angry, cortisol is released so that we can respond to the danger. Cortisol shuts off the frontal lobe so we can't think rationally or make good judgments. This means we react instinctively and impulsively.
   - oxytocin: pleasure hormone. Oxytocin causes us to feel happy, relaxed, excited. Along with the chemicals serotonin, dopamine, and endorphins, oxytocin helps us feel joy, pleasure, and peace.

3. Give students scenarios appropriate to their age (e.g., you get a present on your birthday, your boyfriend/girlfriend breaks up with you). Ask students what they think happens in their brain (e.g., serotonin levels drop).

4. Have students represent things that release oxytocin for them, and things that cause cortisol release. Discuss the idea that what one person finds stressful (e.g., running a marathon), someone else might find enjoyable.

Figure 7.6 Student collage illustrating things that make them happy (above) and things that cause them stress (below).

Lesson 5: Brain Reactivity

Essential Understanding #1: The brain has chemicals called "neurotransmitters" that control our emotions, attention, memory, and general well-being.

Essential Understanding #2: Our thoughts and perceptions cause the brain to release chemicals, and those chemicals affect our feelings.

Essential Question: Why do we have feelings?

1. Place some berries, water, oil, and ice cubes in a blender. Have students imagine the blender is their brain, with all the different chemicals, feelings, and ideas in it. Turn on the blender until everything is swirled together. Then, observe what happens over time (the mixture settles into layers).

2. Explain that when we think we are in danger – when we feel scared or sad, our brain is like the blender. It mixes up a whole bunch of things, and we can't see clearly what's going on. If we can learn to calm ourselves and not make quick decisions, our brain will settle down and we will be able to see all the pieces.

3. Show students a video about the fight-or-flight reaction (see YouTube, Edutopia, and other sites). Choose an age-appropriate video for your students. Discuss how when the brain perceives danger, either emotional or physical, it stops thinking, and just wants to defend and protect us. That's why we feel like we want to get away, or why we get angry and lose our temper.

4. Show students the graphics below of event, reaction, action. Discuss how certain strategies can be used to interrupt the cycle of cortisol, thereby calming us down, and changing our thoughts and feelings before we react.

Figure 7.7 The ERA Cycle

Figure 7.8 An Example of an ERA Cycle

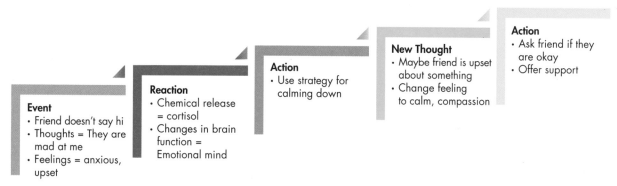

Figure 7.9 Self-Regulated ERA Cycle

5. Have students create scenarios with various starting points, or read a book in which a character encounters something stressful (see appendix A). Ask students to draw or write to represent both cycles – one without strategic intervention, and one with. For example:

- You walk into class, and the teacher announces a test.
  - Thought = "I'm going to fail"; feeling = panic; brain reaction = cortisol release; behaviour = anger, swear at teacher.
  - Thought = "I'm going to fail": feeling = panic; brain reaction = cortisol release; action = deep breathing, positive self-talk; new thought = "I know as much as anyone here. Everyone is surprised. I just need to do what I can"; feeling = calming down, determined; action = take test successfully.

Discuss the importance of recognizing when we are feeling stressed, because then we can self-regulate our emotions by using strategies to calm down.

Many great activities are available to help students explore their feelings and learn how to recognize and regulate them. You can have students identify a feeling they have had in the last 24 hours, draw/write/discuss how they knew they were feeling that way (e.g., tears in their eyes, a knot in their stomach), and tell what they did to deal with it. You can also show photographs or videos, have students identify the emotion(s) a character is feeling, and encourage them to talk about how they know what the person is feeling.

The website *Education World* provides several sample lessons, including one titled "The Feeling Guy" at <http://www.educationworld.com/a_lesson/lesson-plan-managing-feelings.shtml>.

It is important for students to understand feelings are natural and okay. However, feelings can be made worse if we react impulsively or search for reasons why we are upset. This is a critical point to make! For those students who struggle with anxiety, in particular, having them learn how to interrupt the cycle is the greatest gift you can give them.

Give students some scenarios. For example:

- I'm out with friends when I start to feel really nervous – like something's wrong.
- I'm lying awake at night and feel anxious and upset, but I don't know why.

Discuss with students that sometimes our brains become overstimulated and release cortisol. If we do something to relax, the cortisol will go away in 15 to 20 minutes. However, if we focus on trying to figure out what's wrong and why we are upset, we will focus on all the negative things in our life, and cause the brain to release more cortisol, making the situation worse!

Lesson 6: The Senses and Their Effects on the Brain

Essential Understanding: Our senses transmit information to the brain, which triggers memories and reactions.

Essential Question: How do our senses affect our emotions?

What we see, hear, feel, taste, and smell send signals to the brain. Our senses can cause the release of oxytocin or cortisol. A sound, smell, sight, sensation, or taste can trigger instincts or memories that result in pleasure, fear, joy, or anger.

The senses are all linked to the hippocampus – our memory. That's why a whiff of bacon might suddenly trigger a memory of breakfast at Grandma's. Or the smell of cleaning fluid might remind us of hospitals. Similarly, a tune from a song, the taste of home-cooked food, the feel of sand sifting between our toes, or the sight of an oncoming thunderstorm can all trigger memories. Some of these memories are positive, so when thoughts of them are triggered, the brain releases oxytocin. Some memories, though, may be negative; if we feel endangered emotionally or physically, it can cause the release of cortisol.

It is important for students to understand that the mechanism of sensory triggers – memories – cause chemical release. Later, we will talk about this mechanism in relation to Post-Traumatic Stress Disorder (PTSD). In this lesson, we will introduce students to the pathways of the senses, and help students identify triggers in their own lives.

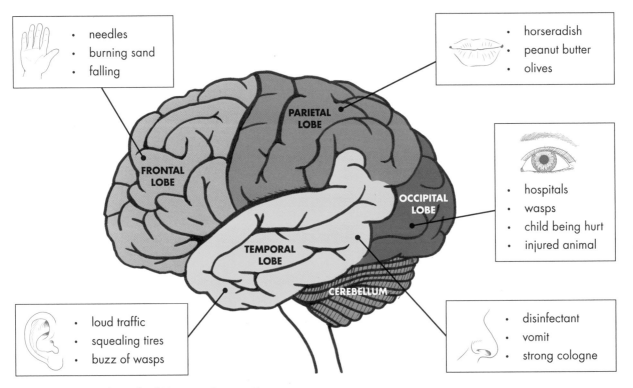

Figure 7.10 Sample Web of Negative Sensory Triggers

1. Have students cycle through some centres related to the senses.
   - Smell: Place a few objects with strong smells (e.g., pepper, rose petals, coffee beans) in opaque containers. Ask students to identify the smells, and to indicate how each makes them feel (e.g., happy, repulsed, sad).
   - Sight: Display photos that will elicit emotions, both positive and negative.
   - Taste: Have students sample various tastes and record their reaction to each. Be aware of any allergies students may have before bringing foods into the classroom.
   - Touch: Have students feel a variety of textures (e.g., soft fur, something prickly) and record how they react to each.
   - Sound: Play audio clips of sounds, both pleasant and unpleasant, and have students record how each sound makes them feel.
2. Show students the graphic of the brain and senses. Have students make two webs – one for things that cause them stress, and the other for things they find pleasurable. Remind them that triggers are usually based on memories. For instance, when I was 12, I was hospitalized for an extended period of time after suffering a ruptured appendix. As a result, certain sights, smells, and sounds trigger unpleasant memories of that hospital stay. The same sights, smells, and sounds might not be triggers for someone else.

Once students identify their unconscious triggers, they can use strategies they are learning to manage the triggers (e.g., the breathing exercises on pages 132–134; the scripts from DBT on pages 156 and 158). For me, when I realized the sound of squealing tires triggers negative memories (I was in a car accident), I recognized why I am triggered. Whenever this happens now, I am able to use breathing techniques, mantras, or other strategies to settle myself down.

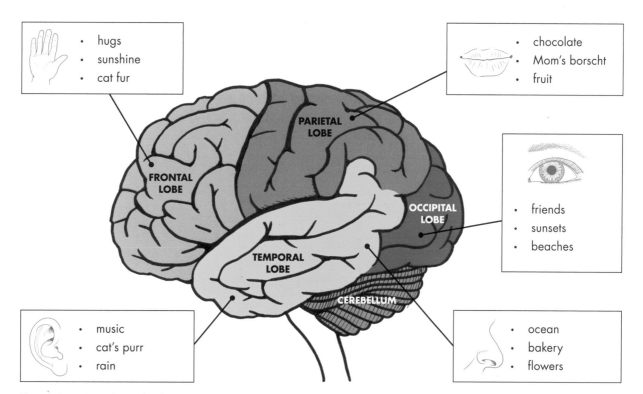

Figure 7.11 Sample Web of Positive Sensory Triggers

Lesson 7: Mental Health and Mental Illness

NOTE: The sections in this lesson may be broken into several lesson periods.

Essential Understanding #1: The definition of mental health, or well-being, has some common agreed-upon elements and some personal definitions.

Essential Understanding #2: Mental health is not static – we all have good times and hard times throughout our lives.

Essential Question: What does it mean to be mentally healthy?

Now that students have an understanding of the brain and how it works, we need to introduce the idea of mental health. So far, everything we have done can be used with K–12 students. The RD program, Spirit Buddies, Class Meetings, and the Brain Unit have been presented to all ages, including at the university where I now teach. I have taught the Brain Unit in my own grade 1/2 class, and the kids loved it! I have also taught it in a high-school biology class.

Mental-health literacy programs have been successfully delivered to many, many students around the world. However, before you begin using the programs below, you need to consider the age of your students and the degree to which students in your class have experienced trauma or mental illness. This is not to make it sound scary –Rather, it is to encourage you to make choices based on what you believe is appropriate for your class. For instance, discussions of addictions may not be appropriate for the youngest kids in elementary schools. On the other hand, identifying simple emotions may not be appropriate for high-school students. The grade suggestions below are just that – suggestions.

Part I: Defining Mental Health

The Mental-Health Continuum (K–12)

1. Introduce students to the words *flourishing* and *languishing*. For younger students, these can be explained as going from happy and content (flourishing) to sad and discouraged (languishing). Place the words *flourishing* and *languishing* on a vertical continuum (so that we can then add the horizontal later). (See figure 7.12.)

2. Put students into small groups. Give each group the list of emotion words (appendix G). Ask students to place the words along the continuum.

3. Discuss with students the idea that health fluctuates. Sometimes we are healthy, and sometimes we get a cold or the flu. Have students share stories of times when they have been mentally healthy (e.g., happy, at peace, flourishing), and times when they have been unhealthy (e.g., sad, angry, languishing).

Flourishing

Languishing

Figure 7.12
The Mental-Health Continuum

The Components of Well-Being

1. Brainstorm with students what well-being means to them. What are the components of a healthy person? Use the Four Spirits (e.g., sort into mental, physical, emotional, and spiritual; see page 24), the well-being clouds (see page 108), or another organizer to help students create a framework with which to think about well-being and flourishing.

2. Discuss with students the two elements to well-being: strategies and outcomes. Give the example of someone who is well. A well person is calm, peaceful, and happy. Strategically, someone who is well uses positive self-talk, develops their interests, and makes time for fun and relaxation to become calm, peaceful, and happy. Have students create a visual representation of what wellness means to them, and how they can achieve it.

3. Share the well-being clouds with students {see page 108}. Review any terms students aren't familiar with. Have students set a goal for interpersonal well-being and one for intrapersonal well-being. For instance, a student may say: "I would like to develop a more positive voice and be less critical of myself; for a few minutes once a day, I am going to use a mantra meditation with a positive affirmation."

4. Present students with the questions from the spiritual cloud. Explain that research shows the biggest factor in well-being as an adult is feeling that your life has meaning and purpose. Discuss the ideas that childhood and adolescence are times for discovering their gifts, developing them, and figuring out how to use their gifts to live a life that is meaningful and purposeful. Have students respond to the questions in a private journal: they can draw, write, or use tech, to record their thinking. (Make sure students revisit their journal or technical device often throughout the year and make revisions as they develop their thoughts.)

Part II: Understanding Mental Illness

Essential Understanding #1: Mental illness is the same as physical illness.

Essential Understanding #2: Mental illness has significant impact on individuals and their families.

Essential Question: What is it like to have a mental illness?

The Mental-Illness Continuum (Grades 4–12)

1. Introduce students to the term *mental illness*. Explain that all of the organs in the human body have a function (or several functions), and use chemicals and structures to carry out that function. Discuss the following example with students: The pancreas produces insulin to regulate sugar in our blood. When the pancreas does not produce enough insulin, high levels of sugar build up in the blood. We call this condition "diabetes." Because high levels of sugar in our blood can cause damage, doctors give patients with diabetes insulin to replace the insulin the body cannot produce.

2. Connect the diabetes example to mental illness. Students need to understand that the brain is just another organ in the body. It, too, produces chemicals that have a function, actually several functions, in the body. When the brain produces too much or not enough of a chemical we need, we call it a mental illness, even though it is actually a physical illness, just as diabetes is.

3. Explain to students that each of the following illnesses comes from either too little, or too much, of an important chemical:
   • Depression: too little serotonin, norepinephrine
   • Schizophrenia: too much dopamine
   • Attention Deficit Hyperactivity Disorder (ADHD): too little dopamine
   • Bipolar: fluctuating serotonin
   • Addictions: related to dopamine
   • Obsessive Compulsive Disorder (OCD): related to serotonin
   • Eating disorders: reduced serotonin
   • PTSD: related to norepinephrine and serotonin
   • Tourette's: excess levels of dopamine

Photocopy and distribute the cards for students with the words for some of these mental illnesses (see appendix H.)

4. Have students create a mental-illness continuum (see figure 7.13 below). Have students place each word where they think it should go on the continuum. You may need to explain to students why the "high mental illness" is on the left. Normally we think of the left as low and the right as high (like on a ruler). However, because high mental illness means someone is unwell (a negative state), Keyes places it on the left.

    Note that we are trying to spark some serious conversation here. We want students to differentiate between clear mental illness (like schizophrenia), conditions that can be related – such as homelessness, and normal personality or emotional differences – such as shyness or having a sad day. Although there is no right answer for what is the "highest" mental illness, it is usually defined by the degree to which it interferes with being able to maintain health, jobs, and positive relationships. Thus, something like schizophrenia is considered high mental illness because it is life-long and significantly affects functioning, where as something like ADHD, while affecting life, does not necessarily prevent an individual from holding a job or having relationships.

High Mental Illness   **Low Mental Illness**

Figure 7.13 The Mental-Illness Continuum

5. Take the two continua and combine them (see figure 7.14). Discuss the idea that we all experience hard times, but someone with a mental illness struggles more deeply than the average person (someone with normal levels of chemicals). Use anxiety disorder as an example. Many people will be nervous before an exam, but someone with an anxiety disorder may be nervous at other times, as well, with no trigger (at least not one that's obvious).

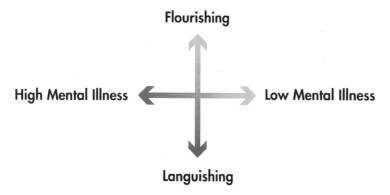

Figure 7.14 Dual Continuum of Mental Health and Mental Illness

6. Divide the class into groups. Have them do some research about one of the illnesses, and then report back. There are many websites, videos, books, and so forth students can use. You could also bring in guest speakers.

Harmony

Is harmony that hard to find?
How could that thought slip his mind,
While on that horrid battlefield,
Killing with the sword he wields.

While training at the camp assigned,
Is harmony that hard to find?
War is not a solution,
When will there be a resolution?

The war is over, and he wins,
Yet he asks god to forgive his sins.
Is harmony that hard to find?
In the cruel society human's designed?

Finally, he goes home at last,
He finds his home wrecked in a blast.
Tears flow freely, he puts that behind.
Is harmony that hard to find?

Figure 7.15 A poem written by a student studying PTSD.

Impact of Mental Illness on Individuals and Families

Students need to understand the impact of mental illness on individuals and their families, as this develops compassion and reduces bullying, alienation, and stigmatization.

1. Ask students to think about media (e.g., movies, books, television shows) that depict people with mental illness. As a class, create a T-chart: on one side list characters students think are valid representations of mental illnesses; on the other side list characters students think are inaccurate/ unfair (e.g., the film *Psycho*).

2. Introduce the term *stigma*. Ask students to define it. Discuss the following definition:

   Stigma refers to a cluster of negative attitudes and beliefs that motivate the general public to fear, reject, avoid and discriminate against people with mental illnesses. Stigma is not just a matter of using the wrong word or action. Stigma is about disrespect. It is the use of negative labels to identify a person living with mental illness. Stigma is a barrier. Fear of stigma and the resulting discrimination discourages individuals and their families from getting the help they need (SAMHSA 2004).

3. Ask students if there was ever a time when they wanted to do something, or wear something, and didn't because they were afraid people would make fun of them. Discuss the idea that fear can stop people from doing the things they need to do to be happy and get well. For instance, seeing a counsellor might be helpful for someone with a mental illness, but if they are afraid someone will make fun of them, they may not see the counsellor to get the help they need. In this way, stigma becomes discrimination – because people with preconceived ideas about what someone with a mental illness is like will reject them socially. Thus, people with mental illnesses are discriminated against when looking for jobs, seeking friendships, and more.

   Have students brainstorm words that are often used in relation to people with mental illnesses (e.g., *loony, psycho, sicko, crazy, crybaby*). Write the quotes from the reproducible (see page 129) on the board, or reproduce and provide each student with a copy. Select a student (or students) to read the quotes aloud one at a time.

4. Have students discuss each quote and respond to it in any way they like. This can be extended to developing service projects, creating information communications (e.g., ads, newspaper articles), and through activities in other curricular areas.

5. Introduce literature and/or show students videos that depict people with mental illnesses (e.g., *Girl, Interrupted; A Beautiful Mind; The Fisher King; The King's Speech; Rain Man; The Perks of Being a Wallflower*). Share video clips of famous people such as Robin Williams, Howie Mandel, and others who have publicly discussed living with a mental illness. Discuss what it must be like to live with a mental illness, and what it is like for friends and families. Be sure to be evenhanded – there are gifts that people with mental illness bring, and there are challenges. We do not want students to pity people with mental illnesses, anymore than they should pity someone in a wheelchair or with diabetes. However, we do want them to recognize the challenges people overcome, and to have respect for them.

Revisiting the Continua

Have students revisit the combined continua (see page 126). Discuss why placing everyone with a particular mental illness on the mental-health continua is not possible: It is possible to have a diagnosed mental illness, such as ADHD, and be flourishing on any given day or period of time. People with mental illnesses are not always ill, nor are they always languishing, but they have to work much harder to flourish, just as someone who has a physical disability has to work harder to be independent physically.

Stigma, Violence, and Mental Illness

Although studies suggest a link between mental illnesses and violence, the contribution of people with mental illnesses to overall rates of violence is small, and further, the magnitude of the relationship is greatly exaggerated in the minds of the general population *(Institute of Medicine 2006)*.

…the vast majority of people who are violent do not suffer from mental illnesses *(American Psychiatric Association 1994)*.

People with psychiatric disabilities are far more likely to be victims than perpetrators of violent crime *(Appleby, et al. 2001)*.

People with severe mental illnesses, schizophrenia, bipolar disorder or psychosis, are 2 ½ times more likely to be attacked, raped or mugged than the general population *(Hiday et al. 1999)*.

The effects of stigma and discrimination are profound. The President's New Freedom Commission on Mental Health (2003) found: "Stigma leads others to avoid living, socializing, or working with, renting to, or employing people with mental disorders – especially severe disorders, such as schizophrenia. It leads to low self-esteem, isolation, and hopelessness. It deters the public from seeking and wanting to pay for care. Responding to stigma, people with mental-health problems internalize public attitudes and become so embarrassed or ashamed that they often conceal symptoms and fail to seek treatment.

Portage & Main Press, 2018, *Ensouling Our Schools*, ISBN: 978-1-55379-683-1

Part III: Supporting People with Mental Illnesses

Essential Understanding #1: Having a support network is critical to the healing of people who are ill.

Essential Understanding #2: We can positively or negatively affect the lives of people with mental illness.

Essential Question: How can we create a support system for people with mental illnesses?

- Remind students that interactions with others change brain chemistry. When we call someone a name, reject them, or otherwise react negatively, their perception of this interaction causes them to release cortisol, and to be unwell. When we smile at someone, are friendly, give them a hug, or just have fun together, the interaction causes them to release oxytocin and serotonin. *How we treat people can either hurt them or help them!*

- Ask: Knowing what we know now, how could we create a supportive community in our class, and in our world, for people with mental illnesses?
  - Prompt students, when needed, to consider the following:
    - If your friend had a physical illness, what would you do?
    - How could you help someone reduce cortisol and increase oxytocin?
      - give a hug; offer to do yoga or breathing, or some other positive feedback to make them feel better
      - not try to fix, try to support
  - What would you do if you were working in a group with someone who gets distracted easily, can't sit still, or gets anxious about speaking out?
  - How would you reduce stigma or stop bullying?
  - How would you know when it was time to get help for a friend?

- Have students work in small groups to create a role-play, video, or information campaign to share their learning. For instance, they could make a video about "what to do when your friend is sad."

- Give each student a copy of the handout "Warning Signs of a Mental Illness" (appendix I). Explain that everyone will sometimes experience the feelings/issues listed on the handout. For instance, everyone will sometimes not feel like going out with friends, and just want to hang out at home. These warning signs are only a concern when:
  - They happen consistently over a period of at least two weeks.
  - They are not triggered by an event when it would be normal to be sad for more than two weeks (e.g., someone's grandparent died). However, if the sadness persisted for months, then it is a concern.

- Ask students if they know who to speak to if they are worried about a friend, or about themselves. Make sure they know about local resources (e.g., counsellors, suicide-prevention lines).

- Give students the mental-health scenarios found in appendix J. Ask them if they think these are times when they should get help for their friend or themselves. Although students may think it's "not their business," they need to know when it is time to get help – even if a friend has sworn them to secrecy.

Strategies for Well-Being

It is important to note the difference between using strategies to maintain well-being, and using them to numb or repress emotions. Teaching children that when they're upset they should do something to get rid of the feelings is a dangerous message: in later years, students may use alcohol or drugs to avoid feeling bad. Students should be told their feelings are genuine and okay. Strategies are used to cope with the feelings, but not to deny or numb them. There is a reason why so many religions have "lamentations" – it is healthy to recognize, acknowledge, and express emotions. Students need to be taught how to do the following:

- Ask themselves whether the feelings they are experiencing are healthy and need expression. For instance, there is a difference between needing to calm down because they're nervous about a test and grieving the loss of someone near and dear. Crying when sad is healthy!

- Find appropriate ways to express feelings of anger. For instance, call a friend to talk, or ask for time alone. Violence is not okay.

While acknowledging and expressing feelings is healthy and necessary, there is a time to begin moving through them. Use the strategies that follow in one or more of these ways:

- as a daily practice to maintain well-being

- to help cope with acute issues of stress or distress

- to take breaks and rebalance oneself before attempting something challenging or facing the next part of the day

You.
Buried.
In that dark, silent coffin.
The you that cannot be seen.
Will we lose it someday? The light we held onto.
The memory of you. The memory of me.
As I watch people bury you
A single tear.
Two tears.
Three tears. Many tears that cannot be counted
Trickles down my cheek.
My tears, cry for me.
Family friends around me
Rubs my shoulder.
"Don't cry"
They tell me.
I ignore them.
They don't understand.
How much I need them.
My family.
I think.
It is unfair.
People I love die first.
Buried.
Alone in the silent darkness
The you that cannot be seen.
I shoulder the burden.
And leave it behind me.
I force on a smile.
And wave farewell.

Figure 7.16 A poem written by a student about an experience of "buried feelings."

Breathing and Its Effects on the Brain

Breathing is an unusual process in the body, because it is automatic (it happens when we aren't thinking about it), and we can control it (we can choose to speed up or slow down our breath).

Scientists have known for a long time that stress affects our breathing (American Psychological Association 2017). The release of cortisol causes our heart rate to rise, resulting in quicker, shallower breathing. Until recently, what we didn't know (although Eastern cultures have recognized this for millennia) was that our breathing can also regulate our stress. When we slow and deepen our breathing, we oxygenate the brain, which causes the release of "pleasure chemicals" such as oxytocin. Deepening our breath signals the brain that it is time to calm down. We can explain this to our students, then we can teach them several different kinds of breathing.

- Breathing to a count

  Using a count that slows our inhale, holds, and then slows the exhale counteracts the hyperventilation of stress. One common technique is 4–7–8, promoted by many yoga and meditation teachers.

  1. Exhale completely through your mouth, making a "whoosh" sound.
  2. Close your mouth and inhale quietly through your nose while silently counting to four.
  3. Hold your breath for a count of seven.
  4. Exhale completely through your mouth, making a "whoosh" sound to a count of eight.
  5. This is one breath. Now inhale again, and repeat the cycle three more times for a total of four breaths.

- Breathing to a mantra

  A mantra is a phrase that is repeated over and over, like a chant. Traditionally, it was considered to have a sacred resonance to it – either because of the actual sound or the meaning of the words. The idea of mantra breathing is to set an intention, or to use a phrase that one is hoping to achieve (e.g., "I am happy and relaxed." "I am safe; everything is okay.") to tell the brain to stop producing cortisol, and instead produce the pleasure chemicals. Encourage students to choose their own mantras. However, it may be helpful to first brainstorm several ideas, so students who can't think of one can select one from the list.

  1. Select your mantra.
  2. As you say your mantra slowly, inhale. Then, exhale (similar to "breathing to a count").
  3. Repeat several times.

- Breathing using imagery

  1. Sit comfortably in a chair or on a cushion.

  2. Imagine a time when you were angry or anxious. Create an image of an animal or object in your head that reflects that feeling (e.g., a cat hissing, a black cloud).

  3. Inhale while imagining an animal/object that you like, or something that smells or tastes good and has bright colours, then exhale as you image the animal/object and dark colours leaving your body.

- Belly breathing

  1. Put one hand on your chest, and the other on your belly, and inhale. As you slowly exhale, focus on pushing out the hand on your belly, without moving the hand on your chest.

  2. Belly breathing can be combined with breathing to a count.

Figure 7.17 Imagery Breathing

Figure 7.18 Belly Breathing

- Reverse belly breathing/
  Back breathing

  1. Put one hand on your lower back, and one hand on your belly.

  2. As you inhale, push out the hand on your back, while keeping the hand on your belly still.

  NOTE: To balance the body, alternate back breathing with belly breathing.

Figure 7.19 Reverse Breathing

- Nostril breathing

  Students can use nostril breathing to regulate their breath by inhaling through one nostril, then exhaling through the other. Many different forms of yoga, qi gong, and meditation use this technique.

  1. Press your thumb down on the right nostril, and breathe out gently through the left nostril.

  2. Breathe in from the left nostril, then press the left nostril gently with the ring finger and little finger. Remove the right thumb from the right nostril, and breathe out from the right nostril.

  3. Breathe in from the right nostril, and exhale from the left.

  4. After every exhalation, remember to breathe in from the same nostril from which you exhaled.

Figure 7.20 Nostril Breathing

  5. Keep your eyes closed throughout and continue taking long, deep, smooth breaths without any force or effort.

Managing Our Environment

We are animals, and we take in sensory information, unconsciously, which affects our mood. A space that is dark and gloomy has a different effect on us than a space that is pleasantly lit and painted in warm colours. Too much sensory stimulation can be overwhelming, but too little lowers our levels of neurotransmitters. In our homes, we regularly adjust our environment to meet our needs. We play music, light scented candles, dim the lights, and control other features to either suit our mood or reshape it. As teachers, we design learning environments, but we also design social and emotional environments. Many of us do so collaboratively with our students, but we rarely do so intentionally to support mental health and positive social interactions.

Some questions we need to consider when we design learning environments are:

- What does inclusive design mean from a social standpoint?
- What structures need to exist/be changed for a broader range of social interactions to take place, and be acceptable?
- How can we facilitate our students learning of prosocial skills?

Some questions we need to consider when we design social and emotional environments are:

- How do we make it acceptable to be an introvert?
- What do we do about the student who prefers older or younger peers?
- How do we model acceptance of uniqueness rather than conformity?

Design involves everything from furniture arrangement, to decoration, to lighting, to smells, to amount of light and air, and more. Teachers may put tennis balls on chair legs to reduce the noise of scraping chairs. Dimmers on light switches, plants along the windowsill, visuals, and room set-up all send a message. Is this an exciting place to be? A peaceful one? A chaotic one? Our classrooms are ecosystems, with biotic and abiotic features that interact and affect each other. To the greatest extent possible, I always wanted flexibility in my classrooms. I had dimmers on the lights, a source for music, and working blinds for the windows (I know, rare in schools!) On some days, I wanted to be able to turn up the lights, open the windows, and put on some upbeat music to wake us all up. At other times, I wanted to dim the lights, play soft music, and close the blinds to create tranquility. When the floors had been waxed or washed, I lit scented candles to get rid of the institutional smell (or electric air fresheners if candles aren't safe).

Managing the classroom environment supports the programming you do socially, emotionally, and academically. Teaching students to manage their environment – to realize they are feeling draggy because it's been cloudy outside for several days and they need to get up and move – also helps them to self-regulate.

Dialectical Behaviour Therapy (DBT)

After two youth died by suicide at a high school I was working with, I called my brother, Dr. Laurence Katz, the head of Child and Adolescent Psychiatry at the Health Sciences Centre, and an expert in Dialectal Behaviour Therapy (DBT). I had no idea what DBT was, but I knew he used it with adolescents who attempted suicide or self-harmed (e.g., cutting themselves). I asked him what it was he did to help kids develop the coping and resiliency skills to overcome their distress. As he began to describe DBT, I was shocked. I had expected some very complex, deep psychological process. Instead, what he described was not unfamiliar at all, and much of it was similar to SEL programming schools already do. My brother explained that the complexity was not in the activities within the program, but in being able to do DBT with kids who were very ill and in crisis. DBT is research–based, and there is a great deal of evidence that it is effective. Some parts to the program are unique and fit well with universal design, Indigenous perspectives, and spiritual education. So what is DBT?

DBT is an expansion of cognitive behaviour therapy (CBT). It was developed by Dr. Marsha Linehan in the 1980s. DBT adds a spiritual and psychosocial component to CBT. Proponents of DBT believe some people are highly sensitive to social situations; arousal levels in their brain increase far more quickly, may be more intense, and may sustain for longer periods of time than in most people.

Although DBT was originally used to treat individuals with borderline personality disorder, it is now used to support youth who struggle with emotional well-being in many different ways. DBT is a therapy, conducted by psychiatrists, with people who have a serious mental illness. DBT can be a Tier 3 intervention for some students, and in that case, should be conducted *only* by experts. At a Tier 1 level, which is how we are using it, DBT can be used to build coping skills in all students at the classroom level; it is not being used therapeutically, but preventatively.

> The word *therapy* can give us pause, because teachers are not therapists.
>
> However, we are not doing the therapeutic parts of this program.
>
> We are only engaging with the preventative parts of the program!

James Mazza wrote a book called *DBT in Schools* (2016) in which he developed a DBT curriculum for teachers and schools. The "STEPS-A" program is described as being an SEL program that "can be implemented at Tiers 1, 2, and 3 in schools using a multi-tiered system of support (MTSS / RTI)". This curriculum demonstrates that DBT can and should be used in schools in a nontherapeutic way.

Rather than treat DBT as a stand-alone program, we can weave aspects of DBT into our programming. We can select aspects of each module that are appropriate for large-group, whole-class settings.

DBT consists of four modules:

1. Mindfulness

2. Interpersonal Effectiveness

3. Emotion Regulation

4. Distress Tolerance

In DBT, mindfulness education is specific to the skills of mindfulness – observing, describing, and participating; to the spiritual functions of mindfulness – nonjudgment, "one-mindfulness" (focusing on one thing at a time, being present, and giving full attention); and to effectiveness – making decisions that are based on what will work to deal with the issue, rather than being stuck in determining who is right/wrong, fair/unfair, and so forth. Many schools have begun to teach mindfulness skills such as breathing exercises, but students also need to understand nonjudgment and effective problem solving. Learning how to let go of "being right," and instead seeking a win-win solution that will achieve the sought-for result is far more satisfying in the end.

The interpersonal effectiveness module focuses primarily on assertiveness and conflict resolution. As teachers, we often try to encourage students to ask for help when they need it, resist peer pressure and make their own decisions, and solve problems in appropriate ways. In addition to assertiveness and conflict resolution, however, interpersonal effectiveness in a universally designed, Indigenous framework also involves the ability to make and maintain relationships, leadership, and community participation.

Emotion regulation is related to self-regulation. Learning to identify emotions and strategies for managing emotions (e.g., anger, anxiety, frustration), and making decisions that are rational and considered, are all critical skills needed to succeed in the social world.

Distress tolerance (see page 109) is the focus I believe schools have not addressed. It is understandable, because we assume a student in crisis requires the intervention of a psychiatrist or psychologist and is a candidate for Tier 3 treatment. But what about prevention? Can we teach students how to tolerate distress *before* they experience it? It is very difficult, even for a trained professional, to teach someone how to deal with distress after experiencing trauma, when cortisol is pumping through their system. It is much better to teach students how to calm their minds and emotions before they are faced with distress.

DBT/Mindfulness Programming	Intra	Intellectual	self-awareness, self-regulation, resiliency, mastery
		Physical	body and sensory awareness, yoga, meditation/breathing exercises
		Emotional/Psychological	emotional regulation, inner peace, calm, environmental mastery, distress tolerance
		Spiritual	interconnectedness, meditation, connection to nature
	Inter	Intellectual	awareness of others
		Physical	
		Emotional/Psychological	supporting others
		Spiritual	altruism, compassion

Figure 7.21 DBT and Mindfulness: Targeted Outcomes for Well-Being

We will use the DBT modules to address each of the mindfulness skills, and extend beyond them into universally designed pedagogy. Some of the DBT modules provide acronyms or phrases that can be taught to children to help them remember what to do when they are in stressful situations. (Apparently, psychiatrists like acronyms as much as teachers do.) We will review all four modules here. However, if your school or you are already implementing programming related to one or more modules, (for instance, if you are doing the MindUP program), you may want to skip that module and select the ones relevant to you.

Keep in mind that DBT is most often used with adolescents. I believe it is possible for us to begin building these skills with very young students (for instance, mindfulness has been taught in kindergarten classes with great success). But not every aspect of DBT may be appropriate for early-years students. As a prevention program, DBT would ideally be started in the late elementary years, so that students enter adolescence equipped with the ability to navigate the emotions and social pressures they will encounter.

Grade-level recommendations:

- Mindfulness Module: Grades K–12
- Interpersonal Effectiveness: Grades 4–12
- Emotion Regulation: Grades 4–12
- Distress Tolerance: Grades K–12

Module 1: Mindfulness

Mindfulness practices have become increasingly popular in school programs. As noted earlier, the human brain is programmed to judge – both ourselves and others. It's a survival instinct: Is this safe or unsafe? Good or bad? Right or wrong? The problem is that our judgments are often wrong. They happen so fast that our experiences are influenced as soon as we get to them. Mindfulness is about being aware of that and taking a fresh perspective. For instance, my friend walks toward me frowning. My judgment – "he's mad at me" – happens so fast, that I look away, or react in some way, and by the time he gets to me, my reaction then influences our connection.

In DBT, students are taught to be mindful of what is underlying their thoughts and behaviours. Three "kinds of mind" are explored: emotion, reasonable, and wise.

1. **Emotion Mind** is when our feelings control our thoughts. For instance, if a person is scared or angry, their thoughts may become defensive, accusing, and confrontational.

2. **Reasonable Mind** is when we can be rational and think objectively about a situation.

3. **Wise Mind** is a combination of emotion mind and reasonable mind. It allows us to recognize our feelings and accept them, while not being controlled by them. Our feelings underlie our intuition – they suggest that we pay close attention to particular cues. Ignoring our feelings is not wise, but neither is impulsively reacting to them.

Becoming mindful is an awareness practice: awareness of the experience of the moment; awareness of how we are experiencing the moment – our thoughts, feelings, and sensations; and awareness of how fleeting the moment can be.

I believe students can best achieve wise mind by first *understanding* the mind and how it works. This is why it is important for students to have done the study of the brain first.

It is also helpful to remind students that the breathing exercises we have shared can be used anytime to calm emotion mind.

Mindfulness Practice

Mindfulness cannot be taught in a single lesson or even in a series of lessons. It is an ongoing practice. Introduce it to students using the activities below, and then make it part of daily life in the classroom. Take breathing breaks, call students' attention to the details of something, and remind them to be nonjudgmental when they are about to be critical of others or themselves.

Mindfulness has two main components: awareness and nonjudgment. Mindfulness is about slowing down, paying attention, and being open-minded before making decisions.

1. Introduce mindful awareness of the senses. Explain that we often get so busy that we stop paying attention to what is going on around us. Engage students in some sensory awareness activities such as the following:

   - Have students close their eyes, and listen to all the sounds around them. Ask them what they heard that they had not noticed when they weren't paying attention.

   - Take students outside, and ask them to look for five different shades of green. Discuss how we sometimes miss the details and beauty of what's around us when we don't look carefully.

   - Give students a small piece of food, such as a raisin or a grape. Ask them to keep it in their mouth, chewing or sucking on it lightly. Ask students to pay attention to the textures and tastes, and how these change over time. Talk about how we often eat so fast, we barely taste the foods we ingest.

   - Have students sit quietly in their chairs. Ask them to notice the feel of the chair on their back and bottom, of the clothes on their bodies, of their breath leaving their nose. Explain that being mindful means being aware of, and paying attention to, things we often don't notice.

   - Take students outside, or have them take out their lunch. Ask them to pay attention to the different smells. Again, explain that being mindful means being aware of, and paying attention to, things we often don't notice.

2. Introduce the concept of nonjudgment. Explain that it means we don't decide whether something is bad or good, whether we like it or don't like it, until we've taken the time to really pay attention and experience it. As an example, show students a food that doesn't look like it would taste good (e.g., dragonfruit, liquid chocolate, shrimp). Ask students if they have eaten foods they initially thought looked "gross," but that turned out to taste good.

   - Have students brainstorm things they didn't think they would like when they first saw or heard of it, but turned out to be good.

- Give students the following examples, and ask them to discuss a mindful/unmindful reaction to it:
  - A new student comes to school wearing weird clothes.
  - A friend brings something for lunch that you have never seen before.
  - Someone is trying to talk to you while you are busy.
  - You walk by someone who is homeless.
  - A friend is texting while driving.
  - You try to do something, and find it is very hard.

NOTE: There are many mindfulness meditations available on the web. Select a few to use with your students.

Figure 7.22 One student's reflection on himself as "different" reflected both the loneliness he sometimes felt, but also the strength and solitude this gave him.

Module 2: Interpersonal Effectiveness

Interpersonal effectiveness in DBT is taught through three acronyms: DEARMAN, GIVE, and FAST.

DEARMAN is the acronym used to develop objective effectiveness. Objective effectiveness refers to the ability to express one's needs in ways that demonstrate self-regulation and avoid conflict or tangential/personal arguments.

The acronym DEARMAN stands for:

Describe your situation.

Express why this is an issue and how you feel about it.

Assert yourself by asking clearly for what you want.

Reinforce your position by offering a positive consequence if you were to get what you want.

(Be) **M**indful of the situation by focusing on what you want and ignore distractions.

Appear confident even if you don't feel confident.

Negotiate with a hesitant person and come to a comfortable compromise on your request.

GIVE is the acronym used to develop relationship effectiveness. Relationship effectiveness refers to the ability to make and sustain relationships.

The acronym GIVE stands for:

Gentle: Use appropriate language, no verbal or physical attacks, no put downs, avoid sarcasm unless you are sure the person is all right with it, and be courteous and nonjudgmental.

Interested: When the person you are speaking to is talking about something, be interested in what they are saying. Maintain eye contact, ask questions, and so forth. Do not use your cellphone while having a conversation with another person!

Validate: Show that you understand a person's situation and sympathize with them. Validation can be shown through words, body language, and/or facial expressions.

Easy Manner: Be calm and comfortable during conversation, use humour, smile.

My Reflection

My reflection
I look into the mirror
I see myself
I blink
How amazing
I say
Mirrors
Where you can see yourself
Like water
Where it casts your reflection
Like a shadow
That copies your every movement
Like an illusion
Not real, but deceivable
Like another me
But at the same time, not another me
I nod
The person that is my reflection nods, too
Even though she is my reflection
We have many differences
I have friends and family and all my other things
But
The me in the mirror is lonely
She has no friends
No family
Just herself
Alone inside the mirror
But
Then someone steps in
And their reflection shows up in the mirror
The me in the mirror isn't lonely anymore
It's got a friend

Figure 7.23 This poem reflects a student moving from feeling isolated to having a friend.

FAST is the acronym used to develop self-respect within social interactions. Self-respect refers to the ability to draw boundaries, not be victimized, and behave with integrity.

The acronym FAST stands for:

Fair: Be fair to yourself and to the other party to avoid resentment on both sides.

Apologize: Apologize less, taking responsibility only when appropriate.

Stick: Stick to your values, and don't compromise your integrity to gain an outcome.

Truthful: Be truthful, and avoid exaggerating or acting helpless to manipulate others.

The interpersonal-effectiveness acronyms are best implemented using role-plays, bibliotherapy, or videotherapy. *Bibliotherapy* is "the use of books to help people solve problems" (Aiex 1993, 1) or "the use of books as a type of therapy" (Wilson 2004, 32). Historically, educators have used literature to teach and explore social skills and morals. Today's teachers are using videos in similar ways. Bibliotherapy and videotherapy work well because they:

- develop self-concept, nurture, and heal self-esteem
- develop self-awareness, reflective skills
- guide children to discover new interests
- relieve emotional pressures, anxiety
- demonstrate to the child that they are not the only one to face a specific challenge
- demonstrate there is more than one way to solve a problem
- depersonalize the discussion of the problem, thereby increasing children's willingness to engage

Aiex (1993) identified nine potential reasons a teacher may choose to use bibliotherapy or videotherapy with students:

1. Show an individual they are not the first or only person to encounter such a problem.
2. Show an individual there is more than one solution to a problem.
3. Help a person discuss a problem more freely.
4. Help an individual plan a constructive course of action to solve a problem.
5. Develop an individual's self-concept.
6. Relieve emotional or mental pressure.
7. Foster an individual's honest self-appraisal.
8. Provide a way for a person to find interests outside of self.
9. Increase an individual's understanding of human behaviour or motivations.

Interpersonal-Effectiveness Lesson

Since DEARMAN is about how to meet one's needs in a socially appropriate way, we can choose books or videos with various scenarios, such as a character asking for a raise at work or asking to do an assignment in a different way than the teacher has assigned. Role-playing how the character might approach the boss/teacher, asking for what they want respectfully, explaining why this will help them, and being open to a win-win compromise assists many students who may be shy or hesitant to clearly express their needs. Because we are portraying the character, and not the student themselves, there is less chance of stigma or fear of talking about what the character might be feeling.

Here is one way of implementing interpersonal effectiveness in the classroom:

1. Have students pose scenarios where they might need to ask for something that makes them nervous, for instance:
   - Ask a group member to do their part of an assignment.
   - Ask a teacher for an alternative assignment.

2. Role-play or hold a class meeting to discuss how to manage the situation. Conflict resolution, using the GIVE acronym, can be done during meetings. Remind students to not make issues personal attacks, to listen empathetically to each other, and to think about how their words and actions will make others feel.

Module 3: Emotion Regulation

Emotion regulation in DBT is taught through the phrase "story of the emotion," and the acronym, PLEASE MASTER.

"The story of the emotion" is based on mental-health literacy and cognitive behaviour therapy. Emotion regulation helps students learn that all feelings are normal and acceptable, but how you think about them, and the situation, will control the response. Students can be taught to understand the process of emotional response using the following example:

1. Scenario: A trigger in the environment: for instance, a rainy day, or a friend walks by without saying hello

2. Interpretation of the event: As individuals, we assign meaning to the event. What is the story we tell ourselves about what's happening? Rainy days are depressing to some, and meditative to others. The friend walking by appears to be ignoring or angry at us, or we think they may be stressed and in a hurry.

3. Body response: Our thoughts trigger chemical release. A thought that evokes sadness, fear, or anger results in cortisol and depressed levels of oxytocin and neurotransmitters. A thought that evokes peacefulness, joy, or empathy does the opposite. We can learn to perceive this based on sensory feedback – heart pounding, flushing, knotted stomach, and so forth are signs of stress. Smiling, a burst of energy, and muscle relaxation tell us we are happy.

4. Communication: Identify the emotion: "I am feeling _____," and then communicate it to ourselves and possibly to others. Doing so allows us to determine an appropriate response.

5. Action: We act upon the emotion.

When we understand this chain of emotion, we can intercept it at various points along the way. For instance, we can learn to question our interpretation of the event: "Is he really mad at me? Maybe he's just having a bad day." "Okay, it's raining – maybe this is a good day to read that book I've been wanting to." Changing our interpretation changes the steps that follow: we manage the cortisol release, and interrupt what may become a negative behavioural response. If we can't change the interpretation, we can then recognize the body's response, label the emotion, and then use the skills we learned in the mindfulness module (see page 138) or the distress-tolerance module (see page 153) to manage the emotion. We can also reach out to someone and express how we are feeling.

Emotion regulation is linked to chapter 7, lesson 5 (see page 120) in our Brain Unit; return to this so students can practice reframing thinking when they are exhibiting stress reactions.

Prevention and Mastery Lessons
Dr. Linehan (who developed DBT) uses a chart with the acronym PLEASE MASTER to also point out that we are more vulnerable to negative emotions when we don't take care of our physical health.

The acronym PLEASE MASTER stands for:

treat **PhysicaL** illness

balance **E**ating

avoid mood-**A**ltering drugs

balance **S**leep

get **E**xercise

build **M A S T E R**y

Mastery comes from the following:

1. developing skills and interests, thus experiencing success and a positive sense of self

2. using the skills taught in other modules and in the story of the emotion learning, which allow students to feel mastery over their emotional health and well-being

We will address the need for academic success in the section on instructional practice (see page 180).

To address the need for physical health, have students explain what physical health means to them. We have Western ideas in our society, but sociocultural expectations of what healthy eating is, what "normal" body weight is, and so forth differ around the world.

The Relationship Between Physical Health and Mental Health

The definition of physical health is based on science, culture, and socioeconomic status. Science tells us about illnesses and ideals, culture tells us about aesthetics and expectations, and socioeconomic status makes the definition of health relative. Take, for instance, a person who is overweight, but not obese. According to science, this person has only a slightly higher risk of illness than a person of healthy body weight. But culture determines, in many cases, how someone feels about body size. In Western cultures, this person may feel disproportionately negative about their body because, although the health risk is minimal, the norms about attractiveness are harsh. Socioeconomic status often determines what is realistic. The availability of fresh food, ability to pay for organic food or healthy proteins, access to health care, and exercise opportunities (e.g., gym memberships, the cost of team sports for kids), and so forth are all affected by economic resources.

So what do students need to know?

Nutrition, exercise, and sleep all affect our well-being, including our emotional and social well-being. Most school systems have some type of health curriculum that teaches basic nutrition and physical education. What isn't taught is the link between nutrition and emotions. What follows provides this missing piece.

The Science of Nutrition and Well-Being

Students need to know and understand the role nutrition plays in brain development, emotional regulation, and physical health. I always started teaching nutrition with two simple lessons (see next page).

Lesson 1: Categories of Foods

Most health curricula explore things like the Canada Food Guide, which focuses on food groups. From a health perspective, though, the roles of carbohydrates, fats, and proteins are equally if not more important than the food groups.

1. Explain to students that food can be sorted into three groups, and each plays a role in the function of their body and brain:

   • **Proteins.** Proteins are the building blocks of the body. Muscles, organs, hair, nails, and ligaments are all composed of protein. Proteins generally come from animal sources – meat, poultry, fish, eggs, and dairy are the primary sources of protein – but vegetables and legumes also provide some protein. Eating proteins also affects our mental health, because proteins affect neurotransmitter and hormone production and communication. For instance, eating protein raises the levels of an amino acid called "tyrosine," which prompts the brain to manufacture norepinephrine and dopamine – neurotransmitters that promote alertness and activity. Increased tyrosine has been shown to affect emotional resilience (Lieberman 1994). Another protein derivative, called "tryptophan," helps the brain develop serotonin. Lowered levels of tryptophan have been associated with aggression and depression, most likely mediated by the lack of serotonin (Young 1996). Clearly, protein is important for both physical and mental health.

      Proteins can be divided into two categories: lean and high fat. Lean proteins contain less saturated fat, and include low-fat dairy, white meat in poultry, seafood, and soy. Regular beef, dark meats, and full-fat dairy contain more saturated fats, which are less healthy but can still be eaten in moderation.

   • **Carbohydrates.** Carbohydrates play a role in energy production. The brain is the greatest consumer of energy in the body. With billions of neurons sending electrical signals all day and night, the brain requires a great deal of energy. The primary source of energy for the brain is called "glucose," a chemical derived from carbohydrates. Without sufficient glucose, the brain develops hypoglycemia – which leads to confusion, light headedness, loss of balance, slurred speech, and distorted vision. Left unchecked, it can eventually become fatal (for example, as the result of a diabetic coma).

      Carbohydrates can provide the fuel for you to stay alert and awake, or they can make you feel tired because they increase the brain's level of the amino acid tryptophan, which in turn spurs the brain to make the calming neurotransmitter serotonin. Serotonin is important for normal sleep patterns and normal blood pressure, learning, and a healthy appetite, among many other functions. Getting the right balance of carbohydrates is, therefore, very important for brain function and mental health.

      Like proteins, carbohydrates can be loosely divided into two categories: simple and complex. Simple carbohydrates convert to glucose rapidly in the body and, therefore, spike the level of sugar in the blood. They provide a short term burst of energy, but then crash – leaving you feeling exhausted and sluggish. Complex carbohydrates, which include whole grains, green and starchy vegetables, and legumes, take longer to break down in the body. Like slow-release medication, the body metabolizes complex carbohydrates a little at a time, so our energy level remains consistent. This doesn't mean simple carbohydrates are all bad. Fruit, dairy, and some vegetables are natural, simple carbohydrates. However, the presence of certain vitamins, fibre, and fats slow down the metabolic process, so eaten in moderation, they are healthy.

The carbohydrates to be avoided are those with chemically added sugars. Sugars come in many names, and most companies are smart – they use a little of several different kinds of sugars rather than a lot of one kind, so that they can hide how much sugar is really in the product. Checking ingredient labels is, therefore, critical. Words ending in "ose" (e.g., sucrose, dextrose, fructose), words ending in "ol" (e.g., sorbitol or maltitol), syrups (e.g., malt, corn, rice syrup), and fruit-juice concentrates are all added sugars.

- **Fats.** Like carbohydrates, fats play a role in energy production in the body. The body burns fat to give us energy. Our brains are made up of significant amounts of fat. What's important for students to know is that not all fats are bad. Trans fat and saturated fat not only have negative effects on the body, they also negatively affect emotion regulation (Holt et al. 2015). Diets high in trans fats reduce the brain's ability to think clearly and regulate emotions. On the other hand, diets low in healthy fats, especially monounsaturated and Omega-3 fats, result in lower brain function and negatively affect learning, memory, and problem-solving ability.

2. Give students pictures of common foods, and have them sort the foods into the three categories: proteins, carbohydrates, and fats. Within these categories, students can sort the foods into healthy and non-healthy examples (e.g., lean meat vs. processed meats, nuts vs. potato chips, ice cream vs. yogurt). Discuss two additional criteria for recognizing health:

- In natural form (single natural ingredient or made by nature) versus processed with additives (made by chemists)

- Proportion: Serving sizes are recommended for a reason!

Lesson 2: Investigating Food Claims and Reading Food Labels

Have students bring products from home or distribute food labels from common items. Examine the ingredients list (how many chemicals can't you pronounce?), and the numbers (how many grams of protein/carbohydrates/fat in each portion?).

Discuss with students the following:

- **How food is classified.** Food is classified by the largest amount it contains. For instance, quinoa contains 25 grams of carbohydrates and 6 grams of protein per serving. Producers try to sell it as being high in protein, but, in truth, you would have to eat 100 grams of carbohydrates to get a full serving of protein from it! Similarly, nuts have far more fat than protein – so they are classified as a fat, not as a source of protein.

- **Appropriate serving sizes for people their age.** How many grams of protein/fat/carbohydrates should they have per meal and per day?

- **Advertising tricks.** Labels must have ingredients listed by amount – from highest to lowest. If producers used only one type of sugar, most products would have sugar listed as the first ingredient. Instead, companies use smaller amounts of several different kinds of sugar (e.g., honey, maltitol, sugar, brown rice syrup) and can list them separately. By doing this, the amount of sugar in most products appears lower on the list and the consumer doesn't realize how much sugar is actually in the item.

HEALTHY EATING

EXERCISE FOR HEALTH

THE HUMAN BODY

HUMAN BODY SYSTEMS

The Science of Exercise and Well-Being

It is well known that exercise affects mood. This is because exercise causes the release of endorphins – brain chemicals that lift mood – and because exercise supports physical health and fitness, which, ultimately, also affects emotional well-being in a number of ways:

1. When we feel energetic and healthy, we are happier. Feeling sick, lethargic, or fatigued affects sour moods.

2. When we feel healthy and fit, we feel better about ourselves and have a sense of pride in our appearance, and this affects our mood.

3. Exercise affects the immune system and the cardiovascular system, resulting in improved brain function due to improved oxygenation and reduced chances of illness.

Exercise also connects us with our environment, and thus improves well-being. We often exercise outdoors, where fresh air, light, and contact with nature all improve mood. As well, exercise can lead to social opportunities and connections, which provide community and belonging. Conversely, a lack of exercise can mean less time outdoors, and withdrawal from group activities. For instance, overweight people may withdraw from social activities that involve exercise or expose body-image issues (e.g., a trip to the beach, going on a hike).

Lesson 3: Exercise

Introduce students to the underlying aspects of exercise, such as speed, flexibility, strength, agility, coordination, balance, and cardiovascular system (cardio). By doing so, we allow all students to find strengths and challenges within their kinesthetic profile, as we did within their learning profile. This is, in effect, an effort to universally design health curricula, and particularly physical education. For too many students, the gym is a place of failure and humiliation. Helping all students learn to live a healthy lifestyle means helping all kids make connections to activities they can enjoy and can be successful at. Outside of school, there are competitive opportunities for serious athletes, as there are for musicians, artists, writers, and so forth. In school, we need to be designing for the diversity of our students. This is critical for students' physical, and mental, health.

1. Ask for three volunteers. Have one volunteer stand on one foot, another hold a squat, and the third do jumping jacks. Who can do their task the longest? Place all students in pairs. Have them time each other doing each of the above exercises. Which was hardest for them? Which was easiest?

2. Explain the meaning of each of these terms: *speed, flexibility, strength, agility, coordination, balance, and cardio.*

3. Ask students which aspects of fitness are most involved in each activity (squats, balancing on one foot, jumping jacks). Have them name two additional activities involving each of these aspects of fitness (e.g., flexibility: yoga, dance, stretching; cardio: running, skating).

4. Create a whole-class chart listing activities that develop/use each aspect (see example below).

Speed	Flexibility	Strength	Agility	Coordination	Balance	Cardio
track	yoga	weightlifting	martial arts	baseball	gymnastics	hiking
football	dance	shotput	basketball	juggling	cycling	tennis
				volleyball	skating	

Lesson 4: Goal Setting

As with the RD program (see page 82), students need to learn to set two kinds of goals: strength-based goals and challenge goals.

- Strength-based goals involve both developing and using one's strengths and interests. For instance, if someone is strong and enjoys being in nature, they may want to set a goal to go rock climbing once a week, beginning with easier climbs and working up to more challenging climbs. This allows them to do an activity they enjoy and can be successful at, which supports their well-being.

- Challenge goals are set to help someone develop resilience and overcome challenges. Rock climbing, for example, requires strength and flexibility. For someone who struggles with flexibility, rock climbing may be a challenge goal for them – they will be motivated to improve since it will support something they care about.

Students need to learn to set goals that support their well-being. When they recognize that exercise supports their mental health, they will understand the need to set goals for regular exercise – in whatever form they choose.

Awareness of the roles of nutrition and exercise in mental health supports students when they create visual scripts in the next module, where they are asked to select activities they enjoy to cope in times of stress.

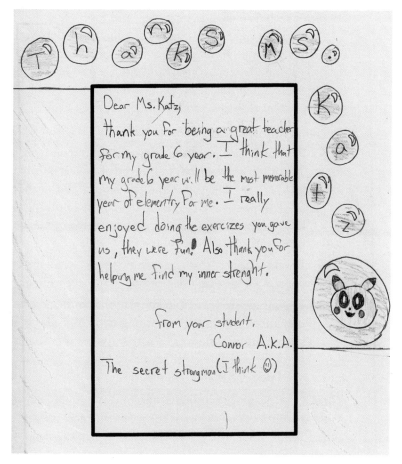

Figure 7.24 Letter from a grade 6 student who decided strength was his goal, and later made the connection to inner strength.

The Role of Culture

Culture affects our beliefs and our behaviours. Healthwise, culture influences our eating habits, daily activities, body image, and sleep routines. Almost all cultures have feasts that celebrate important times and milestones. The message from feasts is that food is a reward or symbol of love and joy. Many cultural foods are also high in fat or carbohydrates, and cultures vary in their beliefs about what makes a person attractive. North American culture's images of beauty are often of very thin bodies, in many cases unhealthily so. In other cultures, especially those where food is scarce, being overweight is a sign of prosperity and health. Where someone lives, or has lived, may also affect their experience with physical activity. In Canada, skiing and water sports, like surfing and kayaking, are common on the West Coast. On the Prairies, cycling and winter sports may be more common. Culture and gender roles can also affect behaviours. Women's hockey is now popular, but for a long time hockey was not thought to be a girl's sport. Similarly, in some cultures, gender stereotypes may exist about activities such as dance, gymnastics, and football.

There is no right or wrong set of beliefs and behaviours. However, it is important to have open conversations about these issues with students. Just as we explore media influence in technology and language arts, students need to be aware of the influences on their choices and beliefs regarding physical health and body image. Such awareness enables them to determine to what extent they accept these influences.

Some Ideas for Lessons/Activities

- Provide ads or portraits of women and men from around the world and across the ages. These images can spark a powerful conversation about what is expected of each gender in terms of appearance and behaviour, and of the pressures to conform to these norms. Stereotypes of the rugged man and the feminine woman, the muscular male body and the waif-thin female body, all have great influence on eating disorders, steroid use, and other unhealthy behaviours.

- Provide recipes of several ethnic foods. Students can use these to consider portion control for certain celebrations that serve unhealthy foods.

- Encourage students to recognize that influences of culture and experiences may convince them to try something new. As a class, watch videos of games and sports played around the world, sort activities into male/female, and then question the reasons behind these divisions. Invite students to be "trainer for a day" and design creative workouts for their classmates.

The Role of Socio-Economic Status

Most students are unaware of the role affluence, or lack of it, plays in choices related to well-being. When students explore the costs of healthy food, playing some team sports, and buying sporting equipment, they develop compassion for those who have fewer opportunities than they do.

I often had students do budgeting activities tied into the math curricula. These activities explored the costs of healthy living, including daily meal plans (and their costs), family grocery budgets, mileage of driving to practices/games for team sports, costs of equipment, and more. Many students then get involved in service projects for raising money, donating healthy food to food banks, or other contributions to their community.

If you are working with students living in poverty, help them recognize the challenges, and try to problem solve around these. Is there a place they can grow some vegetables and fruits? Are there nearby parks where they can hike, cycle, or do other inexpensive activities? What organizations offer support for participating in team sports?

Ultimately, we want students to do the following:

1. Understand that physical health and mental health are related.

2. Understand that different kinds of foods affect their bodies and emotions in different ways.

3. Make informed choices about nutrition and exercise for their health.

4. Understand the role that culture and economics plays in healthy living.

Module 4: Distress Tolerance

Distress tolerance in DBT is based on three concepts: accepting the situation (ACCEPTS), learning to self-soothe, and managing the distress (IMPROVE the moment).

ACCEPTS

ACCEPTS refers to temporarily distracting an individual from the source of distress (i.e., until the cortisol has settled and it is possible to make a wise decision). ACCEPTS refers to the ability to express one's needs in ways that demonstrate self-regulation, and to avoid conflict or tangential/personal arguments.

The acronym ACCEPTS stands for:

Activities: Do positive activities you enjoy.

Contribute: Help out others in your family or community.

Compare: Compare yourself either to people less fortunate than you or to how you used to be when you were in a worse state. This is used to gain perspective and realize the problem may not be as dire as you thought.

Emotions: Allow yourself to feel something different by provoking your sense of humour or happiness with corresponding activities. This can reduce the flow of cortisol, and potentially release oxytocin.

Push away: Put your situation on the back burner for a while. Put something else temporarily first in your mind (break obsessive rumination), by doing an activity.

Thoughts: Force your mind to think about something else. This is an "in-your-head" strategy. Some examples are counting to 10 or singing a song. You can talk to a friend about something else – anything to get your mind off the "broken record" of obsessive "I just can't stop thinking about it" patterns.

Sensations: Do something that gives you a feeling other than what you are feeling – but is just as intense – like taking a cold shower or eating a spicy candy.

Self-Soothe

Self-soothing behaviour involves doing something that is soothing to you – something comforting, nurturing, kind, and gentle. Self-soothing is used in moments of distress or agitation. Children can learn to say and do what a parent or friend would say, or what they would say to a friend who is upset.

IMPROVE

IMPROVE the moment is used to help relax in a moment of distress. It can be used along with mindfulness practices.

The acronym IMPROVE stands for:

Imagery: Imagine relaxing scenes, things going well, or other things that please you.

Meaning: Find some purpose or meaning in what you are feeling. This is similar to finding the lesson (i.e., what you might learn from the experience).

Prayer: Pray to whomever you worship, or, if not religious, chant a positive affirmation, such as: "Everything is going to be okay," or "I can do this."

Relaxation: Relax your muscles, breathe deeply; use with self-soothing.

One thing in the moment: Focus your entire attention on what you are doing right now. Keep yourself in the present.

Vacation (brief): Take a break for a short period of time.

Encouragement: Be your own cheerleader. Tell yourself you can make it through this.

Lessons for Distress Tolerance

Students need to understand that distress tolerance is not about making the pain go away. When something happens that hurts us, our emotions are real and legitimate. However, if we act on them in the moment, we often make impulsive decisions that we regret later. Distress tolerance helps us tolerate the hurt, so we have the time to make wise decisions about how best to deal with the situation, rather than making it worse. Be sure to explain this to students, and remind students of this at the start of each lesson.

Lesson 1: ACCEPTS

The ACCEPTS strategy helps students deal with critical moments of distress in their lives, but it can also be used for everyday kinds of stress.

1. Discuss the concept of acceptance. Accepting when something has happened (e.g., the death of a loved one, the breakup of a relationship, failing at something of importance), is the first step to healing. Students need to have the perspective that:

   - Acceptance *does not* mean forgiveness for what someone, or something, has done. I can accept that my boyfriend has broken up with me, without forgiving him or even letting go of the hurt. Acceptance *does* mean I am not trying to undo it – like trying to persuade him not to leave me.

   - Acceptance means forgiveness for myself. Letting go of self-blame and accepting that everyone goes through hard times (e.g., has relationships end, fails at something they try), allows me to begin the process of healing.

2. Show students the acronym ACCEPTS. Explain that ACCEPTS is a temporary strategy. It is used to give oneself a chance to calm down, gain perspective, and get out of the rut of obsessively thinking about what has occurred. Once that happens, it is time to come back to the issue to deal with one's feelings, and if necessary, problem solve.

3. Have students write the word *ACCEPTS* down the side of a page to make an acrostic with the words for each letter. Going one line at a time, have students create a personal visual script for the acronym, similar to the one on the next page. Each student's script will be different, as they select things they find relaxing/pleasurable. They can use clipart or draw their own pictures, but the visuals are important at all ages, because in a moment of crisis we recall images better than words.

Waiting

I stare out the window
Waiting for you
You said you'd come
But I've already heard that too many times
Why won't you come?
Just once, I'd like you to keep your promises
Be here
But on time
A tear slides down my cheek
You'll never come, won't you?
Don't promise me
When you can't do it
Don't hurt me like that
Waiting
So many days
So many nights
So many tears
It's useless
You'll never come
I give up
I'm leaving
Leaving you behind
Throwing it away
The memory
I throw the memory of you away
I'll find some other friend
So
Goodbye
Goodbye
Goodbye

....Forever

Figure 7.25 A poem written by a grade 7 student about accepting and letting go.

When I am upset, I can...		
Activities	Listen to music or ride my bike	
Contribute	Help my mom	
Compare	Read blogs about people who are struggling	
Emotions	Watch a funny movie	
Push-away	Focus on a task, do a workout	
Thoughts	Talk to a friend	
Sensations	Cook or eat something spicy	

Figure 7.26 Visual Script for Distress Tolerance

As a follow-up to the above activity, discuss with students:

- The goal of the visual script is to interrupt the cortisol cycle, and give someone a chance to calm down and heal before making decisions about actions. Eating spicy food or taking a cold shower, for instance, wakes up the sensory system and turns the brain's attention to the experience, and away from obsessing about the issue that is concerning them.
- They need to regularly revisit their script, so that it is in their mind when something happens and cortisol is rushing through them.
- They can be a good friend or group member by prompting others to refer to their script when they are upset. For instance, when they are arguing with a friend, they could suggest they each do one thing from their own script, and then come back together and try to solve the problem.

4. Use the scripts in class regularly. For instance:
- Suggest to students that when they take a break they select something from their script.
- Prompt a student who is frustrated to take out their script.
- Discuss times when you use your script.

Lesson 2: Self-Soothe

Self-soothing is one of the most important concepts/skills when it comes to maintaining mental health. Many of us know what we would say to someone who is going through what we are struggling with, but we are not nearly as kind to ourselves. We criticize and judge ourselves far more harshly than we do someone else.

Learning to self-soothe has two components:

1. Be kind to oneself. Ask ourselves what a parent or someone who loves us would say to us in the moment, or ask ourselves what we would say to someone else who is going through the same thing.

2. Interrupt the cycle of brain reaction. Use strategies we know for calming ourselves.

Self-Soothe Activity

1. Ask students to think of a time when they were angry with themselves about something. What did they say to themselves? Were they kind? Did what they say help them feel better – or worse? If students can't think of something, ask them if they have ever told themselves they are stupid, or no good, or a loser.

2. Explain that soothing means to make someone feel better, calmer, more peaceful. Mothers soothe crying infants by rocking them, talking softly to them, and holding them. Self-soothing means taking care of ourselves in the same kind way we would someone else. It means being mindful – paying attention to what we are feeling and to what we are saying to ourselves, and not judging ourselves harshly.

3. Ask students to go back to a memory they have of a time when they were angry with themselves. Have them imagine a self-soothing response.

4. Give students some possible scenarios, and ask them how a person could self-soothe in these circumstances. What could they say to themselves? What could they do? For instance:

   - You fail a test.
   - You lose a game because you made a mistake (e.g., let in a goal, take a penalty).
   - You say something critical to a friend, which embarrasses them in front of others.
   - You gain some weight and your jeans don't fit.

Lesson 3: IMPROVE the Moment

IMPROVE the Moment is similar to the ACCEPTS strategy. ACCEPTS is used as a distraction; IMPROVE the moment is used to shift our feelings while still dealing with an issue. Students write the word *IMPROVE* down the side of a page to make an acrostic with the words for each letter. Going one line at a time, have students create a personal visual script for the acronym, similar to the one below (see figure 7.27). Each student's script will be different, as they select things they find relaxing/pleasurable. They can use clipart or draw their own pictures. Alternatively, they can create a rap song about what they could do to improve the moment, or write a story about a character in distress and how the character handles the situation.

When I am upset, I can...		
Imagery	Imagine myself on the beach in Maui.	
Meaning	Find a "silver lining". What can I learn from this?	
Prayer	Ask the universe to give me strength.	
Relaxation	Do some yoga.	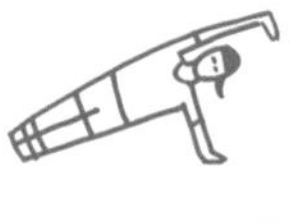
One thing in the moment	Read a book.	
Vacation	Take a nap, or go for a walk.	
Encouragement	Tell myself I am strong, I will be okay.	

Figure 7.27 Visual Script for "Improve the Moment" Strategy

Assessment of Well-Being: An Oxymoron or a Necessity?

Perhaps both. It depends on how we define assessment. If we believe assessment involves evaluation, as in grading, ranking, and so forth, then it is an oxymoron to assess well-being. However, if we understand assessment to be the desire to check in with students about how they are doing, what they are understanding, and what more we can do to support them, then assessment *is* mental-health programming – and a necessity. Thus, assessment *of* well-being makes no sense, but assessment *for* and assessment *as* well-being do make sense.

So, how do we assess well-being? There are empirical scales of things such as self-concept, resiliency, sense of belonging, and so forth, but they cannot capture the depth that we are seeking. These scales can be useful as a system to get a big picture. A school district may choose to have students fill these scales out anonymously to see how they are doing in general and what might need to be considered as needs and goals. However, these scales are not useful to teachers.

On the other hand, assessment *for* well-being and assessment *as* well-being have a variety of purposes:

- to check in with students about how they are feeling in our classrooms and schools
- to assess students understanding and use of the concepts and strategies we have taught them
- to set goals for our teaching, the classroom community, and for individual students (i.e., to have them set goals and assess their progress with our support)

There are several ways we can check in with our students to see how they are doing.

- **Journals.** My students kept personal journals, as a time and venue for reflection and inner work. Sometimes these were curricular, like reflecting on themselves as a mathematician – what were their strengths and challenges? Other times they were social and emotional reflections – what were they grateful for? How were they feeling that day? Sometimes I gave them a topic; other times it was open ended. Students could choose to share their journal with me or not. They could mark pages they wanted me to read, or didn't want me to read. It was their choice.

- **Conferencing.** I conferenced with my students once every two weeks or so during silent reading or during project work time. Conferencing gave me a chance to ask general questions such as:

  ◦ How's it going?

  ◦ Where is your stress level from one to ten? Joy?

  ◦ What's working, and what's not working, for you right now?

  We can also ask more specific questions like:

  ◦ Have you used strategy *x* lately? How did it work for you?

- What strategies are you using to manage your attention?
- Who do you trust as a friend in the class?

- **Provincial & Territorial Resources.** Some provinces and territories provide resources for student self-assessment and/or teacher assessment. In British Columbia, for instance, the new curriculum includes core competencies related to positive personal and cultural identity, personal awareness and responsibility, and social responsibility. The accompanying documents lay out a continuum of development using "I can" statements such as:

  - I can describe different aspects of my identity. I have pride in who I am.

  - I can identify how my challenges can be opportunities for growth.

  - I can contribute to group activities that make my classroom, school, community, or natural world a better place.

  We can use these statement to have students self-assess, and then conference with them about their responses. We can also use the statements as journal prompts: give one to students, and ask them to reflect on (then write about) why it is or is not true for them (see https://curriculum.gov.bc.ca/).

- **Behavioural Observations.** Behaviour communicates, and so does learning. A student who is flourishing relates positively to others, is able to self-regulate their learning, and is willing to persist through challenges. When a student displays evidence of distress, such as anti-social behaviours, moodiness, and an inability to self-regulate, they are telling us they are languishing. This is a critical time to have conferences with students and invite them to share. When we react with annoyance/power, we shut down the lines of communication. If a student is unwilling to share with you, ask if there is someone else they can talk to, and/or what strategies they can use.

  As an example, one day I noticed that one of my grade 7 students seemed distracted and agitated. I waited until the other students starting working, then asked him to conference with me. Since all my students were used to me calling them for conferences, I knew it wouldn't make him stand out for me to call him over. When we sat down, I calmly said to him: "You don't look like your usual self today. Is everything okay?" His eyes grew teary, but he didn't reply. I asked him if he wanted to talk about it, and he shook his head no. I asked him if there was someone he could talk to about it, and again he shook his head no. So, I asked him if there was anything we could do to support him: Would he like us to do some yoga in class today? Go for a walk? No one had to know why we were doing it that day. He told me he didn't know what would help. I told him that was okay; he could do some breathing exercises and be kind to himself for the rest of the day. I infused more breaks than usual into the day. As a class, we went outside to shoot some hoops, did some guided imagery, and generally kept it low key. At the end of the day, he came to me and thanked me. I asked him if it was safe for him to go home that night, and he said yes. I told him to email me if he needed anything. The next day he asked if he could talk to me. I, of course, said yes, and we were able to talk about what he was struggling with (an issue with an older brother).

When I was a classroom teacher, I scanned my room every morning and noted anything unusual about my students. I had some students who were experiencing distress every day. That was their norm. In those cases, the regular use of trauma-informed programming such as DBT and mindfulness practices was critical. I found using it even for a few minutes a day made a difference between a day of challenging behaviour and stress for everyone and a day in which the student coped, if not perfectly, at least in a way that allowed the classroom community to be peaceful.

Keep your eyes on your students, and never assume their behaviour is just deliberate and unnecessary. There is *always* a reason.

Tier 2/3: How Do I Know When to Be Concerned?

The question most teachers have when they first introduce mental-health programming to their students is: "How do I know if there is a serious problem?" They are concerned they may do more harm than good. It is an excellent question, and, unfortunately, the answer is: "There is always that possibility." We could trigger a student who has had traumatic memories – through the smell of someone's lunch, the sound of someone's voice, or a novel we read.

There is never a guarantee that we won't bring back a memory for a student that is painful and triggers a traumatic episode for them. Even a trained psychiatrist can have this happen – there are too many possible triggers. However, the programming suggest in this book will *not*, in and of itself, cause harm. If you teach for a long time, it is likely students will be triggered, even if you never find out that it did happen. Perhaps the student tells you they feel sick and leaves. Maybe they stop coming to class or even school. Likely, this has already happened in your career.

> The truth is, even if we never did any mental-health programming, there is always the possibility of a student being triggered in our classrooms. In fact, it's probably less likely if we do mental-health programming, because the creation of a safe space and a supportive community and the teaching of coping strategies means it is less likely to happen.

What matters isn't that they have been triggered; what matters is how you respond. Responding with compassion and nonjudgment can be healing for someone who has experienced trauma, stigma, and negative reactions from people. When someone is triggered, and then becomes agitated or defensive, they often are wounded anew by the reactions of those around them, who are angry, create a power struggle, or withdraw warmth and support from them when they most need it.

One of the most gifted teachers I ever saw was in the midst of dealing with a student outburst. The young man was screaming and threatening her, and she was trying to get him to leave the classroom. He refused. Suddenly, she paused, looked at the other students, and at him, and said, "Paul (not his real name), would you like a hug? I know I would." He looked startled, and so did the other kids. This was a young adolescent, certainly not used to teachers offering him a hug in the middle of a class. He shook his head no, which I think she expected, but the whole situation diffused. He sat down, put his head in his hands, and became quiet. One of his friends nudged him on his shoulder – his way of giving him the hug.

I'm not suggesting we all go that route. Affection, too, can be a trigger if the student has experienced sexual abuse. But the key here is she asked, she didn't initiate. Paul retained power over his body, and the right to refuse. The teacher honoured his choice, but the message was received. Assuming that a student who is fighting is in a fight-or-flight state makes sense. Reacting to them as we would to a scared puppy growling at us makes sense, too. That she cared was healing for Paul, even if he couldn't show it in front of everyone. That he sat down tells us he no longer felt threatened.

When a student shows signs of fight-or-flight, we should be concerned. We are better off talking to a counsellor, telling them what happened, and asking their advice than we are doing nothing and regretting it later. So, how do we know when a student is not just having a bad day? We can watch for the following:

- behaviours that persist, generally for more than two weeks
- behaviours that change from previous patterns
  - changes in academic achievement, attention, engagement, ability to remember and process information
  - changes in personal hygiene, appearance, body weight (significant gains or losses);
  - withdrawal from friends, activities (e.g., quits the team, stops showing up to an extracurricular activity)
  - seems tired, stressed, confused, distracted
  - experiences new physical illnesses, especially younger children (e.g., headaches, stomachaches, backaches, nausea)
  - feelings of hopelessness, sadness, anxiety; cries often
  - frequent displays of aggression and disobedience; lashes out verbally
  - overly suspicious, accuses others of things, irrational

No one sign is necessarily indicative of a mental illness, and many students, especially adolescents, may sometimes exhibit some of the above. However, it is a red flag if this is not a normal pattern for them and if it persists beyond two to four weeks.

If a student shows overt signals of distress that may seem like attention-seeking behaviours – suicidal statements, threats, self-harm – seek help immediately. What may be a cry for help and attention initially can quickly become tragedy. Don't wait. It's better to err on the side of caution. In such situations, do any of the following:

- Quietly, and privately, prompt the student to use the strategies you have taught, or lead the whole class through a breathing break, without aiming the strategy at the student in distress.

- Call the student aside, or have a private conference with them. Let the student know if they want to talk, you are there to listen. Make sure they know who else they can go to – the counsellor, help lines, and so forth.

- Ask them if they are safe. If they are in danger – either from themselves or from someone else – let them know you want to make sure they are taken care of.

- Talk to the school counsellor and your principal. Let them know what is going on and why you're concerned. Document it in case it comes up again later.

- Remember you are not their therapist, just someone who cares. If the person in distress was your son or daughter, niece or nephew, think about how you would react. According to the Supreme Court, teachers are *in loco parentis* – in place of parent. Teachers are expected "to act in accordance with what a concerned parent would do." (Myers vs. Peel County Board of Education 1981).

If you want to know more about how to respond to students with mental-health problems, I urge you to look into courses in mental-health first aid. They are offered across Canada.

Chapter 8

Programming for Reconciliation and Education for Reconciliation

There is a need for some specific programming related to Indigenous peoples, the history of Canada's relations with Indigenous peoples, and the treaties.

It is critical this programming be done with *all* students, and by *all* teachers, because:

- We cannot change the experience of racism many Indigenous youth still face without changing the attitudes of non-Indigenous Canadians.

- We cannot move forward until we grow comfortable talking to each other, sharing our worldviews and experiences, and finding ways to connect.

- Students need to see both Indigenous and non-Indigenous teachers model sensitivity, respect, and healthy relations.

Reconciliation is not possible until we understand what it is. The dictionary defines *reconciliation* as:

1. The restoration of friendly relations

2. The action of making one view or belief compatible with another

3. The action of making financial accounts consistent: harmonization

So, how do these definitions of reconciliation apply to education, to schools, and to our work as teachers?

To restore friendly relations, we have to create "a culture of mutual respect," as the Truth and Reconciliation Commission (TRC) Calls to Action indicate. Racism and discrimination have to be addressed, and removed from our systems and from our interactions. This requires us to address the second definition – making one view or belief compatible with another. Canadians hold widely disparate attitudes and perspectives about Canadian history and modern Canadians' responsibilities in relation to that history. Many believe Indigenous peoples need to "get over it" and "fit in." Many others feel a sense of shame and guilt.

How does one reconcile with a friend we have wronged? Reconciliation begins by acknowledging what happened, recognizing our role in it (in this case, as colonizers, and people who benefitted from the stealing of the land and the

> Everything we have talked about up to now is relevant to the TRC, and *necessary*. The TRC Calls to Action included the need to teach students empathy and caring, and the need for trauma informed care particularly in regard to the intergenerational impacts of residential schools. As we are doing the brain unit, DBT, RD program, spirit buddies, and class meetings with all students, Indigenous learners will also benefit. This also creates a trauma informed classroom, in which students can feel safe, and learn to manage stress and distress.

settlement since), and apologizing. Second, we have to make restitution. How can we make up for our mistakes? Reconciliation is not about guilt and shame; it is about doing the right thing now to foster healing and well-being for all. This is definition three – making financial reparations. Doing so will allow Indigenous peoples the same opportunities non-Indigenous people have. Here, we need to understand the difference between equality and equity. The same opportunities do not mean everyone needs the same thing. For some students to learn, they need books in Braille; others do not. Equal means giving everyone the same book (either in Braille or print), because equality is a mathematical concept. Equity, however, recognizes that if we offer only one book, one group will have an advantage over the other. For Indigenous peoples to overcome generations of inequity, they may need additional supports beyond what non-Indigenous Canadians need.

Students of all ages can come to understand we wronged a friend, and need to make up for that. They can learn that equity and equality are not the same thing, and fair does not always mean equal.

TRC Resources and Lesson Ideas

A great deal of time and effort has been put into resources created for teachers by a variety of provincial and territorial organizations. Manitoba, Ontario, and British Columbia, to name a few, have units for teachers on treaties, the residential schools, Indigenous cultures and worldviews, and more. We believe the instructional goals behind them make sense. For instance, the Treaty Relations Commission of Manitoba (TRCM) has a K–12 treaty education continuum that is excellent. However, many of the resources do not fit a UDL model in their delivery (e.g., many are blackline masters – worksheets). We will need to "UDL" them – redesign the way in which the content is delivered, while maintaining the instructional content they intended.

The following are examples of how this can be done.

TRCM Alphabet Book (K–2)

The Treaty Commission of Manitoba (TRCM) has provided an alphabet book that is available online, titled *Treaty ABC's.*[10]

The instructional manual lists 26 words related to treaty education that students should learn. The instructions do differentiate responses, suggesting using imagery and games, as you can see.

Vocabulary instruction benefits from six steps:

1. The teacher explains a new word, going beyond reciting its definition (tap into prior knowledge of students, use imagery).
2. Students restate or explain the new word in their own words (verbally and/or in writing).
3. The teacher asks students to create a nonlinguistic representation of the word (a picture or symbolic representation).
4. Students engage in activities to deepen their knowledge of the new word (compare words, classify terms, write their own analogies and metaphors).
5. Students discuss the new word (pair-share, elbow partners).
6. Students periodically play games to review new vocabulary (Pyramid, Jeopardy, Telephone).

However, there is more to UDL than just differentiation. How do we make this accessible to all learners? How do we make history come alive, so students can understand the feelings, not just the facts? So students can analyze, not just memorize? We can respect the instructional goals here:

- to develop students' vocabulary to support learning about the treaties
- to introduce some important understandings related to treaties, such as
  - Treaties were an agreement between two nations that agreed to cooperate and share.
  - The Canadian government made promises to First Nations peoples when they signed the treaties.
  - First Nations peoples believe that what you say is as important as what you write down.
  - The treaties are still law in Canada today.

From these essential understandings we can design activities that support students' well-being and learning.

As a teacher, if my goal is to have students understand the experience of offering to share with someone, of them promising to share with you, and then having that promise broken – how can I do that? We could use role-plays, books about sharing, and so forth. It is also possible to design an experience. You may want to try the following:

One day, give half the class a treat or snack. Tell those students they are allowed to share with those who don't have anything. The next day, give only the other half of the class a treat or snack, and quietly instruct those students they cannot share. Have a class discussion about how this makes both groups feel (you can then give the other students the treat). This exercise might seem harsh, but the experience of sharing, and then not having the sharing returned is one many students will experience in their lives. Building understanding of this, and relating it to the TRC, and also to positive interpersonal relations, can be powerful. We can also use it as a time to teach students how to deal with frustration or anger, how to ask themselves whether they feel good when they do not act with integrity, and so forth. The point is for students to truly understand how the breaking of the treaties has negatively affected all Canadians.

10 See: http://www.trcm.ca/wp-content/uploads/26891-TR-Treaty-ABCs-book-web.pdf>.

Treaty Education Activity (Grades 3–6)

By about grade 3, students are able to understand the concept of a treaty within a governmental structure. In the early years, we can help students understand treaties as friends making promises to share and cooperate. Now, students can understand treaties were made nation to nation, and embedded legally in the founding of Canada. Most middle-years curricula have curricula related to governments, democracy, and human rights. Some essential understandings here might be:

- Governments negotiated treaties, and passed laws, on behalf of the people of their nation.
- Indigenous government systems were well established, and included frequent treaty negotiations between groups.
- Indigenous culture carried an oral tradition – your word was as valid as a signature, whereas British and French governments only recognized written documents as legally binding.
- Indigenous governments agreed to share the land and resources, in exchange for healthcare, education, and a share in the economy of the nation.
- The Canadian government passed a series of laws related to the Indian Act, residential schools, religious freedoms, and land use that were discriminatory and removed the rights of Indigenous peoples.

Again, from the perspective of UDL, we have to make this information both accessible and engaging to diverse learners. Reading texts, doing research, and googling facts to paste on a poster board doesn't cut it.

In one classroom, I did the following to help the students understand the idea of exchange for the good of both sides. I divided the classroom in half (down the middle), and told students on the one side of the line that they couldn't interact with anyone on the other side. Nor could anyone cross over the line for the entire day. Then, I put different supplies on each side of the room (e.g., pencils on one, and paper on the other), and assigned a task to the students that would require use of both sets of supplies. Students quickly became frustrated not having the supplies they needed to be successful. I told them they were going to have to innovate, and use what they had to the best of their ability.

When they returned the next day, they immediately asked if they were going to be allowed to cross the line on this day. I said no, but they could interact with the other side at the boundary. This meant they had to meet in the middle and ask someone on the other side for the supplies they needed.

They began to trade. It was still annoying for them to not be able to get things themselves and to constantly have to ask those on the other side for supplies they needed. As the day wore on, students started forming into groups. They realized they could do bulk exchanges rather than constantly shout to their friends for each item. They came in from recess and one group promptly exchanged a stack of paper for a box of pencils with a group of students on the other side. At that point, I introduced the word *treaty*, and we talked about "making a deal" that helps both groups.

On the third day, students asked if they were now going to be able to cross the line. I said yes, but only one group would be able to do so. The students on the window side of the classroom could go anywhere, whereas the students on the door side of the classroom could not cross the line. They still had to ask. I wanted the students to understand power imbalance and inequality. Some of the students on the window side readily shared with students on the door side, but some started to tease their classmates on the door side – telling others not to give them the paper and laughing about it. Students on the door side then started trying to prevent the window-side students from coming over and "taking their stuff."

That afternoon we had a class meeting. Some students were angry at others for "not being fair" and for "being bullies." We talked about what it felt like to be in each group. We wrote out the feelings:

- Window Side:
  - Day 1: Frustrated

- ○ Day 2: Tired of having to constantly ask, and constantly get things for, the kids on the other side. Easier when they made the treaty.
- ○ Day 3: Relieved to be able to have what they want
  - tired of being asked to go and get things from people on the door side
  - Some felt was unfair and felt bad for those on the door side.
  - Some said they thought it was funny; they were "just joking around."
  - Some thought the door side needed to quit complaining and just deal with it, the way everyone had on the first day.

On the fourth day I reversed the situation. And on day 5, too. I wanted the students on the window side to now see how it is to always have to ask for something. I also wanted the students on the door side to decide whether to have empathy and try to help, or to take revenge.

On Friday afternoon, we had another meeting. Again, students talked through their feelings, which ranged from "They did it to us" to "I knew what it was like." At that point, I introduced the seven sacred teachings shared by many First Nations – wisdom, love, truth, courage/bravery, respect, honesty, and humility – and we talked about the values of each. I asked the students to think about whether they had acted with these values during the week, and to be prepared to share their thoughts on Monday.

The following week, I introduced a timeline of Canadian history from the time of European contact to the present. I divided the class into small groups, and gave each group a cue card about a topic that involved Indigenous peoples – fur trade, treaties, Indian Act, residential schools, powwow ban, and so forth (use topics relevant to the region in which you are teaching). I asked students to research what happened in relation to their topic, and to respond to this question: Was the behaviour of the people in keeping with the seven sacred teachings?

I also had students determine where their event fit on the timeline. I provided them with some resources (articles, websites, storybooks) that were age appropriate. (The group that introduced the topic of residential schools focused on children having to go away to school and missing their families. Depending on the age of your students, you may or may not want to introduce this topic.)

> *Questions*
>
> *What does it mean to be free?*
> *What does walking with dignity mean?*
> *What does fighting for your rights mean?*
> *What does anything mean?*
>
> *Do you know?*
>
> *Do you know the power of your voice?*
> *Do you know the knowledge in your self?*
> *Do you know the dream you have every night will become true?*
>
> *Can you?*
>
> *Can you beat the cruelty of discrimination?*
> *Can you know the difference between right and wrong?*
> *Can you control yourself when things go way out of hand?*
>
> *You can!*
>
> *You can go tough when the times get tougher.*
> *You can make a difference in situations.*
> *You can believe in yourself stand up for others.*
>
> *You did it.*

Figure 8.1 A poem written by a non-Indigenous student respecting the resiliency of Indigenous peoples and what they had been through.

I also asked the students to think about their experiences of the week before, and to make connections to the experiences of the people involved in these events in Canadian history. Students came to some very powerful realizations about the discrimination Indigenous peoples experienced, the immoral behaviour of the government of the time, and the need to now make things better. Throughout the year, as we studied government, democracy, natural resources, human rights, and environmental issues, students repeatedly came back to "that week where we couldn't cross the line."

Treaty Education and Missing and Murdered Indigenous Women (Grades 7–12)

One day I was working with a grade 11 social studies teacher. She told me she was going to teach the treaties in effect in Manitoba (treaties 1–5). She had decided to put the students into small groups, and give each group a file with information about one of the treaties. Their job was to create a presentation for the class about the treaty they had studied. She asked me if this was how I would teach it, and I said honestly that, no, it was not. She asked me why, and I replied that, first, it required no critical thinking – students were just going to read what was in the file, and regurgitate it. They didn't even have to do any research – she had given it all to them. Second, her method of teaching made the unit boring. Engaging adolescents in their learning requires not only a change from text-based facts and drills, but also an infusion of emotion, social justice, and personal connection. She asked me how I would teach it.

I joined her class and wrote the following timeline on the board:

Figure 8.2 Timeline of Women's Status in Indigenous Communities

I told her students they were going to engage in an inquiry project. I gave them the following information: "In 1871, when Canadian settlers first came to treaty meetings with Indigenous peoples, women in the Cree and Ojibwe tribes were held in high esteem. The Elders and grandmothers' councils were advisors to the chiefs, and violence toward women was punishable by expulsion from the tribe. As of 2016, there were more than 1200 missing and murdered Indigenous women, some killed by Indigenous men."

At the end of the project, I said, they would have to answer the following questions: "How did we go from a place where women's lives were valued, to a place where their lives are devalued? What role did the treaties play in this?"

We provided the students with the files, because I didn't want them to spend their time gathering rote facts – I wanted them to focus on analyzing the treaty process, inferring what must have happened, and considering how they felt about it.

I then put a brief summary of Bloom's Taxonomy on the board, like this:

List Recognize Identify	Describe Explain	Analyze Compare Synthesize	Infer Propose Evaluate
D – 50–59	C – 60–69	B – 70–79	A – 80–90 A+ 91–100

Figure 8.3 A Sample Rubric of Bloom's Taxonomy

I referred to the diagram as I explained to students that if their projects shared the information that was in the files or on Google, they were repeating someone else's thinking. While they would pass, their mark would be a C or a D. However, if they went deeper, and really thought about the information they read about – What must have happened? Why? How did they feel about it? What could be done? – then their mark would be a B or an A.

We gave the students time to read some of the basic information and discuss their thinking. After a while, I stopped them again, and said: "I'm going to give you one more piece of information and two more questions to consider for your projects." This is what I wrote on the board:

> **Fact:** British culture of the time did not hold women in high esteem. When Indigenous people arrived to negotiate the treaties, the British refused to negotiate with women, and ridiculed Indigenous men for "letting women tell them what to do."
>
> **Question 1:** Would Canada be better or worse off today if settlers accepted Indigenous culture, rather than trying to force assimilation?
>
> **Question 2:** Where do we want to be in the future, and how might we get there?

I purposely did not frame the questions around gender roles. I wanted to leave open the possibility of students responding in directions we could never have imagined. Gifted students often add complexity beyond what is asked. In this particular instance, some groups stuck to the "women would be better off if..." scenario. One student, however, led his group into a much larger study of Indigenous cultures of the time, related environmental issues, human rights issues, and more.

It is important to not make one culture superior to another. Ultimately, we discuss with the students the idea that every culture has rich history and gifts we can learn from, as well as challenges. The main goal is for students gain an appreciation for the diversity and knowledge of Indigenous peoples, undo the "tepees and loincloths" image, and provide an understanding of the complexity and sophistication that existed before the land became Canada. In doing so, we can help Indigenous students gain respect for themselves and their culture and history, and for non-Indigenous students to gain respect and perspective. As well, we can help all students understand how women must have felt having their value denigrated, and why there might now be resentment and struggle.

These are just a few examples of how we can take the instructional goals put forward by the TRC – such as treaty education, developing empathy, and recognizing the wounds of the past – and bring them to life for all students through a universally designed pedagogy.

We must consider how all of our learners can take part. In the ABC book, students who struggle with writing, vocabulary, and so forth are supported by lived experiences, stories, and imagery. In the treaty-education project, the format for answering the question is left open. Resources can be brought in to support students learning (e.g,, video clips of the TRC sessions and survivors of the residential schools, an Indigenous Elder to answer questions and teach storytelling, and an Indigenous artist to teach students how to tell a story visually). Students can create role-plays, films, and rap songs, or use other media, to support their response to the questions. Sample rubrics for assessing these understandings can be found in Appendix K.

Every Canadian needs to know about residential-schools history for two reasons. First, knowledge helps us to make sure we don't make the same mistakes again. Second, without that understanding, we can't empathize and make sense of the intergenerational trauma and the issues we now face as a country in our relationships. The only question is, at what age should this material be introduced?

As a child, I attended a Jewish private school. Because I was an advanced reader, I was able to go into the section of the library where the chapter books were shelved. When I was in grade 3, unbeknownst to the adults around me, I took out several books about the Holocaust. While I was capable of reading, and comprehending, the books, I was not emotionally ready to handle the material. Learning that seemingly normal people, people who went home to families of their own, were putting babies in ovens and burning them alive was beyond my ability to cope. I shut down. I refused to go to school, to eat, or to leave my room. My parents tried to find out what was wrong, but I wouldn't talk to anyone. I had lost all trust in the world. How could I trust that the people in my neighbourhood wouldn't turn on me the way many people did when they turned their neighbours in to the Nazis? How could I trust that my parents could protect me when the parents in these books couldn't protect their children? I didn't want to live in that kind of world. At eight years of age, I told my mother I didn't want to live anymore. One night, my mother came in and sat on the edge of my bed. Her eyes were teary, which shocked me out of my inner turmoil. She asked me what had happened? I asked her: "How could they do that, Mom?" She asked me what I was referring to. You can imagine her shock when her eight year old replied: "put babies in ovens." I then revealed the pile of books under my bed. I'll leave it to your imagination the conversation she had with the librarian who had allowed me to sign those books out!

My point is, we do need to consider the mental health of the students we are sharing TRC material with. A child could easily be traumatized by the idea that the police might one day come and take them away from their parents and send them to a scary school. Treaty education can begin in kindergarten. Learning that Canada was formed through cooperation and partnership, and that the partnership then began to struggle, is not traumatic. Children understand that friends don't always get along. The dark part of our history, though – the forced resettlements and attempts at assimilation, removal of human rights, residential schools, and ongoing racism and discrimination should not, in my opinion, be taught until students are emotionally ready to manage them. To determine that, consider the following two criteria:

1. Do students understand the concept of time and history?

   A student who understands things that happened in the past are not happening right now can begin to hear about some dark events in human history. Students who do not yet have a sense of time and may think those events are happening right now are not ready.

2. Do students have some sense of how to cope with distress?

   At younger and younger ages, students are being exposed to videos and print information about war, death, violence, poverty, and more. We should not be surprised we are seeing more anxiety in kids, and less joy and wonder. Until students have the ability to discuss their feelings with others, reach out for help when needed, and manage distress, they are not ready.

There is no right age to teach about residential schools. Most resources about residential schools begin somewhere around grade 5. Whether or not to use them at that level is a communal decision. Certainly, in high school, students should be informed. Whenever you decide to introduce this material, be sure you first create a safe space for students to express their thoughts, concerns, and feelings, and have taught students strategies for dealing with them.

The Medicine Wheel and Well-Being

Michael Redhead Champagne has spent nearly two decades as a leader in the Indigenous community of Winnipeg, focusing on youth engagement, facilitation, community organizing, and mobilization. He was recognized as the 2016 Canadian Red Cross Young Humanitarian of the Year and in TIME Magazine as a Next Generation Leader. Michael has also received a Manitoba Aboriginal Youth Achievement Award, as well as recognition as a CBC Manitoba Future 40 leader, a Manitoba Hero, and a Future Leader of Manitoba. He is the founder of AYO – Aboriginal Youth Opportunities and in that capacity shares an activity he uses with Indigenous youth. His teaching on the medicine wheel appears on the next page.

Taking Care of Your Whole Medicine Wheel

The Medicine Wheel is a concept that has been in popular use since knowledge keepers from across Turtle Island came together in the early 1980s and published a book called *The Sacred Tree*. This book, and many of the teachings were shared with urban Indigenous young people such as AYO! (Aboriginal Youth Opportunities) as we were growing up in Winnipeg's North End. The AYO! Movement is a collection of helpers who regularly volunteer their time and gifts to support their community, the families within it, and themselves; they are a board of directors, an executive management team and front line staff all in one individual. AYO! Leaders are urban Indigenous young people themselves, often experiential in terms of living in the inner city, poverty and as a product of various systems (e.g., child welfare, justice, health), and it has become necessary for us to educate our circle on a broad range of systemic and historical challenges. At the same time, we work to build up self-esteem, skills, and the necessary networks and relationships to determine a solution and help Aboriginal youth move their ideas into action. It is difficult for us to accomplish our work if the young leader we are helping is out of balance, and so we use the Medicine Wheel to help us take care of our whole minds, hearts, bodies, and spirit.

Figure 8.4 Medicine Wheel

The many teachings contained within what we now refer to as the Medicine Wheel taught us about our relationship as people to the Earth and natural world around us – including the parts of ourselves, the stages of our lives, and the seasons. For educators who are working on wellness and reconciliation, the Medicine Wheel as a tool for self-care can help us not only take care of ourselves as educators, but to also understand the needs of the learners in our classrooms. Below, you will find an activity you can do by yourself or your classroom to find strategies of self care!

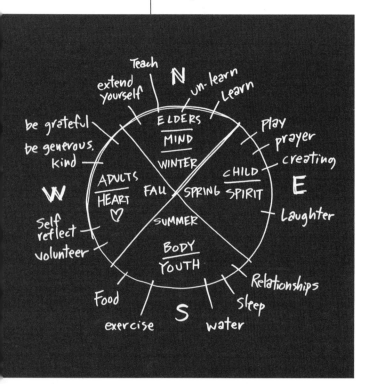

Purpose: to discuss healthy ways of taking care of ourselves with our students, using our own self care strategies as a positive example.

Draw a Medicine Wheel outline on the board and label the 4 directions as follows:

> East – Spirit
> South – Body
> West – Heart
> North – Mind

Explain to students that everyone in the room has a heart, a mind, a body, and a spirit. Emphasize the importance of caring for the many parts of ourselves and remind students that they are experts in their own lives/experiences. Let them know that this is a "lens" with which they can see the world.

You will then go through each quadrant and list the strategies that students share on how to care for that part of themselves.

For each quadrant, ask students to list one strategy per student (minimum four per direction is adequate, but there may be more).

– Michael Champagne

Figure 8.5 Medicine Wheel Activity

Calls to Action and Teacher Responsibilities

The Truth and Reconciliation Commission states three Calls to Action that teachers must play a role in:

1. Develop and implement kindergarten to grade 12 curriculum and learning resources on Indigenous peoples in Canadian history, and the history and legacy of residential schools.

2. Share information and best practices on teaching curriculum related to residential schools and Indigenous history.

3. Build student capacity for intercultural understanding, empathy, and mutual respect.

For elementary-school teachers, you will have done your part if:

- You have instilled in all students an appreciation for diversity, Indigenous culture and history, and Indigenous contributions to Canada past and present.

- You have engaged students in learning about Indigenous peoples in ways that build respect, understanding, and empathy.

- You have introduced treaty education to students, so that they understand we have a partnership that needs to be honoured and hasn't always been.

- You have created a trauma-informed learning environment – a classroom in which students feel safe, develop self-worth and a sense of belonging, and are supported when mental issues arise, not labelled (e.g., oppositional) and punished.

- You have created a classroom that reflects a worldview in which community and interdependence are of equal value to the individual and independence, and in which the gifts in every student are sought.

- You have reached out to Indigenous parents and families without judgment, and built bridges, not walls.

For high-school teachers, you will have done your part if:

- You have engaged students in deep conversations and reflections about issues related to diversity, Indigenous culture, and history (including the residential schools), and Indigenous contributions to Canada past and present.

- You have engaged students in learning about Indigenous peoples in ways that build respect, understanding, and empathy.

- You have connected treaty education and Indigenous perspectives across curricula, so students understand we have a partnership that needs to be honoured, and Indigenous peoples have something to offer all Canadians moving forward.

- You have created a trauma-informed learning environment – a classroom in which students feel safe, are able to develop self-worth and a sense of belonging, and are supported when mental issues arise, not labelled (e.g., oppositional) and punished.

- You have created a classroom that reflects a worldview in which community and interdependence are of equal value to the individual and independence, and in which the gifts in every student are sought.

- You have reached out to Indigenous parents and families without judgment, and built bridges, not walls.

Chapter 9

Moving Toward Joy

Joy, Neurology, and Engagement

Until now, we have focused on well-being. Often, that is interpreted as being content, calm, and peaceful. But what about joy? What about fun, play, love, exhilaration, excitement, adventure – living life to the fullest? Where are these found in our classrooms and schools, for both students and staff?

From a neurological level, joy is associated with the chemicals oxytocin, serotonin, dopamine, and endorphins. This means that joy is not only associated with well-being, it is associated with attention, memory, language processing, and critical thinking!

Somewhere we lost sight of this. We focused on achievement, accountability, rigor – as in *rigor mortis* – and lost sight of the joy and pleasure that should be associated with learning and growing. Rigor and accountability are stiff, stress-filled concepts. Creativity, complexity, intellectual engagement, debate, and learning can and should be fascinating and mind-blowing. Hopefully, as you read this book, an inner voice has occasionally said things like: "Yes! That's cool! What a great idea!" It is that emotion, that elation, that spurs us to invest time and energy in learning something. When we attend a professional development workshop, we appreciate humour, interaction, having fun, and learning something new that connects to our needs and beliefs. Teaching should be enjoyable. So, why do we not want learning to be simple, easy, and exciting for our students? Easy doesn't mean simple, as in dumbed down – it means we are relaxed and engaged in the process. Why is humour, fun, and interaction lacking in so many of our classrooms?

Finding Meaning and Purpose

People who feel their lives are meaningful and have a purpose are far more likely to flourish. Neurologically, we are designed to be social animals. We have mirror neurons in the brain that help us read the emotions of others, and then reflect them back. When we act in a way that makes someone smile, we mirror that emotion – with happiness and gratitude. Helping students, even our youngest ones, see how they can make a positive difference in the world shows them a pathway to flourishing. We can share with our students many examples of young people who have had a positive effect on the world – children's rights' activists such as Craig Kielburger, Om Prakash Gurjar, Iqbal Masih, and Malala Yousafzai to name just a few. They show them they, too, can have a voice. Helping students think about what matters to them, what they think is important, and how their gifts and talents – and their voices – can make the world a better place, sets the stage for a joyful adventure experiencing life.

Talk about current events with your students. In early years, students can learn some children don't have warm clothing or birds and animals are harmed by trash humans leave behind. Even small projects, such as collecting warm clothing and toys for underprivileged children, visiting Elders, or cleaning up the school yard, can give students a sense of contributing to their community. Choice and voice are critical. When we force service on children, it feels like a chore and demand. Instead, we want to introduce students to the issues, and let them engage with those that make their heart beat.

One day in a grade 6/7 class I taught, the subject of the upcoming provincial election came up. Students reflected the voices of their parents, so I decided to introduce them to the issues and platforms that were being debated. That way, they could develop their own ideas. We talked about left wing and right wing as concepts – and what they meant for economics, social programming, and more. I asked people who supported the different parties to come in and explain their thinking and reasons. The students read the parties' election materials. At one point, the issue of homelessness arose. One of the students made the comment that the homeless "needed to get a job." This was a learning opportunity and a chance to teach about mental illness, poverty, and trauma. It was also a chance to teach economics and math.

I gave the students a project of creating a budget for a family of four living in Vancouver. They had to research what a one-bedroom apartment, two-bedroom apartment, and larger home cost. They went to the grocery store and added up what three meals a day for four people would cost. Then there were utilities, transportation, taxes, and so forth. After students had completed their budgets, we looked at job ads. I asked them to calculate what a minimum-wage job would bring in. They were stunned to realize there weren't many jobs, most were not full time, and minimum wage would not allow someone to house and feed a family of four.

I asked a staff member from Covenant House (a shelter for homeless youth) to talk to students about homeless kids and why and how they ended up there. He talked about what their lives were like, the foster-care system, and intergenerational trauma. Slowly, the students began to talk about gratitude, and how lucky they were to live where they did. Many did not come from wealthy families and had had significant challenges of their own. Still, they had food to eat and a roof over their heads. The students decided to put on a concert for the school to raise money for Covenant House. They worked for weeks writing raps and songs, creating music on instruments and computer programs. Each student put together a care package – a bag with a blanket, book, snacks, socks, warm clothing, cosmetics, toys – whatever they wanted. We went down to Covenant House and presented the director with a cheque. Then my students were each introduced to one young person who was living or visiting Covenant House, and gave each a gift package.

Infusing joy into your students can, ironically, also come from confronting significant challenges, both personal and professional. We were able to cover significant portions of the math curriculum, engage in literacy and research, and discuss social issues. My students felt powerful and were affected emotionally, socially, and intellectually in the course of this service project. Years later, one of them emailed me to say he had just taken a job – at Covenant House.

Joy can be found when we:

- pay attention to what we need

- honour our own interests, needs, and experiences

- focus on gratitude for what is good in our life

- do service: feel we have made a positive difference in the lives of others

We talked about each of these in the Brain Unit (see page 112). So, how do we explore them through our learning?

Indigenous Perspectives on Connecting with the Whole

In chapter 3, we discussed the Indigenous worldview related to interdependence. If fulfillment comes from self and community actualization, then how do we infuse this into our classrooms?

We have also discussed the need to help students discover their gifts, and how to use them to contribute to a better world. When students see their community responding positively to their contributions, they develop pride and are empowered to move forward.

Local context matters. Indigenous educational practices teach us that land-based, culturally appropriate education has great meaning for youth, especially in a time of climate change and species extinction. The Indigenous concept of "all my relations" – the idea that we are all connected, to both the living and the nonliving aspects of our world – is a spiritual perspective we need more than ever. The experience of a child growing up in the Maritimes is different from that of child growing up on the Prairies. The social issues they can relate to, their role models, and their relationship to the land they inhabit all differ. What is the same, however, is that people flourish when their lives are filled with joy, meaning, and purpose.

We know that just as we have mirror neurons for reflecting social interactions (see page 177), we also have brain structures dedicated to processing sensory information that is natural. A bird's song activates different brain reactions than does traffic noise, even though both are auditory. Students who live in urban environments often lack a relationship with the land. Finding ways to engage students with the natural world supports well-being. We can take students outside to do breathing exercises, yoga, and qi-gong or tai-chi. Community gardens allow students to dig in the mud and commune with nature.

Some teachers go further. One teacher in a northern Manitoba school taught a unit on the moose hunt. Science topics, such as organ systems, habitats, reproduction, biodiversity and more, were connected. Math was taught through weighing and measuring moose meat, calculating shares for the community, and evaluating the economic impact of the hunt on the community. As well, a study of sustainability used statistics of population size, annual birth rate, and territorial range. Social studies was addressed through studies about traditional Indigenous culture, sustainability, environmental issues, and rights and responsibilities. Students documented their experiences through writing, photographic essays, and film. Ceremonies of music and dance also enriched student experience.

Although some teachers may not go this far, we can all get students out of the classroom, onto the land, and into the community. Learn about the natural environment of your region experientially, and get your students involved in issues that matter to them, their families, and their communities. Experiences don't have to be big – they just have to be meaningful.

Instructional Practices for Well-Being and Joy

At the beginning of the school year, teachers work hard to establish routines, teach organizational structures, and articulate expectations for students' behaviour. Their efforts help establish a classroom climate in which students develop their understanding of the rules of the game and begin to form friendships. The beginning of the school year is a crucial moment in time, a moment in which we can create a spiritual, compassionate space, a magical moment in which students can discover that the new school year might be different, that they themselves might be different. Such a moment is all too easily lost amid the organizational paperwork and the frenzied activity that often accompanies the first weeks of school.

Setting the stage for the magical moments may sound idealistic, but it is not unrealistic. Coaches do it all the time. They tell the students: "Being a star quarterback is great, but if there's no receiver to catch the ball, you can't win the championship." Coaches point out that every member of the team contributes something different: "You can't expect a wide receiver to do what a linebacker does, but both are necessary." They convince even adolescents that they are a team, and that they need to support each other if they want to succeed. Why can't learning, too, be a team sport? (Katz 2012)

> When we take the time to focus on well-being, we also are priming our students brains for the curriculum to come.

We are always learning. Infants learn, dogs and cats learn – all animals learn. Students learn. But what are our students learning in school? How many are learning that learning is boring, unpleasant, exhausting, stressful, and that they are no good at it?

Schools are places of learning. Students discover who they are, what they can do, and what they can contribute in their classrooms and beyond. Instructional design can foster students' self-worth and self-efficacy, or it can create stress and trauma through repeated failure and humiliation. Instruction can develop critical thinkers, socially conscious citizens, leaders, and collaborators, or it can develop worker bees whose jobs will be taken over by machines. So, how do we weave together what we know about mental health, well-being, neurology, and learning with the demands of curricula, assessment, reporting, and "the system." Fortunately, Mother Nature did it for us.

We learn best when we are happy. Thus, when we take the time to focus on the well-being of our students, we are also priming our students' brains for the curriculum to come. When I was in the classroom, I noticed that as I invested more time in social and emotional learning (SEL), my students did better academically, not just on the activities I facilitated, but on the provincial exams, as well. This happened every year. Research bears this out. Meta-analyses show an 11 point gain on standardized exams when SEL programming is present, compared to when it is not (Durlak et al. 2011).

What greater goal is there than our students', and our society's, well-being? It is a bonus that it also allows us to delve into curricula with students who are able to self-regulate their attention and emotions, know themselves as learners, know how to work with others, and are not afraid to take risks and persevere through challenges. The key point is: *success breeds well-being.* When a student constantly fails, no mental-health and SEL programming can protect them from the impact of years of struggle. We have to consider our instruction, as well.

The definition of *inclusion,* according to Merriam Webster, is:

1. The action or state of including or of being included within a group or structure.

2. A body or particle recognizably distinct from the substance in which it is embedded.

This book has very much been focused on the first definition, but what of the second? Have we created a school where "being distinct from the substance in which it is embedded" is valued and celebrated? Do we honor uniqueness, creativity, and divergence, or do we focus solely on getting it right? When we create a classroom in which we regularly highlight uniqueness, we model for students that difference is okay, and that you don't have to be the same to be valued and included. This raises the following questions:

- How has "being distinct" become a negative in our schools?

- What role does our teaching, assessment, behavioural expectations, and so on, play in making difference a problem?

Instruction focusing on products that have a predetermined outcome devalues creativity and innovation. Students' works that all look identical displayed on the bulletin board are perfect examples of this. If all we ever learn is what someone else has already discovered, we would never move forward. One needs some base knowledge, but encouraging innovation is critical. As four- or five-year olds, children are incredibly innovative. They can play in a cardboard box for hours with entire worlds in their minds. By the time they are in grade 4, they just want to know what the right answer is. That needs to change.

> *Innovation* is the process of developing a new method, idea, product, or improving on an old one. Synonyms are *change, alteration, revolution, upheaval, transformation, metamorphosis,* and *breakthrough.*

Revolution. Can we teach our students to be revolutionary? *Revolutionary* does not have to mean rebellious, although there is a time and a place for that, too. Revolutionary minds, however, discovered the human genome, created the iPhone, and fought for civil rights. Can we invite students to create representations of their learning that go beyond regurgitation, and come in formats we can't even imagine? Can we teach students to infer the way an archaeologist and an historian do, design the way a scientist does, visualize the way an astrophysicist or an architect does? Can we give students the initiative to create, compose, build, write, and code in new and revolutionary ways? Three-year-olds do it when left alone to play.

Joy results in innovation.

Most teachers don't think they are creative or innovative. That's because we define creativity only in the artistic realm. Have you ever taught something in a new way? Planned a new lesson or unit? Rearranged your classroom? Used a tool in an unintended way (like a paper clip to...)? If so, you are an innovator. It may not have seemed revolutionary, but it is still innovation. Even if we are not innovators, we can give our students the chance to be. Have you ever had a student say or do something that wowed you? That's what we're aiming for – allowing students to try, fail, try again, and wow us, their peers, and themselves.

Connecting Mental-Health Programming with Curriculum Across the School Year

No matter how much we value our students' well-being, we still have a curriculum to teach. So, when do we have time to do all of this? This is where innovation comes in. Find ways to sneak mental-health programming into subjects, and sneak subjects into mental-health programming. It's all about connections.

NOTE: In the charts on the next two pages, RD stands for the Respecting Diversity program, BU stands for the Brain Unit, DBT stands for Dialectical Behaviour Therapy, and TRC indicates the big picture not only of the TRC's Calls to Action but also Indigenous perspectives and worldviews.

Subject	Topic	Sample Activity
Science	The Senses, Sound, Hearing, Light	• BU: Sensory reactivity, breathing exercises • DBT: Mindfulness activities
	Daily and Seasonal Changes, Weather	• BU: Add in connection between mood and amount of light, weather to brain unit, • TRC: (Indigenous perspectives) on seasons and weather
	Living Things	• RD: Diversity of strengths and challenges, self-awareness, and disability • BU: Lessons on the need for sleep, nutrition, and exercise • BU: Lessons on the need for touch and connection, oxytocin • TRC: All My Relations • DBT: Interpersonal effectiveness (meeting our needs)
	Habitats, Ecosystems, and Communities	• RD: Lessons on interdependence and diversity • BU: Lessons on response to others and the environment • TRC: All My Relations
	Maintaining a Healthy Body	• BU: Connections between mental and physical health • BU and DBT: Self-regulation of cortisol in • BU: Nervous system & brain
	Diversity of Living Things, Biodiversity	• DBT: Mindfulness • RD Program • BU: Differences in reactivity, perceptions, neurochemistry, mental illness • TRC: All My Relations
	Chemistry	• BU: Neurochemistry, regulation of oxytocin, cortisol, and neurotransmitters
	Electricity	• BU: Neuron communication
	Cells and Systems	• BU: All
	Reproduction/Genetics	• BU: Genetics of mental illness • TRC: Epigenetic role in intergenerational trauma
	Homeostasis	• BU and DBT: Relationship to wellness versus stress when changes occur`
	Scientific Theory and Research	• RD: Multiple Intelligences versus "g" – the debate • BU: Mental illness and mental health • TRC: Indigenous perspectives

Figure 9.1 Mental-Health Programming in Science

Subject	Topic	Sample Activity
Social Studies	Me, My Family	• RD: Lessons 1–4, • BU: All
	Community	• RD: Lessons 3, 5–9 • BU: Lesson 7 • DBT: Interpersonal Effectiveness • TRC: All
	Canadian History	• BU: Treatment of people with mental illness • TRC: All
	Geography of Canada	• TRC: All
	Indigenous Peoples and Culture	• TRC: All • BU: Perspectives on well-being and mental illness
	Quality of Life	• RD: Lessons 4–9 • BU: Lesson 7 • DBT: All • TRC: All • Class Meetings
	Ways of Life	• TRC: All • RD: Lessons 4–6 • BU: Lesson 7 • DBT: Mindfulness • Class Meetings
	Ancient Civilizations	• BU: Lesson 7 (explore beliefs and practices related to spirituality, well-being, and mental illness) • DBT: Mindfulness
	Government	• TRC: Treaties, residential schools, Indian Act, etc. • Class Meetings
	The Environment and Sustainability	• TRC: All
	Diversity and Pluralism	• RD: Lessons 3, 4–6, 9 • TRC: All • BU: Lesson 7
	Natural Resources	• TRC: Treaties, land-based education

Figure 9.2 Mental-Health Programming in Social Studies

Everything we do is related to language arts in some way – reading, writing, listening, speaking, viewing, and representing. Texts for literature circles, video and film study, dramatic enactments and plays, visual representations, and so forth can be selected around some of these topics, particularly the TRC, community and interdependence, mental health, mental illness, spirituality, and well-being.

A Sample Unit Connecting Mathematics and Well-Being

In mathematics, connections exist to every curricular strand, but teachers will have to decide when and how to make those connections. For instance, in a grade 9 unit on linear algebra, we can connect social issues to the idea of functions and relations. The intention of this unit is to have students explore the *concept* of a linear relationship, not just recognize or plot one, which is a lower-order level of thinking. The concept of a linear relationship is that one variable is directly (constantly) related to another (e.g., the more you eat, the more weight you will gain). We want students to consider the importance of research that reveals relationships and influences amongst variables in real-life issues. The relationship between poverty and academic achievement, as an example, is more complex than the one between eating and weight gain. This requires students to develop the basic skills (differentiate a linear from non-linear relationship, interpret and create graphs, extrapolate patterns for prediction). But the unit does not end there – it can delve into the importance of understanding relationships, correlations, and causation so students can be critical readers of research and news reports. Mathematical concepts such as constancy, communication, patterns, predictability, and uncertainty are all explored as students learn that while we can make logical predictions (e.g., if the rate of obesity continues to rise, health-care costs will also increase), we cannot be absolutely sure our predictions will come true.

Big Idea

Rate of change is an essential attribute of linear relations, and has meaning in the different representations, including equations.

Essential Understandings

- Algebra is the study of relationships and the solving of mysteries (e.g., why does variable x change? What influences it?)
- Many real-world functional relationships can be represented by equations, which in turn can be used to predict/find the solution to real-world problems.
- Linear algebra allows us to make predictions based on consistent relationships (concept of constancy in mathematics).
- Numbers communicate important information about real-life phenomena.
- Linear relationships can be depicted visually, and graphic representations can aid in prediction.

Essential Questions

- How does recognizing linear relationships in the real world affect our ability to predict outcomes and make informed decisions regarding social issues?
- What do numbers tell us about the magnitude of an issue and the urgency of problem solving?
- How can we represent these linear relationships so they can be understood clearly?

Limited	Basic	Good	Excellent
Understands variables can influence each other in predictable ways	Explains how an equation or graph describes a relationship that is constant, with supporting examples	Demonstrates how a real-world functional relationship can be represented by an equation	Proposes solutions based on patterns/predictability
Understands numbers can indicate a "big problem" or "little problem"	Compares degree of influence, and magnitude of a problem, giving examples	Evaluates solutions to problems based on both mathematical and social variables Justifies importance of resolution (i.e., some problems may affect more people, but be of less severity, and vice-versa)	Communicates the urgency of resolving a social issue with power and impact Uses statistics, equations, and graphs in insightful ways
Identifies examples of linear relations.	Explains and differentiates between linear and non-linear relations.	Analyzes real-life data to determine if the pattern or relationship is linear.	Critiques a local issue that shows a linear pattern and propose a solution to solve it.
Explains the linear pattern in a graph. Lists the components of a clearly labelled graph.	Produces a graph that shows a linear relationship. Interpolates and extrapolate values within a graph.	Generates a linear equation from a pattern. Evaluates whether a graph represents a linear situation or equation.	Creates an infographic, which includes a linear equation and its graph, to present data regarding a local issue.

Figure 9.3 Mental-Health Programming in Math

Stations and Centres (Cooperative Work)

Verbal- Linguistic	Logical-Mathematics	Visual-Spatial	Bodily-Kinesthetic	Musical-Rhythmic
Write a news article to explain an equation for a real-world problem/issue: What does the future foretell if the pattern continues?	Evaluate the statistical claims of an article, reporting influences on a social issue: Are the conclusions logical? How urgent is it for society to respond?	Create an infographic to represent a linear relationship related to a social issue: Persuade people it is important.	Construct a model to represent a linear relationship related to a given problem.	Create an interpretive dance that demonstrates a linear relationship related to a social issue.

Naturalist	Interpersonal	Intrapersonal	Existential	
Illustrate a linear relationship found in nature.	Explore the factors contributing to a social issue, and their magnitude: Indicate whether there are linear relationships within them.	Think about the factors that influence you in your own life; indicate whether there are linear relationships within them: How powerful an influence do they hold? Write an equation to represent their impact.	Look at the data related to spiritual practices (e.g., meditation) and health: Recommend policy for Health Canada.	

Figure 9.4 Sample Activities for an Integrated Math and Social Studies Unit

Examples of Student Products

- **Musical-Rhythmic:** Two students created a dance in which they first portrayed a couple whose movements were gentle and coordinated. They then portrayed the couple drinking alcohol, with movements becoming aggressive and reactive rather than coordinated (depicting relationship between alcohol use/addictions with domestic violence).

- **Bodily-Kinesthetic:** One student created a model showing a car accident at lower speeds, and one at higher speeds (depicting the relationship between speeding and fatalities).

- **Naturalistic:** A student created an artistic representation of pesticide use alongside depletion of bird populations.

- **Verbal-Linguistic:** A student wrote an article in response to the equation $x = 2y$, inferring that if x was the rate of obesity, y could be the rates of pancreatic cancer, given recent research detailing the increased risk of pancreatic cancers in adults who are obese.

3. **Logical-Mathematical:** Students looked at a graph that indicated the closer people live to a landfill, the more likely they are to struggle in school. Students researched the concept of a correlation: Do the toxins from a landfill cause learning difficulties? Are landfills placed in more

impoverished areas, where a series of factors may be influencing learning? (Causation can't be attributed to a relationship, when it is a correlation, not an empirical experiment.)

We could easily have tailored this unit to topics such as mental illness in the community or the TRC. For instance, we could have had students explore the relationship between poverty and depression, Indigenous ancestry and foster-care placement, and so forth. This means that while I am teaching my math, and students are learning about linear algebra, they are also gathering data that further informs them about these important issues.

Teachers who wish to use this sample unit can suggest the following social issues, which may reflect a linear relationship:

- industrialization/emissions with global warming
- human population growth with deforestation, endangered species, and so forth
- socioeconomic status with academic achievement, diabetes, obesity, and so forth
- poverty with infant mortality rates
- rates of gun ownership with mass shootings

Scheduling Programming Across the Year

The following is a sample of a how one teacher designed a program for a year. Teachers can modify the program, based on the depth they wish to go with their students.

Elementary School

Weeks 1–2	Weeks 3–4	Weeks 5–6	Week 7 on
Theme: Self-awareness • RD #1–4, mix in • Brain Unit #1–3 (e.g., when making the community brain, introduce the parts of the brain)	Theme: Self-regulation • Brain Unit #4–6 • DBT mindfulness, emotion regulation, distress tolerance • Class Meeting to establish ethics	Theme: Compassionate learning communities • RD #5–9 • Brain Unit #7 • DBT Interpersonal Effectiveness • Class Meetings • Spirit Buddies	Curricular connections, daily programming (e.g., breathing breaks, mindfulness practices)

Figure 9.5 One Teacher's Implementation Timeline for SEL and Mental Health Programming

Or

Term 1: Sept–Dec	Term 2: Jan–Mar	Term 3: April–June
RD Program	Brain Unit	Supporting people with mental illness
Democratic classrooms and Spirit Buddies		
Strategies for Well-Being		
DBT Modules #1–2	DBT Module #3	DBT Module #4

Figure 9.6 Alternative Implementation Timeline for a Single Class

Or

Grades K–2	Grades 3–5	Grades 6–7
RD Program and Lessons 1–2 of BU	RD review, Lessons 3–6 of BU	RD review, Lesson 7 of BU
Democratic classrooms and Spirit Buddies		
Strategies for Well-Being		
Breathing exercises	DBT: Interpersonal effectiveness, Mindfulness	DBT: Distress tolerance, Emotion regulation, continue Mindfulness
Treaties as cooperation	Treaties as government, power, and human rights Indigenous culture and government	TRC: Treaties as privilege, exploitation, discrimination, Residential Schools Indigenous land claims, modern issues

Figure 9.7 Possible Implementation Framework for an Elementary School

High School

There are a couple of ways to implement these programs in the high-school setting.

- Divide by subject: Science teachers can do the Brain Unit, social studies teachers can do the RD program, health teachers can do DBT. Everyone does Spirit Buddies for five minutes first thing in the morning. Class Meeting occurs once a month or twice per semester in each class. Everyone then connects mental health to their curriculum.

- Workshop style: Do RD in a one-day workshop. Each teacher takes a class of students for the day (e.g., everyone keeps their first period class all day). Do the same thing with the Brain Unit over two days (first day all about the brain, second day about mental health and mental illness). Take a day for each module of DBT, once a month over the semester (total of seven days). Or do the whole thing in a one week schoolwide program during the first week of school, then start the regular schedule.

The Story of Mr. T

While working with a grade twelve English-language-arts teacher, the need to teach students how to write persuasive essays surfaced. Mr. T, as we'll call him, told me he had traditionally taught the five-paragraph essay to students – the one with the introductory paragraph, three paragraphs each with a topic sentence and supporting details, and then a concluding paragraph. Yawn. That's what he, and his students felt, too. So we talked about how we universally design something like essay writing, which so many students find challenging and a barrier to success in school.

I pointed out to Mr. T that, first and foremost, students needed to understand the concept of persuasion. To persuade someone requires an ability to touch an audience in such a way that they are moved to action. Since language arts is about multiple literacies, not just text based, I suggested we first have students explore persuasive communications of a variety of media (e.g., visual, oral, written). We decided that since the Syrian refugee crisis had become an international issue, we would use it as a vehicle for introducing the concept to the students. We began by sharing a series of communications about the Syrian refugee crisis, including info-graphics, editorials, and newscasts, and asked students to raise their hands when they were convinced Canada should get involved. The last piece we showed was the picture of a four-year-old boy, who had drowned, lying on a beach. Everyone's hand went up. We asked students why they had had no reaction to earlier photos, reports, stats, and so forth. We discussed the idea of a powerful, even iconic, communication. We introduced the idea of iconic pieces – things that changed history, beliefs, or perceptions and endured, and discussed whether that photograph was likely to become one that people remembered many years on. We then introduced students to the stations they would be working through. Each station, loosely based on multiple intelligences, contained an iconic piece such as the audio of Martin Luther King's "I Have a Dream" speech, the photograph of a young girl running naked after a napalm attack in the Vietnam war, songs like *Give Peace a Chance* and *Blowing in the Wind,* and the poem *In Flanders Fields.* Students moved through stations analyzing why the pieces were so powerful and the techniques used by the creators. We wanted them to think about what techniques a photographer, artist, lyricist, orator, etc. use to create powerful, persuasive pieces. We talked about colour and imagery, lighting and drama, tone of voice, and pause. For their final projects students were asked to choose an issue that was important to them, and create an "iconic" piece to influence an audience and persuade them of its importance, in any format they chose. Students were given rubrics like these as assessment measures:

Beginning	Approaching	Fully Meeting	Exceeding
Expresses opinions about powerful/not powerful	Explains techniques used to create powerful communications	Analyzes specific pieces, justifies opinions regarding power	Compares and contrasts pieces (e.g., two photos, or a speech and a photo) for power and technique
Communicates ideas, beliefs, values about a specific issue	Applies basic techniques of a genre to revise for power	Insightfully combines genre specific techniques with content to create persuasive communications	Combines genres with content in creative ways to design iconic communication pieces
C– = 50–59%	C+ = 67–72% C = 60–66%	B+ = 80–85% B = 73–79%	A+ = 95–100% A = 86–94%

Figure 9.8 Sample Rows from a Rubric in Grade 12 Language Arts

Beginning	Approaching	Fully Meeting	Exceeding
Recognizes that social injustices affect societies	Describes divergent perspectives regarding a social injustice	Evaluates ways in which the causes of social injustice are complex and have lasting impact on society	Proposes solutions, or provides insight and perspective to highlight the complexity of an issue
Identifies one perspective regarding a social injustice	Describes divergent perspectives regarding a social injustice	Analyzes how social-justice issues are interconnected	Proposes solutions considering multiple needs and perspectives
Identifies one perspective regarding a social injustice	Describes divergent perspectives regarding a past social injustice and its impact today	Explains different perspectives on past and present people, places, issues and events, evaluates critical moments/events	Proposes solutions, or provides insight and perspective to highlight the complexity of an issue and its historical evolution
Recognizes that societies change and grow	Describes one group/society's history noting changes and constants	Compares and contrasts continuities and changes for different groups and individuals in different times and places	Draws inferences regarding the interactions between the continuities and changes for different groups and individuals in different times and places
C– = 50–59%	C+ = 67–72% C = 60–66%	B+ = 80–85% B = 73–79%	A+ = 95–100% A = 86–94%

Figure 9.9 Sample Rows from the Connected Social Studies Unit

One young woman from the Middle East asked if she could paint. She began by sketching.

Figure 9.10 Charcoal Sketches

Then she drew it out on a canvas, and slowly filled it in.

Figure 9.11 The Painting in Progress

Her final product looked like this:

Figure 9.12 The Final Product

She explained that it was about the Palestinian-Israeli conflict. On the left were the grieving mothers of children who had died. On the right, biblical imagery to show that it is an ancient conflict. In the centre, the revelation that they are actually brothers, born of the same mother. This student could not have been successful had we just started with essays. However, she was certainly able to understand the concept of persuasion. More importantly, she engaged with passion and power, innovated and created, and built relationships with her new classmates borne of respect. If we really needed to teach her to write an essay, we could now do so. Telling her that paragraph one is about the left side, paragraph two is about the right side, and her conclusion is the idea of the brothers makes turning this into an essay understandable, and connected to what this student cares about.

Later, in a conversation with Mr. T, he commented that I had "saved his career." I was stunned – he seemed a very gifted young teacher who I would have wanted my own children to encounter. He told me that teaching had "just not turned out to be what he thought it was going to be." It was "missing something, and he couldn't figure out what it was until he came to a workshop and learned about RD, Spirit Buddies, and Class Meetings." Then he realized that was it – the social and emotional aspect of teaching, and reaching, his students was missing. He wanted to connect with and engage his students, not just prepare them for the test.

Creating classrooms and schools that are filled with passion and joy, innovation and creation, is possible, even in our current system. It benefits students and teachers alike, and can only benefit the communities they live in and serve.

Chapter 10
School Culture and Staff Well-Being

Mr. T (see page 190) should never have considered leaving the profession. He is exactly the kind of teacher we need in our system – a high-school teacher who prioritizes his relationship with his students. Teaching the curricula wasn't enough for him; he wanted to teach kids. At the same time, he loved literature and literacy and wanted to share that passion with his students. He was willing to experiment and try new things, let go of how he had done things in the past, and delight in the passion and innovation of his students.

Creating school cultures where teachers like Mr. T feel safe to make these changes, and are valued rather than ridiculed by their peers for implementing them, takes the same investment in well-being that it does for teachers to support their students. You may want to review chapter 4 to remind yourself of the goals and research behind what follows.

Building Staff Culture

Leaders in schools have to consider the same things teachers do in their classrooms – how to develop a positive climate, ensure all members of the community develop a sense of self-worth and belonging, and have opportunities to learn and grow. Teachers balance maintaining a positive relationship with students and knowing when to push them every day. So, too, must educational leaders.

Several key processes are involved in achieving this balance:

- identifying strengths within the staff
- setting vision
- building and supporting collaborative practice and teacher leadership
- supporting teacher professional learning

Team Building: The RD Program for Staff

The RD program can be used as a team-building activity with staff, with some changes. Although teachers may not need to brainstorm what *smart* means (see page 86), a discussion with a prompt like: "It takes as much intelligence to … (e.g., compose a master symphony, survive in the jungle) as it does to write a newspaper article – agree or disagree") can open the conversation about what is valued in schools and in Western culture. Staff can then explore their profiles in the intelligences, and discuss how their profile affects their teaching. The community brain can be developed based on intelligences, or curricular areas of strength, and/or areas of strength related to mental health.

For instance, teachers could place a flag with their name on it stating an intelligence that is their strength. Other teachers can then go to them when seeking ideas or support (e.g., I need a bodily-kinesthetic activity related to ecosystems). Alternatively, teachers could identify a curricular strength they have (e.g., math), and become advisors to others in these areas. The point of this exercise is to create safety – we all have strengths, we all find some parts of what we do challenging, and we can trust and rely on each other for support.

For the lessons about careers, I have often given school staff pictures of famous people (e.g., the Dalai Lama, Salvador Dali, Beethoven, Oprah), or cue cards with occupations listed on them, to prompt a discussion about what is required for success and eminence. The purpose is to create some cognitive dissonance around our beliefs that students can only be successful if they are verbal-linguistic, can sit still, and are "respectful and responsible" – in the traditional definitions of these terms. However, many eminent people likely don't sit still for significant periods of time, don't choose to read novels in their leisure time, and don't spend hours writing stories.

When teachers with heterogeneous strengths are placed into planning teams and challenged to plan a unit or activity that will engage all of their learners, they quickly realize how much more effective it is to work across departments and grades. For instance, I have given teachers case studies about an early-years class that included a highly gifted student, or a senior-years class that had a student with a significant cognitive disability. The expertise of a high-school teacher came in handy when considering enrichment for the gifted student, and an early-years teacher can often help senior-years teachers think about less complex forms of the content they are teaching. When planning a cross-curricular unit, the diversity of voices becomes a benefit.

As well, when the effort to develop programming for mental health, the Truth and Reconciliation Commission (TRC), and Universal Design for Learning (UDL) become a focus, the conversation shifted to staff strengths about these topics, such as having knowledge of Indigenous cultures and worldviews; possessing skills related to mindfulness, meditation, yoga; knowing how to build relationships; and so forth.

Setting the Vision: School Plans for Well-Being

Teachers need to know the *why* of change. Too often in our schools new mandates come down with little explanation, and even less training. Teachers are just supposed to figure it out and do it. No one hands a gamma knife to a neurosurgeon and says, "Just use it." First, a connection has to be made between the needs of the surgeon and her patients, and the new technique. Then, training needs to be provided in how to use the knife. Similarly, we first have to help teachers see the connection between the programming we are suggesting and the needs of the teachers and their students. There are many ways, but I have found the following way effective with teachers:

1. Goals for our students

   a. Give 10 sticky notes to each small group of teachers. In their groups, have the teachers write 10 words (one per sticky note) that reflect what they consider the most important qualities for students to leave their class/school with. For instance, we want students to be respectful, critical thinkers, good citizens.

   b. Ask the teachers to sort the notes into two groups: those that are SEL/mental-health outcomes and those that are cognitive/academic outcomes. Some words may apply to both, but ask teachers to make a decision about where these words best belong.

   c. Have teachers note the ratio: how many goals are SEL/mental health versus cognitive/academic? I have done this exercise with teachers, parents, and students internationally, and the results are the same. There are always more SEL/mental-health goals.

   d. Have teachers discuss these questions: Do our practices match our dreams? Are we devoting time to the things we say are most important? How often are we getting caught up on the little things/small stuff?

   e. Sort the group's sticky notes according to a framework (e.g., TBM, see below; well-being clouds).

STUDENT PROFILE

BLOCK ONE Social & Emotional Learning		BLOCK TWO Inclusive Instructional Practice		BLOCK THREE Systems & Structures (What we do to support students)	
SELF-WORTH	BELONGING	COGNITIVE CHALLENGE	INTERACTIVE LEARNING	SUPPORTING BLOCK ONE	SUPPORTING BLOCK TWO
Confident	Collaborative	Critical Thinker	Works with diverse others	RD Program	UBD
Self-aware	Leader	Perseveres	Contributes	Spirit Buddies	DI
Resilient	Active in school life	Takes Initiative	Leadership	DI	Explicit teaching
Risk taker	Respectful	Passionate	Flexible	Restitution	Flexible groupings
Initiative	Generous	Engaged	Powerful communicator		
Know their strengths	Empathetic	Strives			

Figure 10.1 One school staff's brainstorm of "what's important" for students to develop/become.

2. Ask staff to do the same for themselves. What do they most want for themselves in their professional life? Who do they want to be as a teacher?

STAFF PROFILE

BLOCK ONE Social & Emotional Learning		BLOCK TWO Inclusive Instructional Practice		BLOCK THREE Systems & Structures (What we do to support staff)	
SELF-WORTH	BELONGING	COGNITIVE CHALLENGE	INTERACTIVE LEARNING	SUPPORTING BLOCK ONE	SUPPORTING BLOCK TWO
Confident	Collaborative	Critical Thinker	Works with diverse others	Snack days	Many taking courses
Self-aware	Leader	Life long learner	Contributes	In house PD	Co-plan
Resilient	Active in school life	Takes Initiative	Leadership		
Risk taker	Respectful	Passionate	Flexible		
Initiative	Generous	Engaged	Team Player		
Know their strengths	Empathetic	Creative	Engages with colleagues in prof. dialogue		

Figure 10.2 One school staff's brainstorm of who/how they want to be at work.

3. Hold a group discussion: What are the barriers we face to achieving these goals?

SYSTEMIC	COMMUNAL	STUDENT	PROFESSIONAL
Exams	Poverty	Challenging behaviour	Text-based instruction
Grades	Lack of parent involvement	Diverse range	Isolated
Lack of resources	Arriving on time/ attendance	Can't work together	Stress/ overwhelm
Service delivery – too much in and out	Food security (kids haven't had breakfast)	Passive – just want the right answer	Disrespected/ undervalued

Figure 10.3 Barriers to Achieving the Goals for Students

4. From a strengths-based perspective, have teachers focus on what they are doing well in fulfilling these goals and how they are finding their way around some of the barriers. Rather than focus on the negatives, have teachers set goals for their students and for themselves as professionals, using the wealth of knowledge and skill found in both their professional and neighbourhood communities.

5. Create assessment measures: How will teachers know if they are achieving the goals they have set for their students and their colleagues? I have had teachers indicate:

   - If students were achieving these goals, they:
     ○ can describe themselves as learners
     ○ take initiative, persevere through challenges
     ○ participate in school activities, have voice in democratic classrooms
     ○ can problem solve in pro-social, win-win ways
     ○ engage in service learning
     ○ work collaboratively in heterogeneous groups
     ○ demonstrate passion and engagement in their learning
     ○ take turns assuming leadership, depending on the nature of the activity (i.e., recognize their own and others' strengths)
     ○ seek challenge, inquire, engage in critical dialogue
     ○ understand what it means to analyze, synthesize, make connections, infer, and envision
     ○ self-direct their learning

   - If staff are achieving these goals, they:
     ○ know their strengths, are recognized for them
     ○ feel cared for, support each other
     ○ seek learning from/with each other
     ○ have the "big picture" of the school community, collaborate to solve problems
     ○ feel safe to take risks, try new things
     ○ are inspired, focused, and engaged – remember what matters
     ○ have opportunities for voice and leadership

6. Ask staff to prioritize. Where do they want to start? Put it together into a plan: What are the goals? What are you already doing? What further resources could you tap? How will you know if you have achieved the goal?

GOAL #1:
All students know themselves as learners, take pride in their contributions to the learning community

What we are doing well:
1. Use RD program to intro learning profiles/MI
2. Recognize different ways of learning

Resources we could tap:
1. Community members who have jobs utilizing different strengths
2. Aboriginal Elders

Things to consider adding:
1. Point out (regularly) students varied strengths
2. Notes home – what students are doing well

Assessment:
1. Student self-evaluations of their learning are positive
2. Students offer help to classmates readily (have confidence)

GOAL #2:
Students work collaboratively in groups, can problem solve pro-socially

What we are doing well:
1. Starting to take time to teach group work skills
2. Use restitution as a problem solving method

Resources we could tap:
1. Guidance counselors, social workers to come into classes
2. Parents who work in jobs that involve teaming
3. Sports coaches for team building

Things to consider adding:
1. Class meetings
2. Mind-up

Assessment:
1. Students can work together in class meetings to build consensus and community

GOAL #3:
Students engage in critical dialogue, understand what it means to analyze, synthesize, make connections, infer, question, and envision

What we are doing well:
1. Upper grades using literature circles
2. Increasing dialogue opportunities
3. Explicitly teaching analysis and connections
4. UBD

Resources we could tap:
1. Elders to work on visioning
2. Jen & Faye Brownlie to help out

Things to consider adding:
1. Double entry journals grade 2 & up
2. Visualizing activities with ELA, Math, & Fine Arts

Assessment:
1. Students are able to respond to prompts related to critical thinking such as
   a. What is the big idea here?
   b. What do you wonder about?
   c. What does this remind you of?
   d. Why do you think this is happening?
2. Students can create images from a description, describe an object from multiple perspectives, work with geometrical shapes, patterns, and processes

Figure 10.4 School Plan for Students

GOAL #1:
Staff have opportunities to connect, share, personally and professionally.

What We Are Doing Well:	Resources We Could Tap:	Things to consider adding:	Assessment:
1. Staff meetings have PD component	1. Coaches – team building 2. PLC grants 3. Use PD to visit each other's classrooms, view strengths!	1. Class meeting style staff meetings – what's going well, issues 2. Mini-RD program for staff (our strengths, how we can work together)	1. Staff climate survey? 2. Co-planning/teaching increases

GOAL #2:
Staff see big picture of school as community, problem solve together

What we are doing well:	Resources we could tap:	Things to consider adding:	Assessment:
1. Informal dialogue, problem solving (seek help from each other) 2. Willingness to help, share resources	1. School profile – committee to set priorities 2. RT, Counsellor to give briefs at staff meetings	1. As above re: class meetings 2. Subcommittee with GC, RT, VP & Two CT's	1. Co-planning of school resource use 2. All staff clearly know goals, agreed upon processes

GOAL #3:
Staff engage in professional dialogue, set PD goals and work together to implement new initiatives

What we are doing well:	Resources we could tap:	Things to consider adding:	Assessment:
1. Working on literacy initiative 2. Share ideas	1. Jen & Faye to facilitate visioning 2. School based PLC	1. Mapping areas of strength to develop, areas of concern to address 2. Use TBM as framework, start with Block 1	1. PLC is well attended 2. Staff visiting each other, co-planning/teaching 3. Shared focus and dialogue – creative and engaged

Figure 10.5 School Plan for Staff

7. Have teachers create identity statements, as a school and as individuals.
   - We are a school that:
     - values the community we serve
     - is invested in the mental health of our students
     - cares about each other
     - learns and grow together
     - challenges our students intellectually, through a learning community that values critical dialogue
   - I am a teacher who:
     - is passionate about literacy and social justice
     - cares deeply about the well-being of myself, my students, and my colleagues
     - believes that learning is fun and communal

8. At each staff meeting, revisit these IEPs or school plans and identity statements. If teachers begin to lose sight of what matters, talk about it. Talk about the need to be mindful and refocus on what does matter. Just as we want to prompt students to remember their goals and strategies, teachers can help remind each other, as well.

Another activity I do with teachers is have them write a "professional eulogy." What would they want people to say about them at their retirement? What would their students and colleagues say? What would their legacy be?

Most eulogies include a somewhat predictable format:

- where a person was born, their early years
- significant moments in their life
- their gifts and passions, and the difference they made to those around them
- the legacy they left behind.

Having teachers reflect on their professional journey (even if they're beginners), and what legacy they want to leave behind focuses us again on what matters. Teaching teachers to ask themselves whether this is how they want to be remembered can be a reminder when we lose sight of our own personal values in the midst of a chaotic day or time. It is a powerful exercise!

Building and Supporting Collaborative Practice and Teacher Leadership

Professional learning communities require effort to truly be inclusive and support a positive school culture. The history of teaching has not been one of collaboration. One-room schoolhouses did not provide opportunities to work with anyone else, nor did traditional industrialized education. You worked your part of the assembly line. Leaving it was a disruption to efficiency.

In modern times, we find ourselves at a crisis of human health in our schools. When close to half our teachers leave the profession, something is wrong.

Teachers are human beings, with partners and families, hearts and souls. It's not okay to make them sacrificial lambs. Teachers like Mr. T can be a gift to our society, or we can leave them by the wayside. We must change the ways in which we work together and support each other. The divide between leadership and staff, between teachers and teaching assistants, between teachers and other teachers harms everyone, including the students. Children know when conflict fills the air.

Spirit Buddies for Staff

Adults are no different than kids – we don't like feeling invisible, unappreciated, uncared for. In our schools, there are staff members in a variety of roles who feel isolated and neglected, whose gifts are not appreciated, and who lack friendships with their colleagues.

Schools I have been working with have begun to use Spirit Buddies with staff to create connection and belonging. For instance:

- School A does Spirit Buddies every Monday morning. Coffee and muffins are provided, and teachers meet in their groups to check in, share, and prepare for the week.

- School B was concerned that there was a lack of interaction across departments. It was a large high school, and teachers tended to only connect with people who taught the same subjects as them. So like School A, they started doing Spirit Buddies on Mondays – but they made the groups cross-departmental.

- School C noted that there seemed to be separation across roles. Lunchtime in the staffroom consisted of the educational assistants' table, the teachers' table, and so forth. They started doing Spirit Buddies on Mondays – but they made the groups mixed across staff roles.

Democracy, Distributed Leadership, and Staff Meetings as Class Meetings

Democratic classrooms share leadership opportunities and power across the members of the learning community to the greatest extent possible. The teacher remains as a "government," setting boundaries and ensuring safety during the problem-solving process. Similar processes can be used with staff to distribute leadership and empower teacher leaders.

Distributed leadership encourages multiple sources of influence within any organization, including schools. In schools, the willingness of school leaders to give teachers and staff a voice in the running of the school is critical to the success of any reform. If the teacher is unwilling to share power, student voice and autonomy cannot develop. Similarly, research shows that without the active and full support of those in formal leadership positions in schools, distributed leadership related to teachers is unlikely to flourish or be sustained. Leadership in schools involves two processes: performing tasks such as hiring, budgeting, scheduling and so forth; and influencing others in ways that change how they think and act. Teachers can be involved in both aspects of leadership. When it comes to establishing a spiritual climate, it is critical that leaders support teachers who can influence their colleagues to get on board.

Teachers can use the Class Meeting as a tool for empowering students, and school leaders can use the same structure to run staff meetings, thereby empowering staff. Imagine having staff sit in a circle, going around the circle first to take notice of the good things that have happened since the last meeting – expressing gratitude for each other and the experiences – and then raising concerns and problem solving as a team. In this structure, you are unlikely to have staff members at the back of the room answering their email!

Scheduling and Service-Delivery Models

There are structural realities to creating collaborative teams. We have to make the time to collaborate! In the elementary-school setting this is easier to achieve. The value of collaboration and push-in services has to be communicated to teachers, but the system itself is not a barrier to this. However, in the high-school setting this is not the case. I've always wondered how high schools became such a segregated setting. They are sandwiched by much more inclusive structures. Elementary schools and universities group students into cohorts. My father just celebrated the 60th anniversary of his medical-school class. The bond he and his colleagues shared going through med school together has remained over decades. I was in a cohort for both my bachelors and masters degrees in Education. As with my father, I still have friends today from those times. Yet, in high school, students are scheduled as individuals. They are one of hundreds, sometimes thousands, of students. They do not have the same classmates in each class throughout the day. As a result, teachers don't teach the same students as their colleagues do. So how do you collaborate?

- Ensure teachers, educational assistants, and clinicians understand the reasons for collaboration and the goals, and develop the skills to do so.
  - Student outcomes when co-teaching is present are significantly better.
  - Teachers' well-being is improved in collaborative environments.
  - Pull-out supports result in negative identities, stigma, and social isolation for students. Even young children who initially like it, later refer back and say: "I'm not smart. I went to resource."
  - Students don't generalize skills well from one environment to another, especially those with special needs. Teaching a student a skill in the little room down the hall is unlikely to result in transfer of the skill to the general-education classroom.
  - When we remove students, as noted earlier, we do not develop the capacity in their friends and community to support them. We also miss students in the class who may not be struggling in the moment, or we may not be aware are struggling in that moment, but will at a later time, and would benefit from learning the skills proactively and the expertise of a clinician.

- Arrange students into cohorts. There are several ways, and degrees, of doing this:
  - In some of the high schools I am working with, students are placed in cohorts for their core subjects (language arts, math, science, and social studies). They then diffuse for their electives. This allows teams of teachers to be created who all work with the same students. Add in a few EAs, resource teacher(s), and counsellors, and you have the ability to collaborate. Not only can instruction become more differentiated and engaging, teachers then have the ability to talk about students who are languishing and how to support them, and can support each other, as well.
  - In one high school I worked, in we arranged students in cohorts according to electives. For instance, all the students taking health and beauty as a vocational training then took their core courses together. Again, this allowed teacher teams to be formed. This provided rich opportunities for collaboration and co-teaching. The physics teacher and the power-mechanics teacher teamed up to do a unit on flight and the combustion engine. Students learned the mathematics and principles of flight in physics, and then in power mechanics, built an airplane that would fly.
- Create common planning time. Again, this can be done in a variety of ways:
  - Early dismissals: Some schools add extra time to each day, and then dismiss early one day a week so teachers have the time to meet and plan.
  - Schedule common prep periods for teacher teams so they can work together.
  - Arrange coverage for teacher teams in a host of creative ways. One school I worked with had two teachers, an Elder from the local Indigenous community, and a couple of parents take students on a land-based education project to the local marsh. Three other teachers stayed behind and had time to plan.

Assign EAs to classrooms, just as we do teachers. When we assign EAs to individual students the outcomes can be *very* negative, academically and socially. If health and safety make this necessary, then so be it (e.g., a student with a condition that requires suctioning). The vast majority of students do not need a dedicated educational assistant. It can create stigma and interfere with their opportunity to interact with their peers. It also sends the message to the EA that their job is that child, rather than as part of a team in which every adult is working with all of the students. Mom and Dad bring different things to the table in raising their children. Sometimes one of the kids needs some extra time from one of them. But all the children will sometimes need help from both. The isolation that educational assistants experience, and the resulting desire to connect with other EAs, often results in students being pulled out to a room to where several EAs and "their students" work, giving the adults feel some support and connection. It's understandable, but harmful. Educational assistants need to be part of the classroom team, and connected to the teacher and resource teacher, who are also part of the team.

Supporting Teacher Professional Learning

Like our students, teachers learn at different rates, are ready for different knowledge and skills at different times, and learn best in different ways. Leaders, therefore, need to consider:

- the need to give everyone a vision of where we are trying to go
- an acceptance that not everyone will start at the same time or place, proceed at the same rate, or need the same supports along the way

Leaders need to recognize who the true leaders are among their staff and support them as they begin the change process. As with the change curve we discussed in chapter 4, it is a mistake to focus on the teachers who are not yet ready or willing to change in the beginning. Start with the early adopters and early majority. Provide all the supports and resources they need to be successful in piloting new programming. When other teachers see the results and hear about what is happening, they will slowly come on board. It also means leaders will have to consider how to differentiate the professional learning. Research tells us there are a few common structures that work best, and some that do not (Desimone 2009).

- One- or two-day workshops don't work. Teachers require at least 30 hours of training in any new innovation, spread over the year. If you have the budget to release teachers for 50 days, you are better off releasing 10 teachers for five days (30 hours), than 25 teachers for two days. The latter will not result in sustainable change; the former will.
- Teachers learn in different ways. Some need to "see it," and some need to "do it." To support this, cover classes so teachers can visit each other. Spend the money to bring in a knowledgeable facilitator to work with the first group of teachers. Have the facilitator co-teach with your teachers, demo teach, and debrief. Later, they will become your coaches and you won't need to spend anymore. However, the first group of teachers will need intensive support, as they are first ones to try the new practice. With no one else to support them, they have no one to turn to.
- Identify your teacher leaders. Sometimes these are your early adopters, and sometimes not. If you can convince one leader that this change is important and will help to support teacher well-being, as well as students, they will become your most powerful advocate. When teachers see "Gail is doing it," the majority come on board. You must not only support them to increase their knowledge; you also have to help them develop as leaders.

> Teacher leaders don't only need knowledge of the innovation. They also need training in peer coaching and consulting.

- Find ways to give these leaders the chance to influence change. Let them lead a PLC. Buy the books and support a book club. Release them from one block of teaching, or one afternoon a week, and let them co-plan and co-teach with others.

Finally, Make It Fun!

Teachers need to create classrooms where students want to be, engage, and learn. School leaders need to do the same. Check in with your staff: How are they doing? What do they need? When a teacher is going through a difficult time, put extra supports in. Let them know you have their back. Get staff together socially, not just at winter holidays. Go on retreats, extend lunch hour one day and bring in a surprise buffet. Create a team and join a pick-up league in a sport. Offer wellness activities before school, at lunch, or after school (e.g., bring in a yoga teacher, or an artist, or anyone who inspires, builds collegiality, and leaves teachers feeling renewed.)

Conclusion
A Story of Hope

As we have invited teachers to think about wellness in inclusive classrooms, and the importance of reconciliation for all Canadian students, I am reminded of the optimism I feel every time I speak to a school community – be it the students, staff, or families. As we have already acknowledged, we as Canadians have inherited the wreckage of broken relationships between Indigenous peoples and the state. Canadian children today are growing up in a country where there still is not equity or genuine fairness for all Canadians, where there remains a desperate need for reconciliation. The signs are all around them: poverty, marginalized communities, crime, and racism. Experience has taught me that many Canadians are desperate for solutions, and to find a way to contribute to these solutions. This is especially true with young people. Every time I speak to a school community, the willingness I find to embrace and work toward reconciliation is uplifting. It fills me with a hope that sustains me when the work ahead may otherwise seem insurmountable.

Certainly, there remains much work to do. Canada is a nation that continues to wrestle with a difficult history and its impact on its citizens and children. There are many who grew up hearing only one story about First Peoples. There are those who still don't understand the need for reconciliation, or who believe that Indigenous peoples are unfairly advantaged in Canada. Racism continues to persist. Schools are going to have a central role to play in undoing much of this misunderstanding. Where schools in Canada were once used as weapons against Indigenous peoples, the inclusive schools of reconciliation will be places of healing, empowerment, and hope. Children today are growing up a in nation where more than ever we have the opportunity to hear each other's stories and recognized the commonalities of our shared humanity. It is in these relationships where reconciliation flourishes.

Years ago, I was told a story about my own Anishinabe ancestors. A story about my Kookum's and Mishomis' (Grandmother and Grandfather's) peoples, set long ago in the Anishinabe communities of Manitoba prior to contact with Europeans. It is a story about a drum.

I am told that in those days, in the old days before the *zhaganashi* (English speakers) came, there would often be a ceremony when the people would gather together to see off the hunters who would leave the community in hopes of bringing back enough game to keep their families thriving. Of course, Manitoba is a beautiful province. It is a beautiful expanse of prairie land and Canadian

Shield rich with thousands of lakes and stunning vistas. As beautiful as it is, it is also a place that can be very harsh on its people. Anyone who has lived through a Manitoba winter understands only too well how treacherous the shortest outing can be in the middle of January. I am told that as the people of the communities watched their hunters head out into the Manitoba wilderness, it was the responsibility of someone in that community, an Elder or a Knowledge Keeper, to sound a drum and keep a rhythm until the hunters returned.

As the story goes, it was believed that if the drummer sounded the drum in the right way, in a good way, and if the hunters listened in a good way, they would hear the drum no matter where they were. In this way, they would always know what direction home was.

I suppose that there are many ways to receive a story such as that. In today's modern world, it might be easy to reject the notion that a hunter could hear the sound of a handheld drum while kilometres away from home. To a Western scientific mind, the idea of such a small drum being audible above the howl of winds or the roar of rushing waters is absurd. Others may hear a story such as this and take a more generous position. They may accept that others might believe in such a notion even if they themselves don't share the same conviction. Such people allow for another's belief system as being part of a diverse world filled with diverse people, all of whom are entitled to their own stories. Still others may collect such a story, study it, and categorize it according to anthropological principles and cherish it as an artifact of the past. For our purpose, I will suggest another possible way of understanding such a story – one much more in line with the goals of reconciliation as I understand them.

Sometime after I first heard this story of the drum, I was driving on a highway back toward Winnipeg from a wedding I had attended in Ontario. I received a phone call from my mother regarding my cousin's husband. Like many Canadian families, ours has seen some of its own travel overseas to serve in Afghanistan. Corporal Christopher Klodt was an accomplished and seasoned soldier by the time I received that phone call about him from my Ma. As I watched the highway disappear behind me on the dark stretch of road, she explained to me that Christopher had been on patrol near Kandahar when a firefight broke out between our Canadian forces and the Taliban. As the fighting began, the Canadian soldiers crouched down behind the stone walls of an orchard and began to return fire. I am told that in situations where our forces cannot see the enemy they are trained to watch for the muzzle flashes of enemy fire as an approximation of their position. Christopher raised his head to do just that, when, for him, suddenly everything went black.

My family in Winnipeg received the call while he was in transit, being airlifted from Afghanistan to Germany, which is Canada's closest ally in that region with hospitals capable of responding to such injuries. A bullet had passed through his neck, and his life was in peril. When I finally pulled off that highway, which in those hours of not knowing whether or not Christopher would survive seemed to stretch on forever, I attended my grandmother's church, where the family had gathered. The church's priest had opened the space for us to be together. As a family, we prayed and lit candles in hopes that my cousin's husband, the father of her unborn child, would survive and return home one day.

Looking back on those memories, I can't say whether or not any of us really believed that the act of lighting candles would bring Christopher back home safely. But I don't think that was the point. I think that the point of us gathering and performing that ritual was about hope. It was about bringing a family together and offering comfort through ceremony in moments when everyone felt helpless and afraid. I believe all of us can relate to needing hope sometimes. It is a universal human experience.

When I think about the stories of Anishinabe communities that would gather to hear the sounding of the drum, I believe another way to interpret that story is that the sounding of the drum was all about hope. Manitoba can be a treacherous and dangerous place. I imagine that watching loved ones head out into that unforgiving landscape must have been terrifying. The sound of the drum, that beautiful rhythm kept by a trusted leader who kept vigil while singing and praying, probably offered hope to people who felt helpless and afraid.

Such is the task before us. As educators we have the opportunity to help young Canadians find the commonalities in our shared humanity. We have the opportunity to accomplish what the Truth and Reconciliation Commission's Calls to Action refer to as education for "intercultural understanding, empathy and mutual respect." We have the opportunity to contribute to reconciliation in inclusive classrooms where *all* students see themselves as transformative, of having the tools and compassion they need to help our nation heal and reclaim its identity as a Treaty nation.

Kevin Lamoureux

Appendices

Resource List

Programs/Resource Kits

- Mindfulness
  - Mind-Up
- DBT
  - DBT Skills in Schools
- TRC
  - http://www.fnesc.ca/irsr/
  - http://reconciliationcanada.ca/wp-content/uploads/2014/09/ReconciliationCanada_Dialogue_workshop-guide.pdf
  - https://fncaringsociety.com/shannens-dream-school-resources

Books Mental Health (elementary)

- Anxiety
  - *When I Feel Afraid* – Cheri J. Meiners
  - *David & the Worry Beast* – Anne Marie Guanci
  - *Wilma Jean the Worry Machine* – Julia Cook
  - *The Anti-Test Anxiety Society* – Julia Cook
  - *Sea Otter Cove* – Anne Marie Guanci
  - *I Have Squirrels in My Belly* – Trish Hammond
  - *Panicosaurus* – Kay Al-Hani
  - *Wemberly Worried* – Kevin Henkes
  - *Moving Gives Me a Stomachache* – Heather McKend
- Emotions, Feelings, and Mood (Regulation)
  - *Be Positive* – Cheri J. Meiners
  - *Cool Down and Work Through Anger* – Cheri J. Meiners
  - *Soda Pophead* – Julia Cook
  - *Grief Is Like a Snowflake* – Julia Cook
  - *Blueloon* – Julia Cook
  - *Whimsy's Heavy Things* – Julie Kraulis
  - *When Sophie Gets Angry – Really, Really Angry* – Molly Bang
  - *Yesterday I Had the Blues* – Jeron Frame
- Resiliency
  - *Bounce Back* – Cheri J. Meiners
  - *Be Honest and Tell the Truth* – Cheri J. Meiners
  - *Bubble Gum Brain* – Julia Cook
  - *Don't Be Afraid to Drop* – Julia Cook
  - *The Ant Hill Disaster* – Julia Cook

- *Mama Had a Dancing Heart* – Libba Moore Grey
  - *Voices of the Heart* – Ed Young
  - *Thank You, Mr. Falker* – Patricia Polacco
  - *Bully* – Patricia Polacco
  - *Mieko and the Fifth Treasure* – Eleanor Coerr
- SEL Skills and Attitudes
  - *Feel Confident* – Cheri J. Meiners
  - *Have Courage* – Cheri J. Meiners
  - *Join In and Make a Friend* – Cheri J. Meiners
  - *Talk and Work It Out* – Cheri J. Meiners
  - *Making Friends Is an Art* – Julia Cook
  - *Bully Beans* – Julia Cook
  - *Baditude* – Julia Cook
  - *I Can't Believe You Said That* – Julia Cook
  - *Cliques Just Don't Make Sense* – Julia Cook
  - *The Want Monsters* – Chelo Manchego
  - *Each Kindness* – Jacqueline Woodson
  - *My Many Colored Days* – Dr. Seuss
  - *The Sneetches* – Dr. Seuss
  - *The Hundred Dresses* (bullying) – Eleanor Estes
- Spirituality and Mindfulness
  - *Forgive and Let Go* – Cheri J. Meiners
  - *Reach Out and Give* – Cheri J. Meiners
  - *Stand Tall* – Cheri J. Meiners
  - *The Judgmental Flower* – Julia Cook
  - *Lolli and the Magical Kitchen* – Elena Paige
  - *Relax Kids: The Wishing Star* – Marneta Viegas
  - *Frog's Breathtaking Speech* – Michael Chissick
- ADHD
  - *My Mouth Is a Volcano* – Julia Cook
  - *Shelley, the Hyperactive Turtle* – Deborah Moss
  - *It's Hard to Be a Verb* – Julia Cook
  - *Decibella* – Julia Cook
  - *Cory Stories* – Jeanne Kraus
  - *Baxter Turns Down His Buzz* – James Foley
  - *Joey Pigza series* – Jack Gantos
  - *Some Kids Just Can't Sit Still* – Sam Goldstein
- Bipolar Disorder
  - *Eli the Bipolar Bear* – Sharon Bracken

- Eating Disorders
  - *How to Be Comfortable in Your Own Feathers* – Julia Cook
- Sexual Abuse
  - *The Kid Trapper* – Julia Cook
- Brain
  - *Your Fantastic, Elastic Brain* – Joann Deak and Sarah Ackerly
  - *My Little Brain* – Baby Professor
  - *Think Tank* – Baby IQ Builder books
  - *A Walk in the Rain with a Brain* – Edward Hallowell
- Living with Parents with Mental Illness
  - *Sometimes My Mommy Gets Angry* – Bebe Campbell
  - *Can I Catch It Like a Cold?* – CAMH
  - *Why Is Mommy Sad?* – Paul Chan

Books Mental Health (Young Adult)

- Stigma and Discrimination
  - *Carry the Ocean, Shelter the Sea* (sexual orientation, disability) – Heidi Cullinan
  - *M in the Middle* (anxiety, autism) – Vicky Martin
  - *Fans of the Impossible Life* (depression) – Kate Scelsa
  - *Out of My Mind* – Sharon Draper
- Autism/Asperger's
  - *Eleanor Oliphant is Completely Fine* – Gail Honeyman
  - *The Curious Incident of A Dog In The Nighttime* – Mark Haddon
  - *House Rules* – Jodi Picoult
- Anxiety
  - *Kalix the Werewolf* – Martin Millar
  - *I'm With Stupid* – Geoff Herbach
  - *Dr. Bird's Advice for Sad Poets* – Evan Roskos
  - *Fangirl* – Rainbow Rowell
  - *Finding Audrey* – Sophie Kinsella
  - *Highly Illogical Behavior* (Agorophobia) – John Corey Whaley
- Anger/Rage/Violence
  - *Reality Boy* – A.S. King
  - *Hate List* – Jennifer Brown
  - *Nineteen Minutes* – Jodi Picoult

- Addiction
  - *Clean* – Amy Reed
  - *Cracked Up To Be* – Courtney Summers
  - *Smack* – Melvin Burgess
  - *Finding Home* – Lauren McKellar
- Depression/Suicide
  - *By the Time You Read This, I'll Be Dead* – Julie Ann Peters
  - *I Was Here* – Gayle Forman
  - *All the Bright Places* – Jennifer Niven
  - *The Sea of Tranquility* – Katja Millay
  - *The Memory of Light* – Francisco Stork
  - *Court of Mist and Fury* – Sarah Maas
  - *The Astonishing Adventures of Fanboy and Goth Girl* – Barry Lyga
  - *It's Kind of a Funny Story* – Ned Vizzini
  - *Impulse* – Ellen Hopkins
  - *Looking for Alaska* – John Green
- PTSD
  - *Girl Against the Universe* – Paula Stokes
  - *These Gentle Wounds* – Helen Dunbar
  - *Something Like Normal* – Trish Doller
  - *Use Somebody* – Riley Jean
- Psychosis/Schizophrenia
  - *Mosquitoland* – David Arnold
  - *Schizo* – Nic Sheff
  - *A World Without You* – Beth Revis
  - *Made You Up* – Francesca Zappia
  - *Freaks Like Us* – Susan Vaught
  - *Everything Here is Beautiful* – Mira Lee
  - *The Day the Voices Stopped* – Ken Steele
- Eating Disorders
  - *Wintergirl* – Laurie Halse Anderson
  - *The Downside of Being Charlie* – Jenny Torres Sanchez
  - *Paperweight* – Meg Haston
- Family/Friends with Mental Illness
  - *Things I'm Seeing Without You* – Peter Boganni
  - *Saving Francesca* – Melina Marchetta
  - *The Impossible Knife of Memory* – Laurie Halse Anderson
  - *I, Girl X* – Annalise Grey
- OCD
  - *The Rest of Us Just Live Here* – Patrick Ness

Portage & Main Press, 2018, *Ensouling Our Schools*, ISBN: 978-1-55379-683-1

- *Every Last Word* – Tamara Ireland Stone
- *The Unlikely Hero of Room 13B* – Teresa Toten
- *OCD Love Story* – Corey Ann Haydu
- Bipolar Disorder
  - *Crazy* – Amy Reed
  - *A Tragic Kind of Wonderful* – Kelly Jensen
  - *Marbles: Mania, Depression, Michelangelo and Me* – Ellen Forney
- Borderline Personality Disorder
  - *Girl Interrupted* – Susanna Kaysen
- Abuse
  - *I Hadn't Meant to Tell You This* – Jacqueline Woodson
  - *Speak (Rape)* – Laurie Halse Anderson
  - *Bitter End (Domestic Violence)* – Jennifer Brown
  - *All the Rage (Rape)* – Courtney Summers
- Spirituality
  - *The Opposite of Loneliness* – Marina Keegan
  - *The Alchemist* – Paulo Coehlo
  - *Persepolis* – Marjane Satrapi
  - *The Prophet* – Kahlil Gibran
- Resiliency
  - *Phenomena: The Lost and Forgotten Children* – Susan Tarr
  - *Sorta Like a Rockstar* – Matthew Quick
  - *The Hate You Give* – Angie Thomas
  - *Refugee* – Alan Gratz
  - *Fish In A Tree* – Lynda Mullaly Hunt

Books – TRC

- Residential Schools (with grade levels)
  - *When We Were Alone* – David Robertson (K–4)
  - *Shi-Shi-Etko* – Nicola Campbell (1–4)
  - *Shin-Chi's Canoe* – Nicola Campbell (1–4)
  - *Arctic Stories* – Michael Kusugak (1–4)
  - *When I Was Eight* – Christy Jordan-Fenton and Margaret Pokiak-Fenton (1–4)
  - *Not My Girl* – Christy Jordan-Fenton and Margaret Pokiak-Fenton
  - *Kookum's Red Shoes* – Peter Eyvindson (4–7)
  - *Fatty Legs: A True Story* – Christy Jordan-Fenton and Margaret Pokiak-Fenton (4–6)
  - *A Stranger at Home: A True Story* – Christy Jordan-Fenton and Margaret Pokiak-Fenton (4–6)
  - *No Time to Say Goodbye* – Sylvia Olsen (4–8)
  - *As Long as the River Flows* – Larry Loyie (4–7)
  - *My Name Is Seepeetza* – Shirley Sterling (4–7)
  - *We Feel Good Out Here* – Julie-Ann Andre (4–7)
  - *I Am Not a Number* – Jenny Kay Dupuis (3–6)
  - *Dear Canada: These Are My Words* – Ruby Slipperjack (4–7)
  - *Mush Hole: Memories of a Residential School* – Maddie Harper (6–9)
  - *Red Wolf* – Jennifer Dance (7–12)
  - *Goodbye Buffalo Bay* – Larry Loyie (9–12)
  - *The Secret Path* – Gord Downie (6–12)
  - *Wenjack* – Joseph Boyden (9–12)
  - *Sugar Falls: A Residential School Story* – David Robertson (9–12)
  - *7 Generations: A Plains Cree Story* – David Robertson (9–12)
  - *A Residential School Graphic Novel* – Jason EagleSpeaker (10–12)
- Reconciliation and Intergenerational Trauma
  - *The Outside Circle* – Patti LaBoucane-Benson (10–12)
  - *Betty* – David Robertson (9–12)
  - *The 500 Years of Resistance Comic Book* – Gord Hill
- Indigenous People and Culture
  - *Yetsa's Sweater* – Sylvia Olsen (K–4)
  - *What's the Most Beautiful Thing You Know About Horses?* – Richard Van Camp (K–4)
  - *Storm Boy* – Paul Owen Lewis (K–4)
  - *Fox on the Highway* – Thomson Highway (K–4)
  - *Solomon's Tree* –Andrea Spalding (K–4)
  - *Niwechihaw* – Caitlin Nicholson (K–3)
  - *I Like Who I Am* – Tara White (K–4)
  - *Lessons from Mother Earth* – Elaine McLeod (K–4)
  - *Where Did You Get Your Moccasins?* – Bernelda Wheeler (K–4)
  - *Seven Teachings series* – Katherena Vermette (K–3)
  - *Sockeye Mother* – Brett Huson (5–7) (also environment)
  - *Catching Spring* – Sylvia Olsen (4–6)
  - *Little Voice* – Ruby Slipperjack (4–6)
  - *Piisim Finds Her Miskanow* – William Dumas (4+)

Portage & Main Press, 2018, *Ensouling Our Schools*, ISBN: 978-1-55379-683-1

- ○ *Tales from Big Spirit* (biography series) – David Robertson (4–6)
- ○ *How We Saw the World* – C.J. Taylor (2–5)
- ○ *The Rough-Faced Girl* – Rafe Martin (1–5)

Other Themes

- Diversity
  - ○ *Emmanuel's Dream* – Laurie Ann Thompson
  - ○ *The Other Side* – Jacqueline Woodson
  - ○ *Grandfather Gandhi* – Arun Gandhi
  - ○ *Thank You, Mr. Falker* – Patricia Polacco
  - ○ *Junkyard Wonders* – Patricia Polacco

- The Environment
  - ○ *Mama Miti* – Donna Jo Napoli
  - ○ *The Lorax* – Dr. Seuss
  - ○ *Miss Rumphius* – Barbara Cooney
  - ○ *Where the Wisdom Lies* – Hope Ives Mauran

- Social Justice
  - ○ *A is for Activist* – Innosanto Nagara
  - ○ *Malala Yousafzai* – Karen Abouraya

Multiple Intelligences: Early Years Survey

Part 1

This survey has 9 sections. Each section has 10 statements. Read each statement, and think about whether it describes you, how you think, or how you feel. If you think the statement is true for you, write a 1 on the line beside it. At the end of each section, add up the 1's, and write your total for that section in the space provided.

Section 1

_____   I enjoy sorting things into groups or collecting similar things.

_____   I care about plants and trees.

_____   Hiking and camping are fun.

_____   I like taking care of plants or helping in the garden.

_____   I think we should save parks for animals and trees to live in.

_____   I like putting things in order.

_____   Animals are important in my life.

_____   I recycle cans, bottles, and paper.

_____   I like learning about animals, plants, and science.

_____   I like playing outside a lot.

_____   **TOTAL for Section 1**

Section 2

_____   I hum or sing a lot to myself without even realizing I'm doing it.

_____   I pay attention to noise and sounds.

_____   Dancing to a beat is easy for me.

_____   I am interested in playing a musical instrument.

_____   I like listening to poetry.

_____   I remember things by putting them in a rhyme.

_____   I like listening to music while I'm doing things.

_____   I like lots of different kinds of music.

_____   I like movies with singing and dancing in them.

_____   Remembering the words in songs is easy for me.

_____   **TOTAL for Section 2**

Section 3

_____   I keep my things neat and orderly.

_____   It helps me when people tell me how to do things one step at a time.

_____   Solving problems comes easily to me.

_____   I ask a lot of questions about how things work.

_____   I can do math quickly in my head.

_____   I like trying to figure things out.

_____   I cannot start my work until I know for sure all the things I have to do.

_____   It's easier for me to do new things when teachers or parents tell me exactly how.

Portage & Main Press, 2018, Ensouling Our Schools, ISBN: 978-1-55379-683-1

_____ I like using the computer to do my work.

_____ If something doesn't make sense to me, I get upset.

_____ **TOTAL for Section 3**

Section 4

_____ I like helping people.

_____ I enjoy discussing questions about life.

_____ Religion is important to me, and I like going to church or temple or mosque.

_____ I like looking at paintings and sculptures.

_____ I like to relax and think about things, and I daydream a lot.

_____ I like to visit beautiful places in nature.

_____ I think about what happens to people when they die.

_____ Learning new things is easier when I know why it's important.

_____ I wonder if there are other forms of intelligent life in the universe – like aliens.

_____ Studying about what people used to do and think long ago is interesting to me.

_____ **TOTAL for Section 4**

Section 5

_____ I learn best when I work with others.

_____ I like having lots of people around.

_____ It helps me when I practise things with a partner.

_____ I like "talking" to people on the phone, or in email, or texting.

_____ I have more than three friends.

_____ I am a leader among my friends.

_____ I understand how other people feel, and I try to help them.

_____ I like to teach other kids.

_____ Clubs and extracurricular activities are fun for me.

_____ Lots of people ask me to play with them.

_____ **TOTAL for Section 5**

Section 6

_____ I enjoy making things with my hands.

_____ Sitting still for long periods of time is difficult for me.

_____ I like outdoor games and sports.

_____ I pay attention to the looks on people's faces when they're talking.

_____ I try to keep my body healthy.

_____ I like to take things apart and put them back together again.

_____ I like watching people dance.

_____ I like working with tools.

_____ I do a lot of sports, or I exercise a lot.

_____ I learn by doing and touching.

_____ **TOTAL for Section 6**

 Adapted from www.surfaquarium.com, ©1999 Walter McKenzie

Section 7

_____   I enjoy reading books, magazines, and comics.

_____   I know a lot of words for someone my age.

_____   I like writing, whether letters or emails or poems or stories.

_____   It is easy for me to explain my ideas to others.

_____   I am good at spelling.

_____   I like listening to other people talk or read stories.

_____   I write for fun. OR I keep a diary.

_____   I like riddles and jokes.

_____   I find making up stories is fun.

_____   I like talking in front of the class.

_____   **TOTAL for Section 7**

Section 8

_____   I know what is appropriate to do and what is not appropriate.

_____   I learn best when I care about what I am studying.

_____   Fairness is important to me.

_____   I like playing alone or just being alone.

_____   I am very independent, and I like things that none of my friends do.

_____   I like to work alone.

_____   I need to know why I should do something before I agree to do it.

_____   When I like something, I try my hardest at it.

_____   I know what I am good at.

_____   I tell people when I think something they do is not nice.

_____   **TOTAL for Section 8**

Section 9

_____ I have a good imagination.

_____ I like re-arranging my things in my room.

_____ I enjoy creating art.

_____ I use webs, mind maps, and pictures to remember things.

_____ Watching people perform (act, dance, or sing) is fun for me.

_____ I like creating or working with pictures and graphics on the computer.

_____ I like making things with Lego, K'Nex, and other building materials.

_____ I like puzzles.

_____ I can remember what things looked like months ago and even years ago.

_____ I am a good artist.

_____ **TOTAL for Section 9**

Adapted from www.surfaquarium.com, ©1999 Walter McKenzie

Portage & Main Press, 2018, _Ensouling Our Schools_, ISBN: 978-1-55379-683-1

Part 2

Transfer your total points from each section to this table.

Section + M.I.		Total Points
1	Naturalistic	
2	Musical-Rhythmic	
3	Logical-Mathematical	
4	Existential	
5	Interpersonal	
6	Bodily-Kinesthetic	
7	Verbal-Linguistic	
8	Intrapersonal	
9	Visual-Spatial	

Part 3: Key to Totals

Section 1: This total reflects your Naturalistic strength.

Section 2: This total suggests your Musical-Rhythmic strength.

Section 3: This total indicates your Logical-Mathematical strength.

Section 4: This total illustrates your Existential strength.

Section 5: This total shows your Interpersonal strength.

Section 6: This total tells your Bodily-Kinesthetic strength.

Section 7: This total indicates your Verbal-Linguistic strength.

Section 8: This total reflects your Intrapersonal strength.

Section 9: This total suggests your Visual-Spatial strength.

Multiple Intelligences: Middle Years Survey

Part 1

This survey has 9 sections. Each section has 10 statements. Read each statement, and think about whether it describes you, how you think, or how you feel. If you think the statement is true for you, write a 1 on the line beside it. At the end of each section, add up the 1's, and write your total for that section in the space provided.

Section 1

_____   I enjoy sorting things into groups or collecting similar things.

_____   I care about plants and trees.

_____   Hiking and camping are fun.

_____   I like taking care of plants or helping in the garden.

_____   I care about environmental issues like logging and global warming.

_____   I like putting things in order.

_____   Animals are important in my life.

_____   I recycle cans, bottles, and paper.

_____   I like learning about animals, plants, and science.

_____   I like playing outside a lot.

_____   **TOTAL for Section 1**

Section 2

_____   I hum or sing a lot to myself without even realizing I'm doing it.

_____   I pay attention to noise and sounds.

_____   Moving to a beat is easy for me.

_____   I am interested in playing a musical instrument.

_____   I like listening to poetry.

_____   I remember things by putting them in a rhyme.

_____   I like listening to music while I'm studying or doing homework.

_____   I like lots of different kinds of music.

_____   I like movies with singing and dancing in them, and I like music videos.

_____   Remembering the words in songs is easy for me.

_____   **TOTAL for Section 2**

Section 3

_____   I keep my things neat and orderly.

_____   Step-by-step directions are a big help when I'm trying to do things.

_____   Solving problems comes easily to me.

_____   I ask a lot of questions about how things work.

_____   I can do math quickly in my head.

_____   Word problems and brain teasers are fun for me.

_____   I cannot start my work until I know for sure all the things I have to do.

_____   It's easier for me to do new things when teachers or parents tell me exactly how.

_____   I like using the computer to do my work.

_____   If something doesn't make sense to me, I get upset.

_____   **TOTAL for Section 3**

Section 4

_____   It is important to me to know how I fit in with the world or a group.

_____   I enjoy discussing questions about life.

_____   Religion is important to me, and I like going to church or temple or mosque, and praying.

_____   I like looking at paintings and sculptures.

_____   I like relaxation and meditation exercises.

_____   It is inspiring to visit beautiful places in nature.

_____   I enjoy reading about what ancient and modern people thought about the world.

_____   Learning new things is easier when I know why it's important.

_____   I wonder if there are other forms of intelligent life in the universe – like aliens.

_____   Studying about what people used to do and think long ago is interesting to me.

_____   **TOTAL for Section 4**

Section 5

_____   I learn best when I work with others.

_____   I like having lots of people around.

_____   It helps me when I practise things with a partner.

_____   I like "talking" to people on the phone, or in email, or texting.

_____   I have more than three friends.

_____   I am a leader among my friends.

_____   I understand how other people feel, and I try to help them.

_____   I like to teach other kids.

_____   Clubs and extracurricular activities are fun for me.

_____   Lots of people ask me to play or hang out with them.

_____   **TOTAL for Section 5**

Section 6

_____   I enjoy making things with my hands.

_____   Sitting still for long periods of time is difficult for me.

_____   I like outdoor games and sports.

_____   I pay attention to the looks on people's faces when they're talking.

_____   I try to keep my body healthy.

_____   I like to take things apart and put them back together again.

_____   I like watching people dance.

_____   I like working with tools.

_____   I do a lot of sports, or I exercise a lot.

_____   I learn by doing and touching.

_____   **TOTAL for Section 6**

Portage & Main Press, 2018, *Ensouling Our Schools*, ISBN: 978-1-55379-683-1   Adapted from www.surfaquarium.com, ©1999 Walter McKenzie

Section 7

_____ I enjoy reading books, magazines, and comics.

_____ I know a lot of words for someone my age.

_____ I like writing or texting, whether letters or emails or poems or stories.

_____ It is easy for me to explain my ideas to others.

_____ I can spell words accurately.

_____ I like listening to other people talk or read stories.

_____ I write for fun. OR I keep a diary.

_____ I enjoy playing with words like puns, anagrams, or tongue twisters.

_____ The lyrics in a song matter to me.

_____ I like talking in front of the class.

_____ **TOTAL for Section 7**

Section 8

_____ I know what is appropriate to do and what is not appropriate.

_____ I learn best when I care about what I am studying.

_____ Fairness is important to me.

_____ I like playing alone or just being alone.

_____ I am very independent, and like doing my own thing.

_____ I like to work alone.

_____ I need to know why I should do something before I agree to do it.

_____ When I like something, I try my hardest at it.

_____ I know what I am good at.

_____ I tell people when I think something they do is not nice.

_____ **TOTAL for Section 8**

Section 9

_____ I have a good imagination.

_____ Re-arranging a room is fun for me.

_____ I enjoy creating art.

_____ I use webs, mind maps, and pictures to remember what I learn.

_____ Watching people perform (act, dance, or sing) is fun for me.

_____ I like creating or working with pictures and graphics on the computer.

_____ I like creating models and images.

_____ I daydream more than other kids.

_____ I can recall what things looked like months ago and even years ago.

_____ I am a good artist.

_____ **TOTAL for Section 9**

Adapted from www.surfaquarium.com, ©1999 Walter McKenzie

Portage & Main Press, 2018, *Ensouling Our Schools*, ISBN: 978-1-55379-683-1

Part 2

Transfer your total points from each section to this table.

Section + M.I.		Total Points
1	Naturalistic	
2	Musical-Rhythmic	
3	Logical-Mathematical	
4	Existential	
5	Interpersonal	
6	Bodily-Kinesthetic	
7	Verbal-Linguistic	
8	Intrapersonal	
9	Visual-Spatial	

Part 3: Key to Totals

Section 1: This total reflects your Naturalistic strength.
Section 2: This total suggests your Musical-Rhythmic strength.
Section 3: This total indicates your Logical-Mathematical strength.
Section 4: This total illustrates your Existential strength.
Section 5: This total shows your Interpersonal strength.
Section 6: This total tells your Bodily-Kinesthetic strength.
Section 7: This total indicates your Verbal-Linguistic strength.
Section 8: This total reflects your Intrapersonal strength.
Section 9: This total suggests your Visual-Spatial strength.

Portage & Main Press, 2018, *Ensouling Our Schools*, ISBN: 978-1-55379-683-1

Multiple Intelligences: Adolescent and Adult Survey

Part 1

This survey has 9 sections. Each section has 10 statements. Read each statement, and think about whether it describes you, how you think, or how you feel. If you think the statement is true for you, write a 1 on the line beside it. At the end of each section, add up the 1's, and write your total for that section in the space provided.

Section 1

_____ I enjoy categorizing things by common traits.

_____ Environmental issues are important to me.

_____ Hiking and camping are enjoyable activities.

_____ I enjoy working in a garden.

_____ I believe preserving our National Parks is important.

_____ Putting things in hierarchies makes sense to me.

_____ Animals are important in my life.

_____ My home has a recycling system in place.

_____ I enjoy studying biology, botany, or zoology.

_____ I spend a great deal of time outdoors.

_____ **TOTAL for Section 1**

Section 2

_____ I easily pick up on patterns.

_____ I focus in on noise and sounds.

_____ Moving to a beat is easy for me.

_____ I've always been interested in playing a musical instrument.

_____ The rhythm of poetry intrigues me.

_____ I remember things by putting them in a rhyme.

_____ Concentration is difficult while listening to a radio or television.

_____ I enjoy many kinds of music.

_____ Musicals are more interesting than dramatic plays.

_____ Remembering song lyrics is easy for me.

_____ **TOTAL for Section 2**

Section 3

_____ I keep my things neat and orderly.

_____ Step-by-step directions are a big help.

_____ Solving problems comes easily to me.

_____ I get easily frustrated with disorganized people.

_____ I can complete calculations quickly in my head.

_____ Logic puzzles are fun.

_____ I cannot begin an assignment until all my questions are answered.

_____ Structure helps me be successful.

_____   I find working on a computer spreadsheet or database interesting.

_____   Things have to make sense to me, or I am dissatisfied.

_____   **TOTAL for Section 3**

Section 4

_____   It is important to me to see my role in the "big picture" of things.

_____   I enjoy discussing questions about life.

_____   Religion is important to me.

_____   I enjoy viewing art masterpieces.

_____   Relaxation and meditation exercises are rewarding.

_____   I like visiting breathtaking sites in nature.

_____   I enjoy reading ancient and modern philosophers.

_____   Learning new things is easier when I understand their value.

_____   I wonder if there are other forms of intelligent life in the universe.

_____   Studying history and ancient cultures helps give me perspective.

_____   **TOTAL for Section 4**

Section 5

_____   I learn best when interacting with others.

_____   The more people, the merrier.

_____   Study groups are very productive for me.

_____   I enjoy chat rooms.

_____   Participating in politics is important.

_____   Television and radio talk shows are enjoyable.

_____   I am a "team player."

_____   I dislike working alone.

_____   Clubs and extracurricular activities are fun for me.

_____   I pay attention to social issues and causes.

_____   **TOTAL for Section 5**

Section 6

_____   I enjoy making things with my hands.

_____   Sitting still for long periods of time is difficult for me.

_____   I enjoy outdoor games and sports.

_____   I value non-verbal communication such as sign language.

_____   I think a fit body is important.

_____   Arts and crafts are enjoyable pastimes.

_____   Expression through dance is beautiful.

_____   I like working with tools.

_____   I live an active lifestyle.

_____   I learn by doing.

_____   **TOTAL for Section 6**

Portage & Main Press, 2018, *Ensouling Our Schools*, ISBN: 978-1-55379-683-1   Adapted from www.surfaquarium.com, ©1999 Walter McKenzie

Section 7

_____ I enjoy reading all kinds of materials.

_____ Taking notes helps me remember and understand what I hear or read.

_____ I keep in touch with family and friends through letters, texting, and email.

_____ It is easy for me to explain my ideas to others.

_____ I keep a journal.

_____ Word puzzles like crosswords and jumbles are fun.

_____ I write for pleasure.

_____ I enjoy playing with words like puns, anagrams, and spoonerisms.

_____ Foreign languages interest me.

_____ Debates and public speaking are activities I like to participate in.

_____ **TOTAL for Section 7**

Section 8

_____ I am keenly aware of my moral beliefs.

_____ I learn best when I have an emotional attachment to the subject.

_____ Fairness is important to me.

_____ My attitude affects how I learn.

_____ Social-justice issues concern me.

_____ Working alone can be just as productive as working in a group.

_____ I need to know why I should do something before I agree to do it.

_____ When I believe in something, I will give 100% effort to it.

_____ I like to be involved in causes that help others.

_____ I am willing to protest or sign a petition to right a wrong.

_____ TOTAL for Section 8

Section 9

_____ I have a good imagination.

_____ Re-arranging a room is fun for me.

_____ I enjoy creating art, using varied media.

_____ I use graphic organizers to remember what I learn.

_____ Performance art can be very gratifying.

_____ Spreadsheets are great for making charts, graphs, and tables.

_____ Three-dimensional puzzles bring me much enjoyment.

_____ Music videos are very stimulating.

_____ When recalling things or events, I form mental pictures of them.

_____ I am good at reading maps and blueprints.

_____ **TOTAL for Section 9**

Portage & Main Press, 2018, *Ensouling Our Schools*, ISBN: 978-1-55379-683-1

Part 2

Transfer your total points from each section to this table.

Section + M.I.		Total Points
1	Naturalistic	
2	Musical-Rhythmic	
3	Logical-Mathematical	
4	Existential	
5	Interpersonal	
6	Bodily-Kinesthetic	
7	Verbal-Linguistic	
8	Intrapersonal	
9	Visual-Spatial	

Part 3: Key to Totals

Section 1: This total reflects your Naturalistic strength.

Section 2: This total suggests your Musical-Rhythmic strength.

Section 3: This total indicates your Logical-Mathematical strength.

Section 4: This total illustrates your Existential strength.

Section 5: This total shows your Interpersonal strength.

Section 6: This total tells your Bodily-Kinesthetic strength.

Section 7: This total indicates your Verbal-Linguistic strength.

Section 8: This total reflects your Intrapersonal strength.

Section 9: This total suggests your Visual-Spatial strength.

Portage & Main Press, 2018, *Ensouling Our Schools*, ISBN: 978-1-55379-683-1

My Intelligence Profile

Part 4

Transfer your totals for each section to this table. Then, use your ruler to create a bar graph.

Survey Sections	Section 1 Naturalistic	Section 2 Musical-Rhythmic	Section 3 Logical-Mathematical	Section 4 Existential	Section 5 Interpersonal	Section 6 Bodily-Kinesthetic	Section 7 Verbal-Linguistic	Section 8 Intrapersonal	Section 9 Visual-Spatial
Total 10/10									
Total 9/10									
Total 8/10									
Total 7/10									
Total 6/10									
Total 5/10									
Total 4/10									
Total 3/10									
Total 2/10									
Total 1/10									

The Totals suggest that my intelligence strengths are _____,

_____, and _____.

The Totals also suggest that I need support to strengthen my abilities and interests in _____,

_____ and _____.

Adapted from www.surfaquarium.com, ©1999 Walter McKenzie

Portage & Main Press, 2018, *Ensouling Our Schools*, ISBN: 978-1-55379-683-1

For example:

Survey Sections	Section 1 Naturalistic	Section 2 Musical-Rhythmic	Section 3 Logical-Mathematical	Section 4 Existential	Section 5 Interpersonal	Section 6 Bodily-Kinesthetic	Section 7 Verbal-Linguistic	Section 8 Intrapersonal	Section 9 Visual-Spatial
Total 10/10									
Total 9/10							9		
Total 8/10									
Total 7/10					7				7
Total 6/10									
Total 5/10		5							
Total 4/10						4			
Total 3/10			3						
Total 2/10				2					2
Total 1/10	1								

The Totals suggest that my intelligence strengths are _____ verbal-linguistic _____,

_____ interpersonal _____, and _____ visual-spatial _____.

The Totals also suggest that I need support to strengthen my abilities and interests in _____ naturalistic _____,

_____ existential _____, and _____ intrapersonal _____.

Portage & Main Press, 2018, *Ensouling Our Schools*, ISBN: 978-1-55379-683-1

Brain Diagram (with labels)

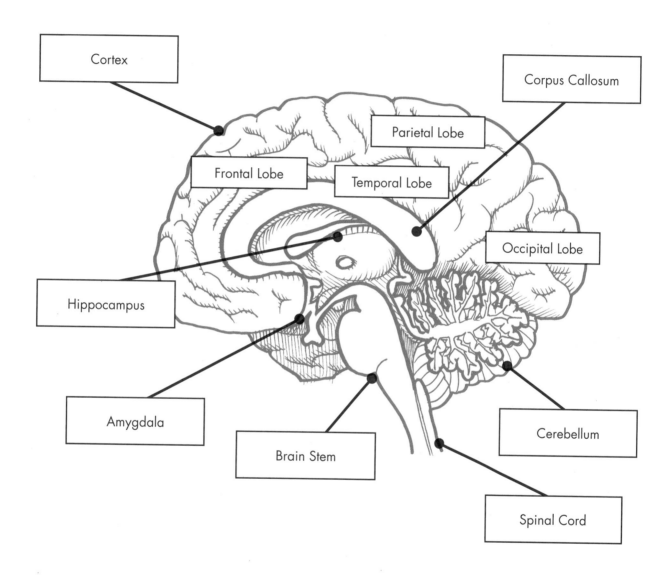

Cortex

Corpus Callosum

Parietal Lobe

Frontal Lobe

Temporal Lobe

Occipital Lobe

Hippocampus

Amygdala

Cerebellum

Brain Stem

Spinal Cord

Portage & Main Press, 2018, *Ensouling Our Schools*, ISBN: 978-1-55379-683-1

Brain Diagram

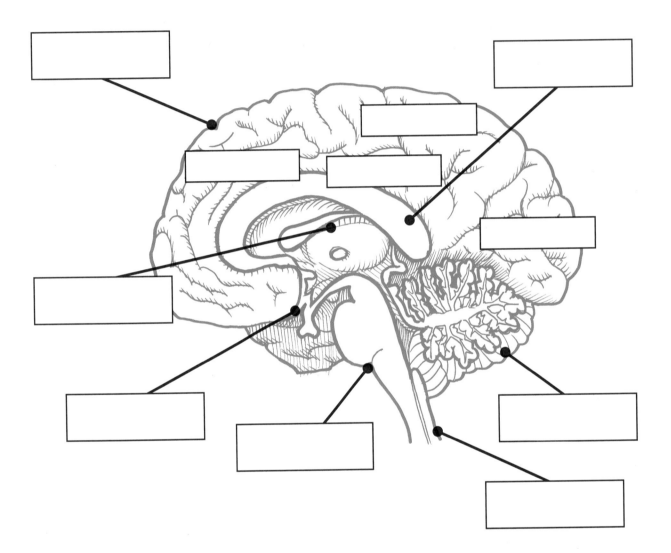

The Brain and the Senses

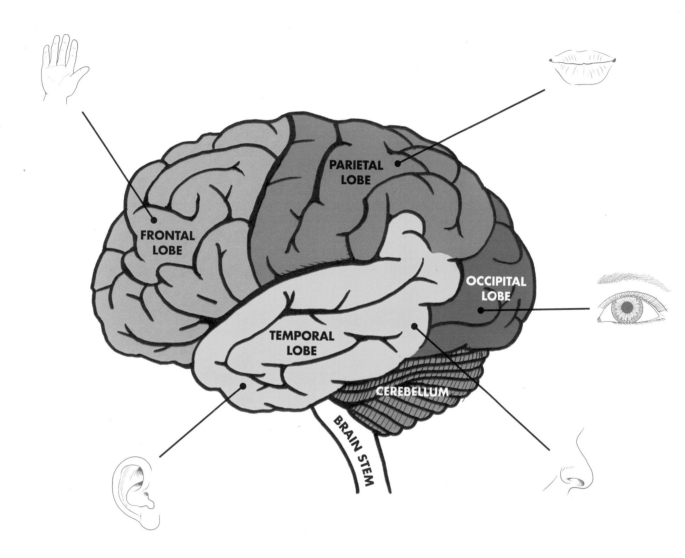

Brain Unit Rubric

Beginning	Approaching	Meeting	Exceeding
Recognizes that the brain helps us think	Identifies major structures and basic functions of the brain	Explains how and why (in terms of evolution, structure, or environment) the brain has specialized areas for different kinds of information and functions	Infers how diversity in humans is reflected in brain development
Recognizes that the brain is made up of cells	Describes the role of neurons in terms of communication	Explains how neurons communicate	Makes connections between neuronal communication and health/illness
Identifies neurotransmitters and key chemicals related to well-being (oxytocin, cortisol)	Explains the relationships between neurochemistry and well-being (e.g., higher levels of cortisol = lower levels of well-being)	Analyzes environmental factors that affect neurochemistry (e.g., sensory triggers, sleep, nutrition)	Evaluates personal triggers and strategies related to self-regulation of neuro-chemistry
Recognizes that there is a relationship between thoughts and feelings	Explains how our thoughts and perceptions cause the brain to release chemicals, and the chemicals affect our feelings	Analyzes how our thoughts affect our feelings and the interdependent, circular relationship between thoughts and feelings	Creates personal strategies for managing well-being

Grade 1 example

"My brain is good at music, because there is always music playing in my house and my mom plays the piano a lot." – *Row 1, Meeting*

Grade 4 example

"My grandpa is in a wheelchair. I guess his neurons don't send messages to his legs." – *Row 2, Exceeding*

Grade 7 example

"I feel best playing hockey, being on the ice, because nothing there – the sounds, sights, smells, and people – reminds me of Africa and what I went through there." – *Row 3, Exceeding*

Grade 12 example

"When I spin out, I just can't stop thinking about what's going on. And the more I think about it, the more upset I get, until I have a total panic attack." – *Row 4, Meeting*

Portage & Main Press, 2018, *Ensouling Our Schools*, ISBN: 978-1-55379-683-1

Beginning	Approaching	Meeting	Exceeding
Identifies basic states of well-being related to emotions (e.g., I'm good, I'm happy)	Describes ways in which mental health is not static – we all have good times and hard times through the course of our lives	Analyzes how the definition of mental health, or well-being, has some common agreed-upon elements, and some personal definitions	Formulates a personal definition of well-being grounded in knowledge, culture, and personal experience
Recognizes that some people live with a mental illness	Describes attributes of specific mental illnesses studied, relates to physical illness	Evaluates ways in which mental illness has significant effects on individuals and their families	Proposes supports for individuals living with mental illness in the classroom, school, and/or community
Describes barriers (e.g., social isolation, bullying) that individuals with mental illness face	Explains why having a support network is critical to the healing of people who are ill, in terms of spiritual, mental, emotional, and physical well-being	Infers how individuals can positively, or negatively, affect the lives of people with mental illness	Demonstrates supportive behaviour, service-oriented perspective – takes initiative

K example

"People should just give homeless people a hug and be nice. Maybe they just had a bad life."
– *Row 3, Exceeding*

Grade 2 example

"Some days I'm happy, but lots of days I'm really sad cause my mom is sick." – *Row 1, Approaching*

Grade 6 example

"Maybe since we all know XXXX is having a tough day, we should just go work outside so we get some light and air and he can move around." – *Row 2, Exceeding*

Grade 8, example

"My family is Buddhist. We don't believe suffering means you're ill. It's your acceptance of it that matters. Healthy people know suffering happens, and you can learn from it. Ill people let it take them down." – *Row 1, Exceeding*

Grade 9 example

"I know it's hard having a mental illness, but I never thought about some of my friends who have parents with issues. One of my friends has to make dinner for his sister and put her to bed cause his mom freaks out at her. I just thought it was unfair and didn't think he should have to do it, but I never thought about having to be the parent cause his mom can't. Wow." – *Row 2, Meeting*

The Neuron (with labels)

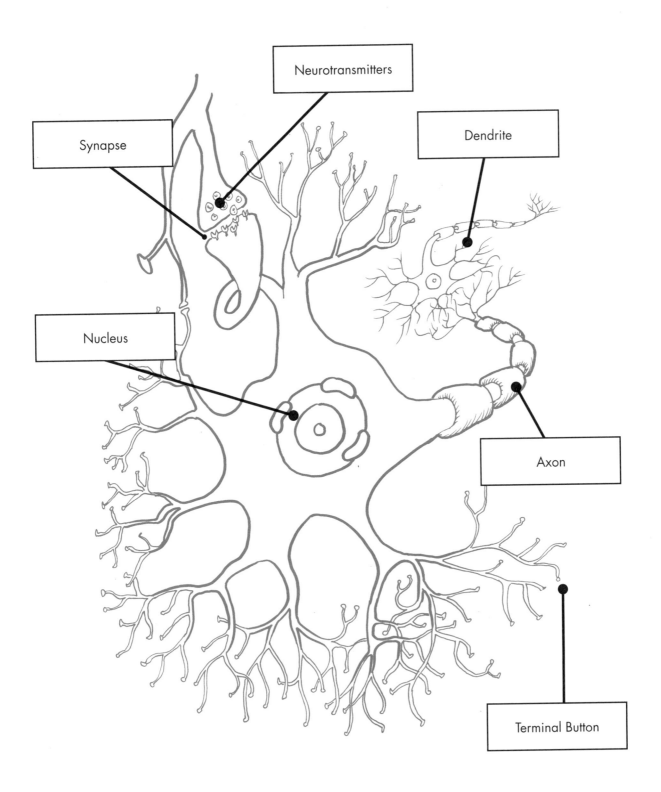

Neurotransmitters

Synapse

Dendrite

Nucleus

Axon

Terminal Button

Portage & Main Press, 2018, *Ensouling Our Schools*, ISBN: 978-1-55379-683-1

The Neuron

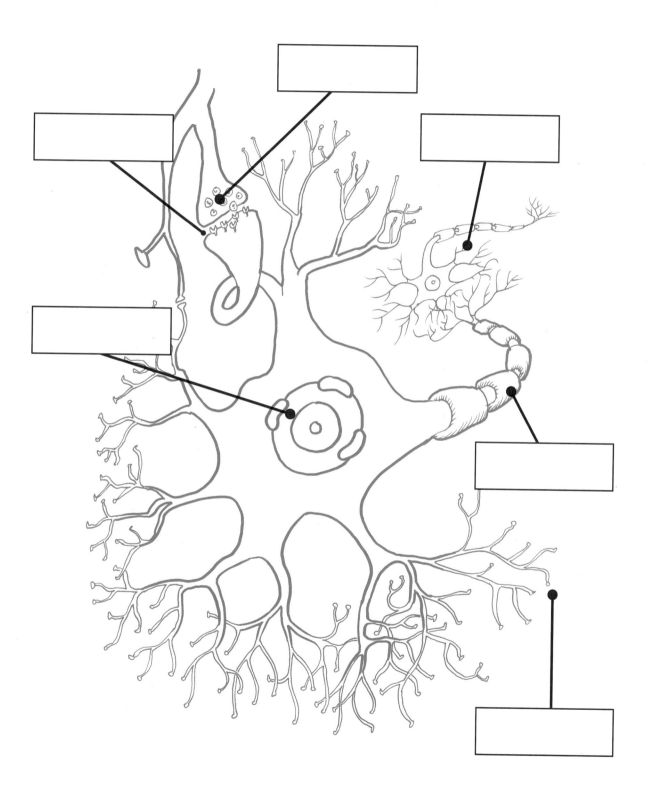

Emotion and Mental Health Words

Elementary Emotion Words

happy	sad	angry	disappointed	frustrated
excited	bored	worried	lonely	hyper
friendly	discouraged	scared	anxious	loving

Middle/High School Words

hurt	depressed	embarrassed	exhausted	irritated
shocked	relaxed	brave	ashamed	alienated
energized	elated	hopeful	insecure	outraged
apathetic	blessed	joyous	exhilarated	confused
proud	amused	dismayed	safe	hopeless
trusting	neglected	rejected	compassionate	calm

Portage & Main Press, 2018, *Ensouling Our Schools*, ISBN: 978-1-55379-683-1

Mental Illnesses

Bipolar Disorder	Depression	Attention Deficit Hyperactivity Disorder (ADHD)	Schizophrenia	Addictions
Tourette's	Obsessive Compulsive Disorder (OCD)	Post Traumatic Stress Disorder (PTSD)	Bulimia	Anorexia

Portage & Main Press, 2018, Ensouling Our Schools, ISBN: 978-1-55379-683-1

Warning Signs of a Mental Illness

1. Feeling anxious or worried

We all get worried or stressed from time to time. But anxiety could be the sign of a mental-health issue if it's constant and interferes all the time. Other symptoms of anxiety may include heart palpitations, shortness of breath, headache, restlessness, diarrhoea, or a racing mind.

2. Feeling depressed or unhappy

Have you noticed that your friend has lost interest in a hobby you used to share? If they've also seemed sad or irritable for the last few weeks or more, lacking in motivation and energy, or are teary all the time, they might be dealing with depression.

3. Emotional outbursts

Everyone has different moods, but sudden and dramatic changes in mood, such as extreme distress or anger, can be a symptom of mental illness.

4. Sleep problems

Generally, we need 7–9 hours of sleep each night. Persisting changes to a person's sleep patterns could be a symptom of a mental illness. For example, insomnia could be a sign of anxiety or substance abuse. Sleeping too much or too little could indicate depression or a sleeping disorder.

5. Weight or appetite changes

Many of us want to lose a few kilos, but, for some people, fluctuating weight or rapid weight loss could be a warning sign of a mental illness, such as depression or an eating disorder. Other mental-health issues can affect appetite and weight, too.

6. Quiet or withdrawn

We all need quiet time occasionally, but withdrawing from life, especially if this is a major change, could indicate a mental-health issue. If a friend or loved one is regularly isolating themselves, they may have depression, be bipolar, have a psychotic disorder, or suffer from another mental-health illness. Refusing to join in social activities may be a sign they need help.

7. Substance abuse

Are you worried a loved one is drinking too much? Using substances such as alcohol or drugs to cope can be a sign of, and a contributor to, mental-health issues.

8. Feeling guilty or worthless

Thoughts like "I'm a failure," "It's my fault," or "I'm worthless" are all possible signs of a mental-health issue, such as depression. Your friend or loved one may need help if they're frequently criticizing or blaming themselves. When severe, a person may want to hurt or kill themselves. This feeling could mean the person is suicidal, and urgent help is needed. Call 911 immediately.

9. Changes in behaviour or feelings

A mental illness may start out as subtle changes to a person's feelings, thinking, and behaviour. Ongoing and significant changes could be a sign that they have or are developing a mental-health issue. If something doesn't seem "quite right," it's important to start the conversation about getting help.

Portage & Main Press, 2018, *Ensouling Our Schools*, ISBN: 978-1-55379-683-1

Mental-Health Scenarios

You can have students read the following scenarios starting with: "A friend is talking to you, and they say…" ahead of the quote, or you can have students read the quotes as though they were in these situations. Ask them whether they think their friend needs help, or whether this is a time when they think they should reach out for help if they were feeling this way.

Scenario #1

"My grandfather died yesterday. I was really close to him when I was younger. We used to hang out and spend a lot of time together. I keep feeling like I disappointed him, cause lately I've been busy with school and friends and I haven't seen him very much. I can't stop crying, and I didn't sleep much last night, either."

Note to teachers: It is normal 24 hours after the loss of a loved one to not be coping well. This is not a case where a mental-health disorder is suspected. It is a time for compassion and care – whether of a friend or toward oneself.

Scenario #2

"I hate Peter. He's always giving me a hard time. Telling me I'm a loser, and I'll never have any friends. Pushing me when I walk by him. Don't tell anyone, but I have a plan, I will get my revenge."

Note to teachers: This is a concern. The word plan moves this from a statement of feelings to a statement of action. Discuss with students that it is normal to wish a bully would leave you alone, or that you wish you could reverse the situation, but that having "a plan" for revenge is a warning sign. This could be a threat or a warning sign of violence, and needs to be followed up. If a friend says this, students can ask about the plan, or choose to just share their concern with a trusted adult. If it is they themselves who are having these thoughts, they should seek help and support.

Scenario #3

"I just don't care anymore. I don't know why. I just don't. I can't focus, can't get out of bed. I want to sleep all the time. I don't feel like hanging out, I just want to be by myself. No offense. I'm just a drag these days. You all should just go without me. You'll have a better time."

Note to teachers: The key to this scenario is how long it has been going on, and whether there is an identifiable trigger. If it is a week after the breakup of a relationship or the loss of a loved one, it is normal. If it has been going on for more than two weeks, with no identifiable trigger, or for more than a month after a trigger, it is time to look for help.

Portage & Main Press, 2018, *Ensouling Our Schools*, ISBN: 978-1-55379-683-1

Scenario #4

"I was always a little different, you know. Like I always wanted everything to match – my clothes, my stuff. I hated it when things were messy and stuff. But now, it's like, crazy. I can't breathe, can't think if everything isn't the way I need it to be. I need everything to be in order, neat, clean. I don't want other people's stuff near mine. I just like my own world the way I like it, and that's it."

Note to teachers: This may be a sign of OCD or an anxiety disorder. Discuss with students the idea of function. That is, a mental-health issue becomes an illness when it interferes with a person's ability to function, and enjoy their life. Someone who prefers things neat and orderly, but can still manage in the regular world does not have a mental illness. Someone who has panic attacks when anything gets changed or is out of order is being impaired in their function – so they need help.

Scenario #5

"Ugh, I am getting so fat. Everyone keeps telling me I'm losing weight, but they obviously need glasses, cause I can see I'm not. I'm going to have to get stricter about my diet, I need to eat way less."

Note to teachers: A student who maintains a belief about their body despite multiple people telling them something to the contrary is unwell. This is a sign of body dysmorphia, and can lead to an eating disorder. When they "have a plan," even though they don't use the word *plan,* it is definitely time to get help.

Portage & Main Press, 2018, *Ensouling Our Schools,* ISBN: 978-1-55379-683-1

Rubrics for Treaty Education

Early Years Treaty Education Rubric

Beginning	Approaching	Meeting	Exceeding
Defines a treaty as a "deal"	Recognizes that the early settlers who came to Canada were helped by Indigenous peoples, and made a deal with them to give back	Describes Canadian treaties as an agreement between two nations that agreed to cooperate and share the land and resources	Proposes solutions to reconciliation of the treaties (developmentally appropriate)
Identifies Indigenous peoples as being the First Peoples of Turtle Island/Canada	Recognizes that the early settlers who came to Canada were helped by Indigenous peoples, and made a deal with them to give back	Explains the promises made to Indigenous peoples by the Canadian government (healthcare, education, and a share of the land and resources in exchange for land and resources for the settlers)	Proposes solutions to reconciliation of the treaties (developmentally appropriate)
Recognizes that Indigenous cultures were an oral culture	Explains the differences between Indigenous law (your word), and British law (your signature on a contract)	Analyzes the different perspectives of the two groups, and explains the resulting conflict in beliefs about what was agreed on	Proposes solutions to reconciliation of the treaties (developmentally appropriate)
Identifies the feelings of Indigenous peoples regarding broken promises	Explains why it is important to "make it right" – i.e., reconciliation	Gives opinions about how to honour the treaties, which are still law in Canada today	Proposes solutions to reconciliation of the treaties (developmentally appropriate)

K example

"The prime minister should share all the money and the parks with the Indigenous people." – *Exceeding*

Grade 2 example

"Indigenous peoples were here first, but then we came and now we're here." – *Row 2, Beginning*

Grade 1 example

"We promised them good schools and good doctors and good places to live so that wasn't fair when they had to go to reserves and couldn't leave." – *Row 2, Meeting*

Grade 3 example

"The Indigenous peoples thought the settlers promised but the settlers tricked them cause they didn't write it down and sign it, so they didn't think it was a promise." – *Row 3, Meeting*

Portage & Main Press, 2018, *Ensouling Our Schools*, ISBN: 978-1-55379-683-1

Middle And Senior Years Treaty Education Rubric

Beginning	Approaching	Meeting	Exceeding
Defines treaties as agreements between two groups	Describes the nature of Indigenous and settler government structures	Evaluates how governments negotiate treaties, and pass laws, on behalf of the people of their nation	Proposes methods of ensuring Indigenous peoples rights are respected going forward through government structures (e.g., new laws, structures)
Recognizes that many Indigenous nations existed in Canada before it was Canada	Describes government systems employed by Indigenous nations in their region	Compares and contrasts various Indigenous government systems, and the processes they used to negotiate treaties between groups (e.g., ceremonies, gift exchanges) and settler formats (business deal)	Evaluates the advantages and disadvantages of the different government structures, treaty processes, and values inherent in the process
Recognizes that Indigenous cultures were an oral culture	Explains the differences between Indigenous law (your word, a gift exchange) and British law (your signature on a contract)	Infers how the power hierarchy affected the outcomes of treaty negotiations in relation to what was legally binding (e.g., only what was written in English carried weight)	Examines the nature of minority rights in Canada today, proposes possible enhancements to protect against future power inequities
Describes basic properties of local treaties	Explains the promises made to Indigenous peoples by the Canadian government (healthcare, education, and a share of the land and resources in exchange for land and resources for the settlers)	Questions the intentions, moral ramifications, and values underlying the treaties, both in the past and in terms of modern-day responsibilities	Makes connections between the issues of the TRC and democracy, humanism, and well-being
Recognizes that Indigenous peoples have been discriminated against by Canadian law, society, and people	Describes the nature of disempowerment and the removal of human rights of Indigenous peoples in Canadian history (e.g., Indian Act, residential schools)	Empathizes with the sense of betrayal and trauma experienced by Indigenous peoples, analyzes modern-day efforts at reconciliation	Proposes new or additional processes/ideas to move reconciliation forward

Portage & Main Press, 2018, *Ensouling Our Schools*, ISBN: 978-1-55379-683-1

Grade 6 example

"I think the Indigenous ways of making treaties was better, because men and women were involved, and it was done with a "win-win" mindset, rather than one group trying to do better than the other." – *Row 2, Exceeding*

Grade 9 example

"It seems to me if Canada caused Indigenous peoples to experience all kinds of trauma, that the only way for reconciliation to happen is for Canada to undo the trauma. We promised healthcare and schools, so we should be sending psychologists and counsellors to all their communities. They should get free training in mental-health literacy and mindfulness using the four spirits. We should build special schools, with environments that look and feel different from how schools normally feel, so they don't get triggered. And their Elders should get a certain number of positions in government, like a council of Elders, to advise the government." – *Row 5, Exceeding*

Grade 11 example

"Well, the treaties seem fair to me. Indigenous peoples shared their land, and settlers helped them with schools and hospitals and stuff." – *Row 4, Beginning*

References

Aiex, Nola Kortner. 1993. "Bibliotherapy." *ERIC Digest*, ED357333
    Retrieved from https://www.ericdigests.org/1993/bibliotherapy.htm

American Psychiatric Association. 1994. "Fact Sheet: Violence and Mental Illness."
    Washington, DC: American Psychiatric Association.

American Psychological Association. 2017. "Stress Effects on the Body." Retrieved from
    http://www.apa.org/helpcenter/stress-body.aspx

Anderson, K.J. and K.M. Minke. 2007. "Parent Involvement in Education: Toward an
    Understanding of Parents' Decision Making." *The Journal of Educational Research*
    100 (5): 311–323. https://doi.org/10.3200/JOER.100.5.311–323

Appleby, L., P.B. Mortensen, G. Dunn, and U. Hiroeh, U. 2001. "Death by Homicide,
    Suicide, and Other Unnatural Causes in People with Mental Illness: A Population-
    based Study." *The Lancet,* 358: 2110–2112.

Brackenreed, D. 2011. "Inclusive Education: Identifying Teachers' Strategies for Coping
    with Perceived Stressors in Inclusive Classrooms." *Canadian Journal of Educational
    Administration and Policy* 122: 1–36.

Brendtro, L., M. Brokenleg, and S. Van Bockern. 2002. *Reclaiming Youth at Risk: Our
    Hope for the Future.* Bloomington, IN: Solution Tree.

Canadian Alliance on Mental Illness and Mental Health (CAMIMH). 2007.

"Mental Health Literacy in Canada: Phase One Draft Report." Retrieved from
    http://camimh.ca/wp-content/uploads/2012/04/Mental-Health-Literacy_-_
    Full-Final-Report_EN.pdf

Clark, D.A., S. Kleiman, L.B. Spanierman, P. Isaac, and G. Poolokasingham. 2014.
    "'Do You Live in a Teepee?' Aboriginal Students' Experiences with Racial
    Microaggressions in Canada." *Journal of Diversity in Higher Education* 7 (2):
    112–125. http://dx.doi.org/10.1037/a0036573

Collaborative for Academic and Social and Emotional Learning (CASEL). 2017.
    www.casel.org.

Collie, R., J. Shapka, and N. Perry. 2011. "Predicting Teacher Commitment: The Impact
    of School Climate and Social-Emotional Learning." *Psychology in the Schools* 48 (10):
    1034–1048. doi:10.1002/pits.20611.

Desimone, L. 2009. "Improving Impact Studies of Teachers' Professional Development:
    Toward Better Conceptualizations and Measures." *Educational Researcher* 38 (3):
    181–199. doi:10.3102/0013189X8331140.

Drummond, D. and E. Kachuck Rosenbluth. 2013. "The Debate on First Nations
    Education Funding: Mind the Gap." Working Paper 49. School of Policy Studies,
    Queen's University.

Durlak, J.A., R.P. Weissberg, A.B. Dymnicki, R.D. Taylor, and K.B. Schellinger. 2011. "The Impact of Enhancing Students' Social and Emotional Learning: A Meta-Analysis of School-Based Universal Interventions." *Child Development* 82 (1): 405–432. https://doi.org/10.1111/j.1467-8624.2010.01564.x

Elias, M. J. 2004. "The Connection Between Social-Emotional Learning and Learning Disabilities: Implications for Intervention." *Learning Disability Quarterly* 27, 53–63.

Fontaine, P., A. Craft, and The Truth and Reconciliation Commission of Canada. 2015. *A Knock on the Door: The Essential History of Residential Schools from the Truth and Reconciliation Commission of Canada.* Winnipeg: University of Manitoba Press.

Freire, Paulo. 1993. *Pedagogy of the Oppressed.* New York: Continuum.

Gardner, H. 1995. "Multiple Intelligences as a Catalyst." *English Journal* 84: 16–18.

Hattie, John. 2008. *Visible Learning: A Synthesis of Over 800 Meta-Analyses Relating to Achievement.* London: Routledge.

Hawkins, J.D., R. Kosterman, R.F. Catalano, K.G. Hill, and R.D. Abbott. 2005. "Promoting Positive Adult Functioning Through Social Development Intervention in Childhood: Long-Term Effects from the Seattle Social Development Project." [Erratum appears in Arch Pediatr Adolesc Med. 2005 May 159 (5):469]. *Archives of Pediatrics and Adolescent Medicine* 159 (1): 25–31. http://ovidsp.ovid.com?T=JS&CSC=Y&NEWS=N&PAGE=fulltext&D=med5&AN=15630054

Hearne, D. and S. Stone. 1995. "Multiple Intelligences and Underachievement: Lessons from Individuals with Learning Disabilities." *Journal of Learning Disabilities* 28: 439–448.

Hertzman, C. 2012. "Putting the Concept of Biological Embedding in Historical Perspective." *Proceedings of the National Academy of Sciences* 109: 17160–17167.

Holt, M. E., J. W. Lee, K. R. Morton, and S. Tonstad. 2015. "Trans Fatty Acid Intake and Emotion Regulation." *Journal of Health Psychology* 20 (6): 785–793. http://doi.org/10.1177/1359105315580215

Hu, P., and J. Zhang. 2017. "A Pathway to Learner Autonomy: A Self-Determination Theory Perspective." *Asia Pacific Education Review* 18 (1): 147–157. https://doi.org/10.1007/s12564-016-9468-z

Hymel, S., K.A. Schonert-Reichl, and L.D. Miller. 2006. "Reading, 'Riting, and Relationships: Considering the Social Side of Education." *Exceptionality Education Canada* 16: 149–192.

"Indian Residential Schools." Indigenous and Northern Affairs Canada (INAC). Retrieved November 2017: https://www.aadnc-aandc.gc.ca/eng/1100100015576/1100100015577

Institute of Medicine. 2006. *Improving the Quality of Health Care for Mental and Substance-Use Conditions.* Washington, DC: Institute of Medicine.

Irvine, A., J. Lupart, T. Loreman, and D. McGhie-Richmond. 2010. "Educational Leadership to Create Authentic Inclusive Schools: The Experiences of Principals in a Canadian Rural School District." *Exceptionality Education International* 20 (2): 70–88.

Jones, E., R. Haenfler, and B. Johnson. 2001. *The Better World Handbook: From Good Intentions to Everyday Actions.* Gabriola Island, BC: New Society.

Katz, J. 2014. "Implementing the Three-Block Model of Universal Design for Learning (UDL): Effects on Teachers' Self-Efficacy, Stress, and Job Satisfaction in Inclusive Classrooms K–12." *International Journal of Inclusive Education* 19 (1): 1–20. http://dx.doi.org/10.1080/13603116.2014.881569

———2017. "The case of Elvin." In *Inclusive Education: Stories of Success and Hope in a Canadian Context*. Edited by A. Aucoin and K. Calder Stegemann. Toronto: Pearson Education.

———2013. *Resource Teachers: A Changing Role in the Three-Block Model of Universal Design for Learning*. Winnipeg: Portage & Main Press.

———2012. *Teaching to Diversity: The Three-Block Model of Universal Design for Learning*. Winnipeg: Portage & Main Press.

Katz, J. and M. Porath. 2011. "Teaching to Diversity: Creating Compassionate Learning Communities for Diverse Elementary School Students." *International Journal of Special Education* 26 (2): 1–13.

Katz, J., L. Sokal, and A. Wu. (in submission). "Academic Achievement of Diverse Learners as Measured By Critical Thinking in K–12 Inclusive Classrooms Implementing the Three-Block Model of Universal Design for Learning (UDL)."

Kessels, H.W. and R. Malinow. 2009. "Synaptic AMPA Receptor Plasticity and Behavior." *Neuron* 61: 340–350. doi:10.1016/j.neuron.2009.01.015.

Keyes, C. 2005. "Mental Illness and/or Mental Health. Investigating Axioms of the Complete State Model of Health." *American Journal of Consulting and Clinical Psychology* 73 (3): 539–548. doi: 10.1037.0022-006x.73.3.539.

Konishi, C., S. Hymel, B.D. Zumbo, and Z. Li. 2010. "Do School Bullying and Student-Teacher Relationships Matter for Academic Achievement? A Multilevel Analysis." *Canadian Journal of School Psychology* 25 (1): 19–39. doi: 10.1177/0829573509357550.

Leithwood, K.A. and C. Riehl. 2005. "What Do We Already Know About Educational Leadership?" In *A New Agenda for Research in Educational Leadership*. Edited by W.A. Firestone and C. Riehl. New York: Teachers College Press.

Lester, L., S. Waters, and D. Cross. 2013. "The Relationship Between School Connectedness and Mental Health During the Transition to Secondary School: A Path Analysis." *Australian Journal of Guidance and Counselling* 23 (02): 157–171. https://doi.org/10.1017/jgc.2013.20.

Levine, M. 2002. *A Mind at a Time*. New York: Simon & Schuster.

Lieberman, H.R. 1994. "Tyrosine and Stress: Human and Animal Studies." In *Food Components to Enhance Performance: An Evaluation of Potential Performance-Enhancing Food Components for Operational Rations*, B.M. Marriott, ed.: 277–299. Institute of Medicine. Washington, D.C.: National Academies Press.

Marzano. R.J. 2009. "Teaching for the 21st Century." *Educational Leadership* 67 (1): 83–84

McEwen, B.S. and P.J. Gianaros. 2010. "Central Role of the Brain in Stress and Adaptation: Links to Socioeconomic Status, Health, and Disease." *Annals of the New York Academy of Sciences* 1186: 190–222. doi:10.1111/j.1749-6632.2009.05331.x.

Messinger-Willman, J. and M.T. Marino. 2010. "Universal Design for Learning and Assistive Technology: Leadership Considerations for Promoting Inclusive Education in Today's Secondary Schools." *NASSP Bulletin* 94 (1): 5–16. doi:10.1177/0192636510371977.

Morrison, W. and P. Peterson. 2013. *Schools as a Setting for Promoting Positive Mental Health: Better Practices and Perspectives.* Pan-Canadian Joint Consortium for School Health.

Mosby, Ian. 2013. "Administering Colonial Science: Nutrition Research and Human Biomedical Experimentation in Aboriginal Communities and Residential Schools, 1942–1952." *Histoire sociale/Social History* 46 (91) (Mai–May):145–172.

"Myers v. Peel County Board of Education." 1981. 2 SCR 21, 1981 CanLII 27. Supreme Court of Canada. https://scc-csc.lexum.com/scc-csc/scc-csc/en/item/2521/index.do

Nelson, H.J., G.E. Kendall, and L. Shields. 2013. "Neurological and Biological Foundations of Children's Social and Emotional Development: An Integrated Literature Review." *The Journal of School Nursing* 30 (4): 240–250. doi: 10.1177/1059840513513157.

Noddings, N. 1984. *Caring: A Feminine Approach to Ethics and Moral Education.* Berkeley: University of California Press.

Organization for Economic Cooperation and Development (OECD). 2007. *Understanding the Brain: The Birth of a Learning Science.* Paris, France: OECD.

Physical Health and Education Canada. "Health-Promoting Schools." Retrieved October 19, 2017. http://www.phecanada.ca/health-health-promoting-schools

Polderman, T., B. Benyamin, C. de Leeuw, P. Sullivan, A. van Bochoven, P. Visscher, and D. Posthuma. 2015. *Nature Genetics* 47 (7): 702–709.

President's New Freedom Commission on Mental Health. "Achieving the Promise: Transforming Mental Health Care in America." Final Report. DHHS Pub. No. SMA-03-3832. Rockville, MD: 2003.

Richards, J. "Are We Making Progress? New Evidence on Aboriginal Education Outcomes in Provincial and Reserve Schools." C.D. Howe Institute. *Commentary* 408 (April 2014).

Rogers, E.M. 2003. *Diffusion of Innovations.* New York: Free Press.

Rose, D. and A. Meyer. 2002. *Teaching Every Student in the Digital Age.* Alexandria, VA: Association for Supervision and Curriculum Development.

Ross-Hill, R. 2009. "Teacher Attitude Towards Inclusion Practices and Special Needs Students." *Journal of Research in Special Educational Needs* 9 (3): 188–198. https://doi.org/10.1111/j.1471-3802.2009.01135.x

Salovey, P. and J.D. Mayer. 1990. "Emotional Intelligence." *Imagination, Cognition, and Personality* 9 (3): 185–211. http://dmcodyssey.org/

Scanlan, M. 2009. "Leadership Dynamics Promoting Systemic Reform for Inclusive Service Delivery." *Journal of School Leadership* 19 (6): 622–660.

Shepard, J.S. 2004. "Multiple Ways of Knowing: Fostering Resiliency Through Providing Opportunities for Participating in Learning." *Reclaiming Children and Youth* 12, 210–217.

Sinek, Simon. "Start With Why: How Great Leaders Inspire Action." Tedx Puget Sound. Retrieved November 2017: https://www.youtube.com/watch?v=u4ZoJKF_VuA&feature=youtu.be

Smetanin, P., D. Stiff, C. Briante, C.E. Adair, S. Ahmad, and M. Khan. 2011. "The Life and Economic Impact of Major Mental Illnesses in Canada: 2011 to 2041." RiskAnalytica, on behalf of the Mental Health Commission of Canada.

Substance Abuse and Mental Health Services Administration (SAMHSA). 2004. "School Materials for a Mental Health Friendly Classroom: Training Package." Rockville, MD: Vanguard Communications, Inc., SAMHSA and the US Department of Health and Human Services.

Sun, J. and K. Leithwood. 2015. "Direction-Setting School Leadership Practices: A Meta-Analytical Review of Evidence about Their Influence." *School Effectiveness and School Improvement* 26 (4): 499–523. https://doi.org/10.1080/09243453.2015.1005106

Troop-Gordon, W. and H. Gerardy. 2012. "Parents' Beliefs about Peer Victimization and Children's Socio-Emotional Development." *Journal of Applied Developmental Psychology* 33: 40–52. doi: http://dx.doi.org/10.1016/j.appdev.2011.10.001

TRC Final Report. Truth and Reconciliation Commission of Canada. 2015. Retrieved October 19, 2017. http://www.trc.ca/websites/trcinstitution/index.php?p=890

Tyson, O., C.M. Roberts, and R. Kane. 2009. "Can Implementation of a Resilience Program for Primary School Children Enhance the Mental Health of Teachers?" *Australian Journal of Guidance and Counselling* 19 (2): 116–130.

United Nations Education Scientific and Cultural Organization. 1994. *The Salamanca Statement and Framework for Action on Special Needs Education*. Spain: UNESCO/Ministry of Education and Science.

Vowel, Chelsea. 2016. *Indigenous Writes*. Winnipeg: HighWater Press.

Widdowson, D.A., R.S. Dixon, E.R. Peterson, C.M. Rubie-Davies, and S.E. Irving. 2015. "Why Go to School? Student, Parent and Teacher Beliefs about the Purposes of Schooling." *Asia Pacific Journal of Education* 35 (4): 471–484. https://doi.org/10.1080/02188791.2013.876973

Wilson, Gloria Lodato. "Using Videotherapy to Access Curriculum and Enhance Growth." *Teaching Exceptional Children* 36 (6): 32–37

Wood, D. 2007. "Teachers' Learning Communities: Catalyst for Change or a New Infrastructure for the Status Quo?" *Teachers College Record* 109 (3): 699–739. https://doi.org/10.1177/002248717502600425

World Health Organization. 2017. "What Is a Health Promoting School?" School and Youth Health. Retrieved October 19, 2017. http://www.who.int/school_youth_health/gshi/hps/en/.

Young, S.N. 1996. "Behavioral Effects of Dietary Neurotransmitter Precursors: Basic and Clinical Aspects." *Neuroscience and Biobehavioural Reviews* 20 (2): 313–323.

Zins, J.E. and M.E. Elias. 2006. "Social and Emotional Learning." In *Children's Needs III*. Edited by G.G. Bear and K.M. Minke. National Association of School Psychologists.

Index